EJB Cookbook

T0130691

EJB Cookbook

BENJAMIN G. SULLINS
MARK B. WHIPPLE

MANNING

Greenwich
(74° w. long.)

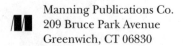

Manning Publications Co.   Copyeditor: Liz Welch
209 Bruce Park Avenue   Typesetter: Dottie Marsico
Greenwich, CT 06830   Cover designer: Leslie Haimes

ISBN 1930110944

Printed in the United States of America
2 3 4 5 6 7 8 9 10 – VHG – 06 05 04 03

To Jenny, Elijah, and Samuel
—Ben

To my wonderful wife, Margie,
and my son, Alexander
—Mark

contents

preface *xv*
acknowledgments *xvii*
about this book *xviii*
author online *xxii*
about the cover illustration *xxiii*

PART I APPETIZERS 1

1 Client code 3

1.1 Invoking a local EJB from another EJB 4

1.2 Invoking a remote EJB from another EJB 6

1.3 Accessing EJBs from a servlet 8

1.4 Invoking an EJB from a JavaServer Page 12

1.5 Invoking EJB business logic from a JMS system 15

1.6 Persisting a reference to an EJB instance 18

1.7 Retrieving and using a persisted EJB reference 20

1.8 Persisting a home object reference 21

1.9 Comparing two EJB references for equality 23

1.10 Using reflection with an EJB 25

1.11 Invoking an EJB from an applet 27

1.12 Improving your client-side EJB lookup code 31

2 Code generation with XDoclet 33

An XDoclet appetizer 35

2.1 Generating home, remote, local, and local
     home interfaces 37

2.2 Adding and customizing the JNDI name for the
     home interface 43

2.3 Keeping your EJB deployment descriptor current 45

2.4 Creating value objects for your entity beans 47

2.5 Generating a primary key class 53

2.6 Avoiding hardcoded XDoclet tag values 56

2.7 Facilitating bean lookup with a utility object 58

2.8 Generating vendor-specific deployment descriptors 62

2.9 Specifying security roles in the bean source 63

2.10 Generating and maintaining method permissions 64

2.11 Generating finder methods for entity
      home interfaces 66

2.12 Generating the ejbSelect method XML 67

2.13 Adding a home method to generated
      home interfaces 68

2.14 Adding entity relation XML to the
      deployment descriptor 70

2.15 Adding the destination type to a message-driven
      bean deployment descriptor 71

2.16 Adding message selectors to a message-driven bean
      deployment descriptor 73

PART II MAIN COURSES 75

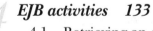
Working with data   77

3.1 Using a data source   78

3.2 Creating EJB 2.0 container-managed persistence   81

3.3 Using different data sources for different users   85

3.4 Using a database sequence to generate primary key
     values for entity beans   88

3.5 Using a compound primary key for your entity beans   92

3.6 Retrieving multiple entity beans in a single step   95

3.7 Modeling one-to-one entity data relationships   97

3.8 Creating a one-to-many relationship for entity beans   101

3.9 Using entity relationships to create a
     cascading delete   104

3.10 Developing noncreatable, read-only entity beans   107

3.11 Invoking a stored procedure from an EJB   109

3.12 Using EJB-QL to create custom finder methods   111

3.13 Persisting entity data into a database view   115

3.14 Sending notifications upon entity data changes   117

3.15 Creating an interface to your entity data   120

3.16 Retrieving information about entity data sets   122

3.17 Decreasing the number of calls to an entity bean   124

3.18 Paging through large result sets   126

EJB activities   133

4.1 Retrieving an environment variable   134

4.2 Implementing toString() functionality for an EJB   136

4.3 Providing common methods for all your EJBs   137

4.4   Reducing the clutter of unimplemented
          bean methods   139

4.5   Sending an email from an EJB   144

4.6   Using the EJB 2.1 timer service   145

4.7   Sending a JMS message from an EJB   147

4.8   Using an EJB as a web service   149

4.9   Creating asynchronous behavior for an EJB client   151

4.10   Creating asynchronous behavior without
          message-driven beans   156

4.11   Insulating an EJB from service class
          implementations   157

4.12   Creating a batch process mechanism   159

5   *Transactions*   *163*

A transaction appetizer   165

5.1   Tuning the container transaction control
          for your EJB   166

5.2   Handling transaction management without the
          container   169

5.3   Rolling back the current transaction   170

5.4   Attempting error recovery to avoid a rollback   172

5.5   Forcing rollbacks before method completion   175

5.6   Imposing time limits on transactions   176

5.7   Combining entity updates into a single transaction   177

5.8   Managing EJB state at transaction boundaries   179

5.9   Using more than one transaction in a method   181

5.10   Managing EJB state after a rollback   183

5.11   Throwing exceptions without causing a rollback   184

5.12   Propagating a transaction to another
          EJB business method   186

5.13   Propagating a transaction to a nonEJB class   188

5.14   Starting a transaction in the client layer   190

5.15   Holding a transaction across multiple
        JavaServer Pages   191

5.16   Updating multiple databases in one transaction   193

Messaging   *197*

6.1   Sending a publish/subscribe JMS message   198

6.2   Sending a point-to-point JMS message   200

6.3   Creating a message-driven Enterprise JavaBean   202

6.4   Processing messages in a FIFO manner from a
       message queue   205

6.5   Insulating message-driven beans from business
       logic changes   209

6.6   Streaming data to a message-driven EJB   210

6.7   Triggering two or more message-driven beans with a
       single JMS message   213

6.8   Speeding up message delivery to a message-driven
       bean   216

6.9   Filtering messages for a message-driven EJB   219

6.10   Encapsulating error-handling code in a
        message-driven EJB   221

6.11   Sending an email message asynchronously   223

6.12   Handling rollbacks in a message-driven bean   225

Security   *229*

7.1   Finding the identity and role of the caller inside
       an EJB method   231

7.2   Assigning and determining EJB client security roles   232

7.3   Passing client credentials to the EJB container   234

7.4   Disabling methods for certain users   235

7.5 Assigning a role to an EJB 238

7.6 Preventing access to entity data 239

7.7 Using EJBs to handle simple authentication with
    an LDAP source 241

7.8 Securing a message-driven bean 242

PART III DESSERTS 245

8 *Logging* 247
    A log4j appetizer 248

8.1 Formatting log messages 251

8.2 Improving logging performance 254

8.3 Using logging to generate reports 257

8.4 Sending log messages to a JMS topic 258

8.5 Logging to an XML file 259

8.6 Creating log file views for the web browser 261

8.7 Creating a centralized log file in a clustered
    environment 263

8.8 Tracking the lifecycle of an EJB 265

8.9 Using a different configuration at runtime 267

8.10 Sorting log messages by client 269

9 *Deploying and unit testing* 273
    A deployment and testing appetizer 274

9.1 Compiling Enterprise JavaBeans 278

9.2 Building the ejb.jar file 280

9.3 Building Enterprise JavaBean stub classes 283

9.4 Creating a stateless session bean unit test 286

9.5 Creating a stateful session bean unit test 290

9.6 Creating an entity bean unit test 292

9.7 Automating test case execution 294

9.8 Executing test cases using a UI 298

appendix A **Mixing it up: related recipes** *303*
appendix B **Second helpings: additional resources** *315*
index *317*

preface

"I did toy with the idea of doing a cookbook.... I think a lot
of people who hate literature but love fried eggs would buy it
if the price was right."
—*Groucho Marx*

As the Java 2 Platform Enterprise Edition (J2EE) gains acceptance among increasing numbers of developers, the resources, tutorials, books, and experts covering Enterprise JavaBeans (EJBs) also grows in numbers. A search at a popular online bookstore using the phrase "Enterprise JavaBeans" turns up 24 books, and these results include only those with the phrase in the title. Using the Google Internet search engine (www.google.com) with the same phrase results in approximately 744[1] pages with a strong relation to EJBs. While the multitude of material is certainly a wealth of knowledge, explanation, and discussion, it often forces EJB developers into lengthy searches for quick solutions. How many times have you needed to answer a specific question and had to search through many pages in a book—or a few books—to find your answer?

Having experienced this problem firsthand, we decided to do something about it. Our goal with this book is to provide an essential problem-solving resource. Just as cookbooks for meals contain step-by-step directions for creating various dishes, this book provides recipes for solving problems involving Enterprise JavaBeans. Here you will find recipes for many types of problems, ranging

---

[1] Google actually listed a potential for 123,000 pages, but cuts off the result after 744 for relevancy.

from simple, everyday quick-reference issues to complex design challenges using EJB patterns.

This book is intended for developers with at least some EJB development experience. With that in mind, you will not find recipes describing the basic construction rules of session and entity beans. We assume that you understand the concepts of enterprise development and the basics of EJB programming. The format used here specifically references problems and issues, avoiding the use of EJB keywords (a look through the table of contents will verify this). For example, rather than looking up "design patterns," look up the actual problem you are trying to solve (for example, "improving network performance"). To maximize the usefulness of the book, the index includes both EJB keywords and problem-area keywords.

The recipes we've concocted are self-contained, referencing other recipes that are related to the solution. We wanted to create a book that you could pick up and start reading at any point. The recipes are short and concise so that you can read them on the subway, in your favorite coffee house, or whenever you find yourself with five minutes to spare.

A useful companion to this book is *Bitter EJB*, also from Manning, which details many antipatterns specific to EJB development. It offers a practical approach to design: how to become a better programmer by studying problems and solutions to the most important problems surrounding the technology.

Now that we have described and set this book up for you, we invite you to partake in our buffet of solutions. You may pick and choose from our nine chapters, or sample them all. Enjoy!

acknowledgments

Many people helped to pull this book together in a very short time frame. We would like to thank Manning Publications for allowing us to work on this project. Thanks to Marjan Bace and Alex Garrett for conceiving and guiding the cookbook idea. Thanks as usual to Susan Capparelle and Mary Piergies for keeping the project on schedule, and thanks to Helen Trimes for getting the word out.

In addition to Manning Publications, we had excellent help from our copy-editor, Liz Welch. She was always ready to work hard with little notice. Likewise, we extend thanks to our reviewers: Karl Moss, Barry Nowak, Lester Martin, Ravi Mathur, Naveen Gabrani, Jeff Sullins, Bruce Tate, and Ganapathy Arunkumar.

Finally, thanks to Cyrus Dadgar for providing his technical expertise and fact-checking ability.

BEN SULLINS—I wish to thank my wife, Jenny. Not only do I get the undying support of a smart, funny, and sexy woman, I also get to live with her for the remainder of my life. I would also like to thank God for giving me this excellent opportunity to provide for my family. Finally, I wish to thank my coauthor, Mark, for working hard and putting up with the pressure to complete this book.

MARK WHIPPLE—I would like to thank my family for enduring the late nights and laptop usage during holiday vacations. Without their patience and support, this book would not be possible. Thanks go to my parents, whose support throughout my life has enabled me to build the skills necessary to succeed. I would especially like to thank my coauthor, Ben. His high level of motivation and enduring drive for success are an inspiration to me, and kept me focused on the completion of this book.

about this book

All but two recipes in this book are based on the EJB 2.0 specification. The recipes on creating EJB web service endpoints and the EJB timer service are based on the EJB 2.1 specification. In a few chapters, the book covers other technologies or frameworks where appropriate. In fact, this book makes use of XDoclet, log4j, Ant, and Cactus. For example, chapter 8 discusses using log4j to provide logging in an Enterprise JavaBeans application. Wherever these outside frameworks or tools are referenced, only the portion that touches the EJB world is described. So even though an introduction may be provided, you might need to consult additional documentation to answer any further questions.

We intend this book for the practicing EJB developer. That said, we don't include many recipes for tasks that we assume you already know how to do. For instance, you won't find recipes describing the basic rules of EJB construction, building, or deployment. Many of the recipes show full examples, whereas others may only show psuedo-code or partial examples. Much of the code can be downloaded from the book's website at www.manning.com/sullins2.

Chapter menu

You can choose to read this book from start to finish, or you can focus on certain topics as you need. The following sections give a short preview of each chapter so that you can jump ahead if you like. In fact, we suggest you jump around in the book for specific solutions to problems you face in day-to-day EJB development. No chapter builds on a previous chapter, so you don't gain anything by reading them in order. We'll bet this is one of the few books on your shelf that allows you to read the last page first without spoiling anything.

Chapter 1   Client code

This chapter presents recipes that deal with problems encountered by Enterprise JavaBean clients. You will work through examples that demonstrate using EJBs with servlets, applets, and JavaServer Pages. This chapter also discusses using EJB metadata to discover information about EJBs before invoking their methods.

Chapter 2   Code generation with XDoclet

Chapter 2 covers code generation by introducing and using an open source tool called XDoclet. XDoclet is quickly becoming the code-generation tool of choice for many Enterprise JavaBeans developers. In this chapter you will learn how to use XDoclet to keep all your EJB files in synch by generating files based off the bean implementation class. XDoclet will generate your deployment descriptors, interfaces, and other classes, such as value objects.

Chapter 3   Working with data

Chapter 3 attempts to cover the most pressing problems that occur when Enterprise JavaBeans work with data. The chapter focuses on using Java Database Connectivity (JDBC) with session beans and with bean-managed persistence entity beans, as well as container-managed persistence entity beans. We also present best practices for using entity beans, and a solution for returning large result sets back to clients.

Chapter 4   EJB activities

This chapter offers a collection of recipes dealing with the day-to-day activities of an Enterprise JavaBean. These recipes are not as closely related as those in other chapters, but you will find unique recipes, such as creating asynchronous processes with message-driven beans and insulating EJBs from business service class implementations.

Chapter 5   Transactions

Chapter 5 deals with transaction-related problems. You will discover recipes working with both container-managed and bean-managed transactions. Along with solutions for creating transactions and propagating transactions, chapter 5 illustrates solutions for working with rollbacks and recovering from errors.

Chapter 6   Messaging

Chapter 6 focuses purely on the messaging aspects of Enterprise JavaBeans applications. This chapter contains recipes dealing with the Java Message Service (JMS) and message-driven beans. You will learn how to send different types of JMS messages to different types of destinations. Also in this chapter are guidelines for encapsulating business logic within message-driven beans, as well as handling errors and rollbacks.

Chapter 7   Security

This chapter contains recipes for solving your security problems by using the security mechanism provided by the EJB container. In addition, chapter 7 includes security guidelines for protecting entity and message-driven beans. The chapter focuses on the EJB declarative security model described by the EJB specification, and describes the various security- and identity-related methods available to each EJB.

Chapter 8   Logging

Chapter 8 covers the open source log4j logging tool. We introduce you to log4j by showing you how to install and incorporate it into your enterprise applications. After the introduction, the chapter provides solutions for some problems related to logging with Enterprise JavaBeans applications. Recipes found here include centralizing logging in a cluster and sorting log messages in a multiclient environment.

Chapter 9   Deploying and unit testing

The two main focuses of this chapter are Apache Ant and Apache Cactus. Several recipes focus on using Ant for building EJB class files, generating stubs, and packaging class files into appropriate JAR files. The second half of the chapter focuses on using Cactus to unit test functionality provided by your EJBs. The chapter provides an introduction to Cactus and testing recipes for entity and session beans.

Appendix A   Mixing it up: related recipes

This appendix renders the recipe titles in a cross reference format. It allows you to easily look up any recipe and find its related recipes. In this manner you will find all the applicable information pertinent to any topic in the book.

Appendix B   Second helpings: additional resources

This short appendix lists some resources for further information on certain topics presented in this book. This is essential as this book is not a detailed tutorial on many of the ideas presented. Use the resources listed here for further explanation and investigation.

Code

The source code is freely available from Manning's website, www.manning.com/sullins2. Many of the recipes include only code fragments to illustrate a point, and these fragments will not be found in the downloadable source code. The downloadable source includes only those examples that contain full listings. In some cases, the entire source is not shown in the recipe.

When we present source code, we sometimes use a bold font to draw attention to specific elements. In the text, `Courier` typeface is used to denote code (XML, Java, and HTML) as well as Java methods and other source code identifiers:

- A reference to a method in the text will generally not include the signature, because there may be more than one form of the method call.
- A reference to an XML element in the text will include the braces but not the properties or closing tag (`<action>`).

How to use this book

This book is not a story—it does not have a beginning or an end. You don't have to read the chapters in order; we recommend you use the index or the table of contents to find the topics you're interested in and jump right to them. Recipe titles are found both in the table of contents and the index. In addition, the major subject areas are referenced throughout the index. The power of this book is its ability to impart solutions in just a few moments. We intend it to be a quick-solutions reference, not an instructional tutorial.

author online

Purchase of the *EJB Cookbook* includes free access to a private web forum run by Manning Publications where you can make comments about the book, ask technical questions, and receive help from the author and from other users. To access the forum and subscribe to it, point your web browser to www.manning.com/sullins2. This page provides information on how to get on the forum once you are registered, what kind of help is available, and the rules of conduct on the forum.

Manning's commitment to our readers is to provide a venue where a meaningful dialog between individual readers and between readers and the authors can take place. It is not a commitment to any specific amount of participation on the part of the authors, whose contribution to the AO remains voluntary (and unpaid). We suggest you try asking the authors some challenging questions lest their interest stray!

The Author Online forum and the archives of previous discussions will be accessible from the publisher's website as long as the book is in print.

about the cover illustration

The figure on the cover of *EJB Cookbook* is a "Paysanne de l'Angoumois," a peasant woman from the Angoumois region in Western France. The Charente Valley, with its excellent vineyards, is the heart of the region and the brandy from the local grapes is known throughout the world as cognac, named after the main distillery.

The illustration, a hand-colored copper engraving, is taken from a French travel book, *Encyclopedie des Voyages* by J. G. St. Saveur, published in 1796. Travel for pleasure was a relatively new phenomenon at the time and travel guides such as this one were popular, introducing both the tourist as well as the armchair traveler to the inhabitants of other regions of France and abroad.

The diversity of the drawings in the *Encyclopedie des Voyages* speaks vividly of the uniqueness and individuality of the world's towns and provinces just 200 years ago. This was a time when the dress codes of two regions separated by a few dozen miles identified people uniquely as belonging to one or the other. The travel guide brings to life a sense of isolation and distance of that period and of every other historic period except our own hyperkinetic present. Dress codes have changed since then and the diversity by region, so rich at the time, has faded away. It is now often hard to tell the inhabitant of one continent from another. Perhaps, trying to view it optimistically, we have traded a cultural and visual diversity for a more varied personal life. Or a more varied and interesting intellectual and technical life.

In spite of the current downturn, we at Manning continue to celebrate the inventiveness, the initiative, and, yes, the fun of the computer business with book covers based on the rich diversity of regional life two centuries ago brought back to life by the pictures from this travel guide.

Part 1

Appetizers

Part 1 of the cookbook deals with two "front-end" topics in Enterprise JavaBeans (EJB) development. Chapter 1 deals with EJB clients, the front end of many EJB applications. Chapter 2 introduces the first open source tool used in the book, XDoclet, for generating EJB-related files and source code.

Chapter 1 covers various problems specifically encountered by EJB clients. In this chapter, you will find recipes working with applets, servlets, and other EJBs acting as clients. In addition, a few recipes deal with problems that transcend the type of client and can be applied in many client situations. Chapter 2 introduces and discusses XDoclet in detail. XDoclet is an open source tool that provides the ability to generate EJB source code and maintain XML deployment descriptors. This chapter examines many of the capabilities of XDoclet pertaining to EJB development.

Client code 1

"Hey man, I'm drinking wine, eating cheese,
and catching some rays."

— Donald Sutherland as Oddball,
from the movie "Kelly's Heroes"

An Enterprise JavaBean (EJB) client is any object that contacts an EJB. For this contact to work, EJBs need to know how to find each other. The recipes presented in this chapter provide solutions for allowing EJBs to locate one another.

EJB clients can be divided into two main categories: remote clients and local clients. This is an important distinction because it affects the way clients find the EJBs they need to use. For example, creating the `InitialContext` instance to look up EJBs in the same virtual machine is completely different from creating an instance for remote EJB lookups. The clients covered in this chapter include Java-Server Pages (JSPs), servlets, applets, and other EJBs. Each client faces its own set of problems.

In this chapter, you'll find recipes for the following tasks:

- Invoking a local EJB method from another EJB
- Invoking a remote EJB method from another EJB
- Contacting an EJB from a servlet
- Contacting an EJB from a JSP
- Using the Java Message Service (JMS) to invoke EJB business logic
- Saving an EJB reference in a persistent format
- Using a persisted EJB reference
- Storing an EJB home object reference
- Determining if two EJB references refer to the same bean
- Getting information about an EJB's methods by using reflection
- Using an EJB from an applet
- Improving EJB lookups

1.1 *Invoking a local EJB from another EJB*

◆ *Problem*

From one EJB, you want to invoke a method on another EJB in the same EJB container.

◆ *Background*

In most EJB applications, completing business logic in one EJB involves invoking another EJB. In addition, entity bean access is usually through a session bean facade. When you're creating an EJB application, it is essential to know how to contact other EJBs in the same EJB container. Solving this problem requires you to know how to find another bean in the same container.

◆ *Recipe*

To invoke a method from another EJB in the same container, from the client EJB, add a method for looking up the home object of the needed EJB. For example, the method shown in listing 1.1 looks up the home object, PasswordHome, for the PasswordBean EJB.

Listing 1.1   A simple lookup method

```
private PasswordHome getPasswordHome() {           Creates a default
                                                   InitialContext
    try {                                          instance
      Context ic = new InitialContext();    ◁─┘
      PasswordHome passwordHome = ( PasswordHome )         Performs JNDI
                   ic.lookup("ejbAccess.passwordHome");    lookup of the
                                                           EJB home
      return passwordHome;                                 object
    }
    catch (NamingException ne) {
      return null;
    }
}
```

◆ *Discussion*

With a reference to the home object, you can invoke any methods declared by the interface. Typically, you would invoke a create() method to acquire a reference to the business interface (remote or local) of the EJB in order to execute business logic or data access.

Finding the home object is only part of using an EJB, of course. Once you have a home object, you can create or locate EJB instances for use (depending on the bean type). With the completion of the EJB 2.0 specification came the concept of *local interfaces.* Typically, if you know that an EJB is only going to be used (or should only be used) in the local EJB container (meaning that it has no remote clients), then the EJB should implement a local home and a local business interface. This is just the same as the home and remote interfaces, except that the local interface is not exposed via Java Remote Method Invocation (RMI) and can only be used in the same virtual machine. Using local interfaces improves the performance and security of EJBs to be used by local clients.

◆ See also

1.1—Invoking a remote EJB from another EJB

1.12—Improving your client-side EJB lookup code

2.1—Generating home, remote, local, and local home interfaces

2.7—Facilitating bean lookup with a utility object

7.6—Preventing access to entity data

1.2 Invoking a remote EJB from another EJB

◆ Problem

From one EJB, you want to invoke a method on another EJB in a remote EJB container.

◆ Background

In most EJB applications, completing business logic in one EJB involves invoking another EJB. In addition, entity bean access is usually through a session bean facade. With most cases, EJB access from another EJB takes place in the same EJB container. However, large enterprise applications may separate business logic across hosts, or may invoke other EJB applications to complete a workflow. In these cases, you might need to access remote EJBs from other EJBs. For this solution, you need to know how to create an initial context for finding a remote EJB container in order to look up or create remote EJBs.

◆ Recipe

Unlike recipe 1.1, you cannot create only the default InitialContext instance and be able to invoke a remote EJB. You must pass in some properties that let the context find the Java Naming and Directory Interface (JNDI) system used for the remote EJBs. For example, the private method in listing 1.2 looks up a remote EJB home object in a Weblogic EJB container.

Listing 1.2   A lookup method using an initialized InitialContext

```
private EquityHome getEquityHome() {

    try {
      // Get an InitialContext
      Properties props = new Properties();      Creates an InitialContext instance
props.put( Context.INITIAL_CONTEXT_FACTORY,    with environment properties
```

```
                    "weblogic.jndi.WLInitialContextFactory" );
        props.put( Context.PROVIDER_URL,
                    "http://MyRemoteHost:7001" );
        Context ic = new InitialContext( props );

        EquityHome  equityHome = ( EquityHome )
                    ic.lookup( "ejbAccess.equityHome" );
    equityHome = ( EquityHome )
        PortableRemoteObject.narrow( equityHome,
        EquityHome.class );

    return equityHome;
    }
    catch (NamingException ne) {
      return null;
    }
  }
```

**Narrows the
return value**

With a home reference in hand, you can find or create a new EJB. The following
code locates an existing instance of the `EquityBean` entity bean:

```
//remote interface of the EJB
Equity equity = null;
String symbol = getSymbol();

try{
  //Use previously acquired home reference
  //to find an entity instance
  equity = equityHome.findByPrimaryKey( symbol );
}
catch(Exception e){
  e.printStackTrace();
  throw new RemoteException("Error Finding Symbol:"+symbol);
}
```

◆ **Discussion**

This recipe shows how one EJB might contact a remote EJB (in a different EJB container). The solution provided here is similar to recipe 1.1 (contacting local EJBs)
except that the JNDI `InitialContext` object must be provided with some properties in order to find the other EJB container. In this example, we provided the
`InitialContext` instance with the correct properties to find a remote Weblogic
EJB container using the following code:

```
props.put( Context.INITIAL_CONTEXT_FACTORY,
                "weblogic.jndi.WLInitialContextFactory" );
        props.put( Context.PROVIDER_URL,
                    "http://MyRemoteHost:7001" );
```

Consult your application server's documentation for the exact properties you need to provide. In addition, to make your beans more portable (and maintainable), you should read the property values in from an environment variable (or similar mechanism).

Notice also that the example EJB uses the `javax.rmi.PortableRemoteObject` class to retrieve the EJB's stub for use. You must always use this class's `narrow()` method when retrieving a remote stub to ensure that the remote stub conforms to the IIOP protocol used now by Java RMI.

◆ **See also**

1.1—Invoking a local EJB from another EJB

1.12—Improving your client-side EJB lookup code

2.1—Generating home, remote, local, and local home interfaces

4.1—Retrieving an environment variable

1.3 Accessing EJBs from a servlet

◆ **Problem**

You want to contact an EJB from a servlet.

◆ **Background**

With the recent push to use web applications for enterprise solutions, servlets have started to perform important roles in business applications. While servlets control the flow and validation of page presentation, they also are the main access point to the back-end business logic contained in EJBs.

◆ **Recipe**

When using a servlet as an EJB client, you might need to contact a local or remote EJB container, so we provide separate recipes for local and remote EJBs. Also, you need to write portable servlets that don't contain hard-coded values for creating the JNDI initial context environment.

Contacting EJBs from the same server

When contacting an EJB in the same virtual machine, you need only make use of a default instance of the `InitialContext` class. For example, the servlet in listing 1.3 contacts a `LoginBean` EJB in order to process a user login.

Listing 1.3   LoginServlet.java

```java
import javax.servlet.*;

public class LoginServlet extends HttpServlet
{
  //home interface for the EJB PasswordBean
  private LoginHome loginHome = null;

  public void init(ServletConfig conf) throws ServletException
  {
        super.init(conf);
        try {
              lookupLoginHome();          Looks up the EJB home
        }                                 from the servlet init
        catch (NamingException e) {
              e.printStackTrace ();
        }
  }

  public void doGet( HttpServletRequest req,
                                 HttpServletResponse res )
  {
    try
    {
      String name = getUserName( req );
      String password = getUserPassword( req );

      Login loginBean = loginHome.create( name );     Creates an EJB and
      Boolean valid  = loginBean.login( password );    validates a login

    }catch( Exception e )
    {
     //handle exception
    }
    //perform further work (not shown)
  }

  public void doPost( HttpServletRequest req,
                            HttpServletResponse res )
  {
    doGet( req );
  }

  private void lookupLoginHome() throws NamingException
  {
    Context ctx = new InitialContext();          Uses the
                                                 InitialContext
    try {                                        class to find an
      if( loginHome == null )                    EJB home
        loginHome = ( LoginHome )3               object
              ctx.lookup( "servletAccess.loginHome" );
    }
```

```
      catch (NamingException ne) {
        throw ne;
      }
    }
  }
}
```

Contacting EJBs in a remote server

The code in listing 1.4 shows the same LoginServlet class, but this time it contacts a remote EJB container to find the LoginBean EJB. The differences appear in bold.

Listing 1.4   LoginServlet.java

```
import javax.servlet.*;

import javax.rmi.PortableRemoteObject;

public class LoginServlet extends HttpServlet
{
  //home interface for the EJB PasswordBean
  private LoginHome loginHome = null;

  public void init()
  {
    lookupLoginHome();
  }

  public void doGet( HttpServletRequest req,
                             HttpServletResponse res )
  {
    String name = getUserName( req );
    String password = getUserPassword( req );

    Login loginBean = (Login) PortableRemoteObject.narrow(
                         loginHome.create( name ), Login.class );

    Boolean valid = loginBean.login( password );

    //perform further work (not shown)
  }

  public void doPost( HttpServletRequest req,
                             HttpServletResponse res )
  {
    doGet( req );
  }

  private void lookupLoginHome() throws NamingException
  {
    Properties props = new Properties();

    props.put( Context.INITIAL_CONTEXT_FACTORY,
                       getInitParameter( "factory_class" ) );
    props.put( Context.PROVIDER_URL, getInitParameter( "url" ) );

    Context ctx = new InitialContext( props );
```

Creates an EJB

Initializes an InitialContext instance with an environment

```
    try{
      if( loginHome == null )
         loginHome = ( LoginHome ) ctx.lookup(
                        "servletAccess.loginHome" );
    }
    catch (NamingException ne) {
      throw ne;
    }
  }
```

Listing 1.5 contains the XML descriptor for the servlet. Notice that it creates the two parameters used by the servlet to build the initial context environment needed to find the remote EJBs.

Listing 1.5   The web.xml for the LoginServlet

```
<servlet>
   <servlet-name>login-servlet</servlet-name>
   <servlet-class>LoginServlet</servlet-class>
   <init-param>
     <param-name>url</param-name>
     <param-value>http://localhost:7001</param-value>
   </init-param>
   <init-param>
     <param-name>factory_class</param-name>
     <param-value>weblogic.jndi.WLInitialContextFactory</param-value>
   </init-param>
</servlet>
<servlet-mapping>
    <servlet-name>login-servlet</servlet-name>

    <url-pattern>/login-servlet</url-pattern>
</servlet-mapping>
```

◆ *Discussion*

The major change for the LoginServlet that contacts a remote EJB is the need to pass environment setting properties into the InitialContext instance used to find the EJB. Notice that in this recipe (as opposed to recipe 1.2) we used initialization parameters to store the values of the properties passed to the InitialContext object, keeping our servlet a little more portable. Notice also that when trying to retrieve the remote object stub of the EJB using the home object we must use the javax.rmi.PortableRemoteObject class to narrow the return value (using the narrow() method). When retrieving a remote stub of an EJB, you must always invoke this method to ensure that the returned object conforms to the IIOP protocol now used by Java RMI.

The properties for the `InitialContext` instance used values retrieved from the servlet's initialization parameters. Doing this allows the servlet to maintain more portability between application servers.

After reading recipes 1.1, 1.2, and 1.3, you will notice that contacting local or remote EJBs is very similar regardless of the client. Because of this, you should start thinking along the lines of developing portable utility classes that can handle EJB lookup for you. By doing so, you can abstract the EJB lookup code away from your client, making your client more flexible and maintainable. Recipe 1.12 shows how utility objects not only abstract EJB lookup code, but can also improve the performance of your clients.

◆ **See also**

1.4—Invoking an EJB from a JavaServer Page

1.12—Improving your client-side EJB lookup code

2.1—Generating home, remote, local, and local home interfaces

2.7—Facilitating bean lookup with a utility object

1.4 Invoking an EJB from a JavaServer Page

◆ **Problem**

You want to contact an EJB from a JavaServer Page (JSP).

◆ **Background**

Just as servlets have become increasingly valuable with the growing popularity of web applications, JavaServer Pages (JSPs) have gained in importance as well. In some cases, developers wish to contact EJBs directly without going through the extra step of contacting a servlet. JSPs are compiled on the server side, and sometimes need to contact an EJB in order to complete the dynamically generated HTML or JavaScript for the end user.

◆ **Recipe**

Using EJBs from JSPs requires knowledge of constructing the correct JNDI initial context and good coding practices. This recipe shows solutions for both remote and local EJBs.

Contacting EJBs in the same container

The code for looking up and using an EJB from a JSP is exactly the same as recipe 1.3 (which describes contacting an EJB from a servlet). Listing 1.6 shows a JSP scriptlet that looks up a home object of the LoginBean EJB.

Listing 1.6   Sample JSP looking up a local EJB

```
<%

  LoginHome loginHome = null;

  try {
    System.out.println("Looking up Home: loginHome ");

    Context localCtx = new InitialContext();
    loginHome = (LoginHome)
                    localCtx.lookup( "jspAccess.loginHome" );
  }
  catch (Exception ne) {
    System.out.println("Unable to look up the EJBHome." );

    throw ne;
  }
%>
```

After creating a home reference, you can create and use a LoginBean EJB instance. The JSP scriptlet in listing 1.7 demonstrates this.

Listing 1.7   Sample JSP using a local EJB

```
<%
    Boolean loggedIn = new Bollean(false);

    String passwd = request.getParameter("Password");
    String username = request.getParameter("UserName");

    System.out.println("JSP Logging in for User:"+userName);

    try{
      Login loginBean = loginHome.create(username);
      loggedIn = loginBean.login(passwd);
      System.out.printIn("Status of Login:"+loggedIn);
    }
    catch(Exception e){
      //process exception, possible go to error page;
    }

%>
```

Contacting EJBs from a remote server

As in recipe 1.3, we also demonstrate the same code, but we're contacting an EJB from a remote EJB container. To successfully find the remote EJB container, you must pass in initialization properties to the InitialContext object constructor. The code in listing 1.8 contacts a remote Weblogic container. The differences from the previous JSP scriptlet are shown in bold.

Listing 1.8   Sample JSP looking up a remote EJB

```jsp
<%

  LoginHome loginHome = null;

  try {
    System.out.println("Looking up Home: loginHome ");

    Properties props = new Properties();
    props.put(Context.INITIAL_CONTEXT_FACTORY,
              "weblogic.jndi.WLInitialContextFactory" );
    props.put( Context.PROVIDER_URL, "t3://localhost:7001" );
    remoteCtx = new InitialContext(props);

    loginHome = (LoginHome)
                    remoteCtx.lookup( "jspAccess.loginHome " );
  }
  catch (Exception ne) {
    System.out.println("Unable to lookup the EJBHome." );

    throw ne;
  }
%>
```

◆ Discussion

The code in listings 1.6, 1.7, and 1.8 is similar to that in recipes 1.1 through 1.3. You should read those recipes for further details on using remote and local EJBs. When using EJBs from JSPs, keep in mind a few good development guidelines: For instance, if you need to contact an entity bean, it is generally accepted practice that you should do so through a session bean. A session façade to an entity bean can provide security for your data and help you improve the performance of your clients. In the same vein, consider wrapping your EJB access code in an object. This will insulate your JSP pages from unnecessary changes due to lookup code changes. Also, it adds a further layer of abstraction to your business logic (and persistence) layer.

In addition, if your EJBs are using bean-managed transactions, take care to avoid starting transactions from the client layer. If a client should start a transaction and walk away, your application might be stuck with locked tables or corrupted data.

Finally, as with the servlet example in the previous recipe, you should consider reading the property values passed in to the `InitialContext` object from a properties file (or similar mechanism). Doing this will improve the maintainability of your code.

◆ See also

1.3—Accessing EJBs from a servlet

3.15—Creating an interface to your entity data

5.15—Holding a transaction across multiple JavaServer Pages

1.5 Invoking EJB business logic from a JMS system

◆ Problem

You want to execute EJB business logic by sending a Java Message Service (JMS) message.

◆ Background

Many complex enterprise applications use a combination of many Java 2 Platform Enterprise Edition (J2EE) technologies, including EJBs and JMS. Using a JMS system, you can trigger back-end business logic in a batch process, from remote clients, or without user interaction. If all of your business logic is encapsulated in EJBs, it would be nice to be able to invoke an EJB using a JMS message. Invoking an EJB with a JMS message requires creating a message-driven EJB and setting up the correct JMS message destination in the application server running the EJB application, as well as configuring the EJB to receive your messages.

◆ Recipe

Create a message-driven bean to receive JMS messages in order to start business logic methods. For example, the EJB class in listing 1.9 defines a message-driven EJB. Notice that it extends a specific EJB interface, and also implements the JMS `MessageListener` interface.

Listing 1.9   MessageBean.java

```
import javax.ejb.*;
import javax.jms.*;                                        Implements
import javax.naming.*;                             MessageDrivenBean and
                                                       MessageListener
public class MessageBean implements                         interfaces
                     MessageDrivenBean, MessageListener {  ◁

  private MessageDrivenContext ctx;

  public void ejbRemove() {
  }

  public void ejbPassivate() {
  }

  public void setMessageDrivenContext(MessageDrivenContext ctx) {
    this.ctx = ctx;
  }

  public void ejbCreate () throws CreateException {
  }

  public void onMessage(Message msg) {   ◁── Implements an
    try {                                     onMessage() method
      String command = (( TextMessage ) msg ).getText();  ◁── Retrieves the
      //perform or delegate business logic                     message
    }
    catch(JMSException ex) {
      ex.printStackTrace();
    }
  }
}
```

To set up a message-driven EJB to receive JMS messages, you need to describe
its functionality in the XML deployment descriptor. For instance, the sample
XML in listing 1.10 describes the message-driven bean, including which JMS
topic it describes.

Listing 1.10   Deployment descriptor for the MessageBean

```
<ejb-jar>
  <enterprise-beans>

    <message-driven>
      <ejb-name>myMessageBean</ejb-name>
      <ejb-class>ejbs.msgbean.MessageBean</ejb-class>
      <transaction-type>Container</transaction-type>
      <message-driven-destination>
        <destination-type>javax.jms.Topic</destination-type>
      </message-driven-destination>
```

```
    </message-driven>

  </enterprise-beans>
</ejb-jar>
```

The XML sample in listing 1.10 ties an instance of the `MessageBean` message-driven EJB to a JMS system using a JMS topic. Each particular application server generally has an additional configuration step for EJB deployment. For example, Weblogic uses an additional XML file to describe the behavior of EJBs. Listing 1.11 contains a sample partial XML document for the message bean that specifies the actual JMS topic for the EJB.

Listing 1.11   Weblogic deployment descriptor

```
<weblogic-ejb-jar>

  <weblogic-enterprise-bean>
    <ejb-name>myMessageBean</ejb-name>

    <message-driven-descriptor>
      <destination-jndi-name>BookJMSTopic</destination-jndi-name>
    </message-driven-descriptor>

    <jndi-name>myMessageBean</jndi-name>
  </weblogic-enterprise-bean>

</weblogic-ejb-jar>
```

◆ *Discussion*

Our example message bean attempts to extract a command string from JMS messages it receives. From this command `String`, it will start particular business processes in an asynchronous manner.

As you can tell from this recipe, you should consult your application server's documentation for the specific way it maps message-driven beans to actual JMS topics and messages. In this example, for Weblogic we needed to create an additional XML file for the message-driven bean that specifies the actual JMS topic for the EJB.

This recipe shows only a small subset of the message-driven EJB capability. When developing message-driven beans, you should consider delegating business logic to other objects rather than tying it to a particular bean. This will allow you to use particular business logic in other places and not tie it to the message-driven behavior. You can read more about this idea in chapter 6.

◆ **See also**

Chapter 6, "Messaging"

1.6 *Persisting a reference to an EJB instance*

◆ **Problem**

You want to serialize a reference to an EJB so that you can avoid looking it up again.

◆ **Background**

One way to improve the performance of the client layer of an EJB application is to avoid repeated JNDI lookup calls to find an EJB. One of the best ways to do this is to save the EJB reference in a persistent format once the client looks it up. Saving a reference to an EJB means creating an object that can rebuild the connection to the EJB object in the EJB container.

◆ **Recipe**

Use an instance of the `Handle` class as the saved reference. Since EJB handles are serializable, we can persist them using an object output stream for later retrieval and use. The EJB specification designed the handle with this in mind. The client code in listing 1.12 implements a method, `saveReference()`, that persists a handle to an EJB.

Listing 1.12   ClientSaver.java

```
public class ClientSaver
{
  private String url;
  private HelperHome home;

  public void runExample()
  {
      home = retrieveHelperHome();        ◁──┘  Retrieves a home
                                                object for the Helper

    Helper goodHelper = null;

    try {
      goodHelper = (Helper)                         ◁───────┐  Creates an
            PortableRemoteObject.narrow( home.create(),     │  instance of the
            Helper.class);                          ◁───────┘  Helper EJB

      saveReference( goodHelper );
```

```
    }
    private void saveReference( Helper helper )
    {
      FileOutputStream   ostream = null;
      ObjectOutputStream objStream = null;

      try{
        ostream = new FileOutputStream( "Helper.obj" );
        objStream = new ObjectOutputStream( ostream );

        objStream.writeObject( helper.getHandle() );
        objStream.flush();
        objStream.close();
      }
      catch(Exception e){
        e.printStackTrace();
      }
    }
  }
}
```

Stores the reference

◆ *Discussion*

Once you have a reference to an actual EJB instance, you can use the getHandle()
method to retrieve a serializable object that contains information for rebuilding
the bean to which it refers. Using an instance of the Handle class, you can store a
reference to an EJB, shut down your application, and then restart and restore the
conversational state between your client and the EJB. EJB handles can be retrieved
only from the EJBObject instance for your EJB. The EJBObject interface is the parent interface to the EJB's remote interface. This means that you can create handles only to remote EJB references, not to local objects.

You can also use an EJB handle to pass an EJB reference to a remote object.
Since the EJB handle instance is a serializable object, it can be passed over an RMI
invocation. This allows you to pass the handle to remote EJBs for callbacks or to
any other remote object. Remote objects receiving the handle will not need to
know how to look up the EJB—they can simply retrieve the EJBObject from the
handle and start using it.

◆ *See also*

1.7—Retrieving and using a persisted EJB reference

1.8—Persisting a home object reference

1.7 *Retrieving and using a persisted EJB reference*

◆ *Problem*

After storing a reference to an EJB (recipe 1.6), you want to retrieve it and use it.

◆ *Background*

Recipe 1.6 illustrates a good way to store a reference to an existing EJB. However, that ability does a client little good if it doesn't know how to retrieve that reference. Retrieving a stored Handle object lets you circumvent the JNDI lookup of the EJB instance. To retrieve a stored EJB handle, you have to deserialize it from its stored location.

◆ *Recipe*

By retrieving a serialized EJB handle, you can re-create the bean that was originally created and that produced the handle (see listing 1.13).

Listing 1.13   ClientLoader.java

```java
import java.io.*;

public class ClientLoader {

    public void runExample() {
        Helper goodHelper = null;

        goodHelper = loadReference();

        //use bean (not shown)
    }

    private Helper loadReference()
    {
        FileInputStream    istream = null;
        ObjectInputStream objStream = null;
        Handle handle = null;
        Helper helper = null;

        try{

            istream = new FileInputStream("Helper.obj");
            objStream = new ObjectInputStream(istream);

            handle = (Handle) objStream.readObject();
            objStream.close();

            helper = (Helper)
                PortableRemoteObject.narrow( handle.getEJBObject(),
                                         Helper.class );
```

Retrieves the
serialized
handle

Gets the
EJBObject
reference

```
        }
        catch(Exception e){
            e.printStackTrace();
        }

        return helper;
    }
}
```

◆ *Discussion*

Retrieving a serialized instance of an EJB `Handle` object is a simple matter of object input/output (I/O). After retrieving the `Handle` instance from its persistent storage, you can invoke its `getEJBObject()` method to obtain the EJB reference that originally created the handle. Using the handle to find the EJB reference lets you skip looking up a home object via JNDI, and then finding or creating an EJB instance.

◆ *See also*

1.6—Persisting a reference to an EJB instance

1.8—Persisting a home object reference

1.8 Persisting a home object reference

◆ *Problem*

You want to serialize an EJB home object reference so that you can avoid looking it up again.

◆ *Background*

By storing a previously retrieved home object reference of an EJB, you can reuse it to create or find new instances of an EJB. You improve the performance of your client by avoiding repeated calls to the JNDI system for the home reference lookup. Persisting the home object will let you shut down your client, restart, and start creating references of an EJB without another JNDI lookup.

◆ *Recipe*

In recipes 1.6 and 1.7, we illustrated the serialization of the EJB handle. Like the `EJBObject` interface (the remote interface parent), the `EJBHome` interface shown in listing 1.14 provides a method, `getHomeHandle()`, that creates a handle for the home object of an EJB. This class invokes some methods whose implementations are not shown.

Listing 1.14   ClientHomeSaver.java

```
public class ClientHomeSaver
{
  private HelperHome home;

  public void runExample()
  {

    //Perform a jndi lookup to get home reference
    home = getHomeReference();        ◁──────┐ Looks up a home
                                             │ object for the Helper
    saveHomeReference( goodHelperHome );──┘

    home = loadReference();

  }

  private void saveHomeReference( HelperHome helper )
  {
    FileOutputStream   ostream = null;
    ObjectOutputStream objStream = null;

    try{
      ostream = new FileOutputStream( "HelperHome.obj" );   Stores the
      objStream = new ObjectOutputStream( ostream );        home object
                                                            reference
      objStream.writeObject( helper.getHomeHandle() );
      objStream.flush();
      objStream.close();
    }
    catch(Exception e){
      e.printStackTrace();
    }
  }

  private HelperHome loadReference()
  {
    FileInputStream   istream = null;
    ObjectInputStream objStream = null;
    Handle handle = null;
    Helper helper = null;

    try{

      istream = new FileInputStream("Helper.obj");
      objStream = new ObjectInputStream(istream);

      handle = (Handle) objStream.readObject();            Retrieves the
      objStream.close();                                   home handle
                                                           reference
      helper = (Helper) handle.getEJBHome();
```

```
        }
      catch(Exception e){
        e.printStackTrace();
      }

      return helper;
    }
  }
```

◆ ***Discussion***

Persisting a home object reference is simple when you create a `HomeHandle` instance. The parent of your home interface provides the `getHomeHandle()` method that returns an instance of the `HomeHandle` class. Only remote home interfaces, not extenders of the `EJBLocalHome` interface, will have the `getHomeHandle()` method. The `HomeHandle` class implements the serializable interface, allowing an instance to be persisted to stable storage.

Using a `HomeHandle` class is useful not only for persisting a reference to a home object, but also for keeping a reference in memory over the lifespan of a client. By keeping the handle around, you can avoid performing further JNDI lookups to retrieve a home reference to the same EJB.

◆ ***See also***

1.6—Persisting a reference to an EJB instance

1.7—Retrieving and using a persisted EJB reference

1.12—Improving your client-side EJB lookup code

1.9 *Comparing two EJB references for equality*

◆ ***Problem***

An EJB client has two EJB references and needs to determine if they are references to the same bean.

◆ ***Background***

A client that uses many EJBs may encounter a situation that requires it to know whether multiple EJB references point to the same bean instance. For example, you may need to know if two entity beans encapsulate the same data, or if two session bean references are identical. Clients cannot use an `equals()` method from an EJB reference because of the nature of EJB deployment. EJB references point to stub objects that may be different stub instances yet point to the same EJB. An `equals()` invocation is not guaranteed to return the correct value.

◆ *Recipe*

Use the `isIdentical()` method from the remote or local interface to compare EJB references. The client program in listing 1.15 creates and compares several `EquityBean` entity EJB instances. A stock symbol makes an `EquityBean` instance unique.

Listing 1.15   A method that compares EJB references

```
public void runExample()
{
     Equity equity1 = null;
     Equity equity2 = null;
     String symbol  = "ACME";
     String description = "ACME Corp";

     try
     {

       equity1 = findEquity( symbol, description );
       equity2 = findEquity( symbol, description );

       System.out.println("Does equity1 equal equity2: " +
                          equity1.isIdentical(equity2) );

       symbol = "CDE";
       description = "CDE Corp";
       equity1 = findEquity( symbol, description );

       symbol = "ACME";
       description = "ACME Corp";
       equity2 = findEquity( symbol, description );

       System.out.println("Does equity1 equal equity2: " +
                          equity1.isIdentical(equity2) );

     }
     catch( Exception e ) {
        e.printStackTrace();
     }
   }
}
```

Comparison
returns true

Comparison
returns false

◆ *Discussion*

When an EJB client retrieves or creates an EJB reference, the EJB container provides a stub object reference that points to the actual bean. That means that the reference contained by the client is actually a reference to the EJB stub object used by the container. Therefore, if you have more than one reference to an EJB, you could have two different stub objects that reference the same EJB. If you were to compare the references using the `equals()` method, it might return false, even if the stubs point to the same EJB. To solve this problem, EJB references implement the `isIdentical()` method. This method compares the two objects (the invoker and the parameter) to see if they both eventually point to the same EJB (through the stub).

1.10 Using reflection with an EJB

◆ **Problem**

You want to examine an EJB using reflection in order to determine its methods, method parameters, and other information.

◆ **Background**

In your EJB application, you would like to examine an EJB reference using reflection. However, since an EJB reference is actually a reference to a stub object in the EJB container (pointing to an EJB), you cannot examine the actual EJB itself. Or you might only have a reference to the EJB home object and you want to determine the EJB's available business methods before looking up or creating one. Using reflection on an EJB reference will not work because the reference points to an EJB stub object inside the EJB container, not to the EJB itself.

◆ **Recipe**

EJB home references implement the `EJBHome` interface, which declares a method `getEJBMetaData()`. This method returns an instance of the `EJBMetaData` class, which provides information about the EJB belonging to the home object. The `Client` class in listing 1.16 demonstrates how to use the `EJBMetaData` instance describing an EJB.

Listing 1.16   Client.java

```
public class Client
{
  private String url;
  private String symbol;
  private String description;
  private EJBHome home;
```

```
public void runExample() {
    Equity equity = null;
    Context ctx = null;

    try
    {
        ctx = getInitialContext();
        home = ( EJBHome ) ctx.lookup( "metadata.equityHome" );
        home = ( EJBHome )
                    javax.rmi.PortableRemoteObject.narrow( home,
                    EJBHome.class);
```
Retrieves the EJB home interface and narrows it

```
        EJBMetaData metaData =
                    home.getEJBMetaData();   ◁—
```
Acquires the EJBMetaData instance from the home object

```
        Class homeClass =
                    metaData.getHomeInterfaceClass();
        Class remoteClass =
                    metaData.getRemoteInterfaceClass();
```
Uses the metadata to get the home and remote class objects

```
        System.out.println("---------[ MetaData Info ]-----------");
        System.out.println("Home Class Type:"+homeClass.getName());
        System.out.println("Remote Class Type:" +
                                    remoteClass.getName());

        home = ( EJBHome )
            javax.rmi.PortableRemoteObject.narrow( home, homeClass );

        System.out.println("Primary Key  Type:"
                + metaData.getPrimaryKeyClass().getName();
        System.out.println("Is this a Session "
                + "Bean:"+metaData.isSession());
     System.out.println("Is this a Stateless Session Bean:"
                + metaData.isStatelessSession());
```
Determines if the EJB is an entity, stateful session, or stateless session bean

```
        Method[] methods =
                homeClass.getDeclaredMethods();
        Method[] remoteMethods =
                remoteClass.getDeclaredMethods();
```
Uses reflection to determine methods

```
        System.out.println("---------[ Home Methods ]-----------");
        for( int i = 0; i < methods.length; i++)
        {
            System.out.println("Method Found:"+methods[i].getName());
            Class[] params = remoteMethods[i].getParameterTypes();
            System.out.println("  Has "+params.length+" Parameters");
            for(int j = 0;j < params.length; j++)
            {
                System.out.println("    Param:"+params[j].getName());
            }
        }
        System.out.println("---------[ Home Methods ]--------\n\n");
```

```
      System.out.println("---------[ Remote Methods ]-------");
      for(int i = 0; i < remoteMethods.length; i++)
      {
        System.out.println("\nMethod "
            + "Found:"+remoteMethods[i].getName());
        Class[] params=remoteMethods[i].getParameterTypes();
        for(int j = 0; j < params.length; j++)
        {
          System.out.println("       Param:"+params[j].getName());
        }
      }
      System.out.println("-----[ Remote Methods ]--------\n\n");
    }
    catch(Exception e) {
      e.printStackTrace();
    }
    System.out.println("End of the example...\n");
  }
```

◆ *Discussion*

The EJBMetaData class is intended to be used by tool developers. For example, an integrated development environment (IDE) application or deployer tool can use the metadata from an EJB for a richer user experience for the EJB application developer .

However, using the EJBMetaData class, you can expose your EJB instances to the reflection API. This allows you to use reflection with EJBs for the same advantages and decoupling as you would for normal applications.

1.11 *Invoking an EJB from an applet*

◆ *Problem*

You want to invoke an EJB from an applet.

◆ *Background*

Java applets can be useful front ends to an EJB application. Unlike servlets, JSPs, or standalone Java applications, applets can easily contact a single remote host (the one that delivered it to the user). To contact an EJB from an applet, you need to package some special classes for it to function correctly. In addition, you must consider the special security restrictions imposed on an applet.

◆ *Recipe*

Due to execution restrictions and environment, you have to take specific factors
into account when developing and deploying an applet from which you want to
invoke an EJB. The simple applet in listing 1.17 contacts a session bean to start a
business function.

Listing 1.17   EJBApplet.java

```java
import javax.swing.*;
import java.awt.event.*;
import java.awt.*;
import java.util.*;
import javax.naming.*;
import javax.ejb.*;
import java.rmi.*;

public class EJBApplet extends JApplet
{
  private JButton button = null;

  public EJBApplet(){}

  public void init()
  {
    setSize( new Dimension( 400,100 ) );

    button = new JButton( "Start" );

    button.addActionListener( new ActionListener()
        {
            public void actionPerformed( ActionEvent event )
            {
              callEJB();
            }
        }
    );

    getContentPane().setLayout( new BorderLayout() );
    getContentPane().add( button, BorderLayout.CENTER );
  }

  public void callEJB()
  {
    try
    {
      InitialContext ctx = getInitialContext();

      SampleSessionHome home =
        ( SampleSessionHome) PortableRemoteObject.narrow(
          ctx.lookup( "ejb/sampleSession" ), SampleSessionHome.class );
      SampleSession bean = home.create();      Calls the
      bean.doProcess();                        SampleSessionBean EJB
```

```
    }catch( Exception e )
    {
      e.printStackTrace();
    }
  }

  private InitialContext getInitialContext() throws Exception
  {
    Properties props = new Properties();          Builds the URL to the
                                                  applet's parent host
    String theHost = getCodeBase().getHost();
    props.setProperty( Context.PROVIDER_URL, theHost + ":7001" );
    props.setProperty( Context.INITIAL_CONTEXT_FACTORY,
                "weblogic.jndi.WLInitialContextFactory" );

    return new InitialContext( props );          Completes the JNDI
  }                                              environment for the
}                                                Weblogic container
```

This applet uses the Swing user interface (UI) components, so the Java plug-in must be installed in your browser for it to work. (Go to http://java.sun.com/ docs/books/tutorial/information/examples.html#plugin for more information on installing the plug-in.) The HTML used to start the applet should also provide the necessary dependent JAR files needed for execution. We created the HTML shown in listing 1.18 by using the plug-in HTML converter program.

Listing 1.18   HTML file for the EJBApplet class

```
<html>
<!--"CONVERTED_APPLET"-->
<!-- HTML CONVERTER -->
<OBJECT
    classid = "clsid:8AD9C840-044E-11D1-B3E9-00805F499D93"
    codebase = "http://java.sun.com/products/plugin/autodl/jinstall-1_4-
  windows-i586.cab#Version=1,4,0,0"
    WIDTH = 400 HEIGHT = 100 >                      Packages
    <PARAM NAME = CODE VALUE = "EJBApplet" >        necessary classes
    <PARAM NAME = CODEBASE VALUE = "." >            for the applet
    <PARAM NAME = ARCHIVE VALUE = "necessaryClasses.jar" >  ◁─┘
    <PARAM NAME = "type"
          VALUE = "application/x-java-applet;version=1.4">
    <PARAM NAME = "scriptable" VALUE = "false">

</OBJECT>

<!--
<APPLET CODE = "applet.EJBApplet" CODEBASE = "."
    ARCHIVE = "necessaryClasses.jar" WIDTH = 400 HEIGHT = 100>
```

```
</APPLET>
-->
<!--"END_CONVERTED_APPLET"-->

</html>
```

◆ *Discussion*

Notice that the applet code used to look up the EJB is very similar to what you find in other remote clients. However, remember that applets can contact only a single remote host—the host that contains the applet class files. For this example, we assume the EJB container also resides on this host and that the applet can therefore contact it. If the applet was a signed applet, it could contact other hosts. To ensure that this applet creates the correct JNDI environment for the InitialContext instance, we use the getCodeBase() method to retrieve the correct URL information.

The second important item for this example is contained in the HTML used to launch the applet. An applet that launches an EJB is going to need the EJB classes (stubs and interfaces), as well as vendor-specific classes used to create the JNDI environment. For instance, our applet uses Weblogic classes. All the necessary classes should be packaged into a JAR file or files and listed in the ARCHIVE attribute of the applet HTML.

We created our HTML file by running a simple HTML file through the Java plug-in HTML converter utility. Doing this generated the necessary browser tags that force a client download of the Java plug-in (which the applet requires).

When you are developing applets that must contact EJBs, consider developing a servlet for the applet. When the applet needs information contained or created by an EJB, it can contact the servlet, which will handle the actual EJB work. Using a servlet decouples your applet from the EJB container, building in more flexibility for your applet. In addition, browsers will have to download less code (your code and third-party JARs) when the applet contacts a servlet rather than an EJB container.

◆ *See also*

1.2—Invoking a remote EJB from another EJB

1.3—Accessing EJBs from a servlet

1.4—Invoking an EJB from a JavaServer Page

1.12 Improving your client-side EJB lookup code

◆ *Problem*

You want to improve the performance of a client that makes multiple EJB lookup invocations.

◆ *Background*

Typical EJB applications make use of a client layer that invokes one or many EJBs several times. This is true for many web applications as well. When your client layer must use a particular bean multiple times, you'll want to make an effort to improve the performance of the JNDI call that looks up the bean. In addition, it would be nice to reduce duplicated code.

◆ *Recipe*

To improve client performance, create a utility object that encapsulates the JNDI lookup of EJB home object reference. In addition to performing home lookups, the utility object can cache the home reference for reuse. For example, listing 1.19 contains a utility object that looks up the home object for an EJB `UserBean`.

Listing 1.19 UserUtil.java

```
import javax.naming.NamingException;
import javax.naming.InitialContext;
import javax.rmi.PortableRemoteObject;

import java.util.Hashtable;

public class UserUtil
{
    private static EquityHome remoteHome = null;

    public static EquityHome getHome( Hashtable env )
                        throws NamingException
    {
        if( remoteHome == null )
        {
            InitialContext initialContext = null;

            if( env == null )
                initialContext = new InitialContext();
            else
                initialContext = new InitialContext( env );

            try
```

Tests for an existing EJB home reference

Builds an InitialContext object with or without environment

```
        {
            Object obj = initialContext.lookup(EquityHome.JNDI_NAME);    ◁─┐
            remoteHome = (EquityHome)
                PortableRemoteObject.narrow(objRef, UserHome.class);
                                                               Uses the JNDI name
        } catch(Exception e) {                                  declared in the EJB
                //handle error                                    home interface
        }
    }
    return remoteHome;
}
}
```

◆ *Discussion*

The utility class in this recipe declares a single static method that you can use with
or without an environment for the internal InitialContext instance. This
method looks up the EJB home reference after checking its class member variable
for an already set value. Since the home variable is static, all instances of the utility
class will share a discovered home reference.

Building a utility class like this one improves EJB client code by providing convenience methods for EJB lookup code, reducing duplicate code, and increasing
performance by caching the EJB home object reference. If you know that this is
only a local EJB, you don't have to narrow the home reference.

To further improve this class, you can add a static method to retrieve local
home interfaces. If you don't want to write a new utility class for each EJB, you
could instead create a generic utility class that contains static methods and static
variables (for home object caching) for each bean. In that case, one class encapsulates all of your EJB lookup code.

◆ *See also*

2.2—Adding and customizing the JNDI name for the home interface
2.7—Facilitating bean lookup with a utility object

Code generation
with XDoclet

"It's so beautifully arranged on the plate—you know someone's fingers have been all over it."

—*Julia Child*

Developing EJBs today entails the creation of a bean class, multiple interfaces, possible helper data access classes, primary key classes, and even lookup utility classes. In addition, each new bean requires changes and additions to the XML descriptor. With each new bean developed, the possibility for out-of-synch files increases. For example, a change to an EJB local interface would require similar changes to the remote interface, the implementation class, utility classes (data access object, value objects, etc.), a facade class, and the XML deployment descriptor.

Now, take that single change and multiply it across all your EJBs. The final result is that a development team must manage the synchronization of multiple files across multiple beans in order to keep the most basic tasks, such as compilation and deployment, working successfully. Without a doubt, experienced developers can ultimately handle this file management problem, but you must also consider the development time consumed by the trivial task of repeating code from interface files to implementation files. Time is a valuable commodity, and most projects struggle to have enough in all phases.

Increasingly, developers are turning to tools that automate much of bean development. For instance, more and more tools provide support for descriptor generation and manipulation. Rather than cover the multitude of IDE tools, we've chosen to cover XDoclet, an open-source tool that is rapidly gaining acceptance. Simple and easy, XDoclet saves you time and energy while generating excellent code.

In this chapter, we present the most common uses of XDoclet, including the following tasks:

- Generating EJB interfaces
- Adding JNDI names to your home interfaces
- Maintaining the XML descriptor
- Creating value objects for entity beans
- Creating primary key classes
- Customizing XDoclet tags with Ant properties
- Generating a utility object
- Adding security roles to the bean source
- Creating method permission XML
- Generating finder methods
- Creating the XML for ejbSelect methods
- Adding home methods to home interfaces

- Generating entity relation XML
- Generating XML descriptors for message-driven EJBs

An XDoclet appetizer

XDoclet requires the use of Ant, a build tool from Apache, which you can find at http://ant.apache.org. This chapter assumes that you have a working knowledge of Ant, including writing build.xml files for compiling and packaging your EJB files. If you have not used Ant for a build system, you can find specific recipes for those tasks in chapter 9.

Specifically, XDoclet relies on the Ant task `<ejbdoclet/>`. Once inserted into the build.xml, the `<ejbdoclet/>` task allows you to specify subtasks for file generation, method construction, and more. Tasks execute a section of code within Ant. Ant contains many predefined tasks for such jobs as generating documentation and compiling, but it lets you build your own tasks as well. In fact, the `<ejbdoclet/>` task is a custom task that executes certain code in the XDoclet library.

For this book, we used XDoclet beta version 1.2. Table 2.1 lists the JAR file dependencies needed by this version of XDoclet, as well as the URL for their download. The JAR files listed in table 2.1 must be in the classpath of the `<ejbdoclet/>` task added to your build.xml file before you execute the `<ejbdoclet/>` Ant task. (Some of the JAR files will not be needed if you don't use certain features of the 1.2 version of XDoclet.)

Table 2.1   The JAR file dependencies for the 1.2 version of XDoclet. These jars should be placed in the `<ejbdoclet/>` Ant task classpath in order for you to use XDoclet 1.2.

Framework/application	Needed JAR files	URL
Ant 1.5	ant.jar	http://jakarta.apache.org/ant/
Log4j 1.13	log4j-1.1.3-jar	http://jakarta.apache.org/log4j/
Commons logging	commons-logging-1.0.jar	http://jakarta.apache.org/log4j/
XML APIs	xml-apis-2.0.2.jar	http://xml.apache.org/xerces2-j/
Velocity	velocity-1.4-dev.jar	http://jakarta.apache.org/velocity/index.html
JUnit	junit-3.7.jar	http://junit.org

After your environment is set up, you need to perform only three steps to generate code:

1 Add the necessary XDoclet tags to your source files (similar to JavaDoc comment tags).

2 Modify the `<ejbdoclet/>` task in the build.xml file to generate the desired files.

3 Execute the Ant task using a command similar to ant `ejbdoclet`.

With three steps, XDoclet can make your EJB development more efficient and streamlined.

Before moving on to the actual recipes, let's quickly examine the pieces of the `<ejbdoclet/>` task contained in the build.xml file. The task basically contains three sections: setup, source file selection, and subtask declaration. The following XML is only a portion of a larger build.xml file and shows an example `<ejbdoclet/>` task definition:

```
<target name="ejbdoclet" depends="init">

<taskdef name="ejbdoclet" classname="xdoclet.modules.ejb.EjbDocletTask">
    <classpath>
        <fileset dir="${xdoclet.lib.dir}" includes="*.jar"/>
    </classpath>
</taskdef>
                                       Defines the new <ejbdoclet/> task>  ❶

    <ejbdoclet  destdir="${src}" ejbspec="2.0" >   ❷ Sets up
                                                       the task
      <fileset dir="${src}">
        <include name="**/*Bean.java" />
      </fileset>

      <remoteinterface/>                  Adds subtasks to  ❸
      <homeinterface/>                    generate code
      <localhomeinterface/>
      <homeinterface/>

      <deploymentdescriptor destdir="${build}/ejb/META-INF" />

    </ejbdoclet>
</target>
```

❶ The first section of the target declares the task and provides the name of the implementing class that will perform the functions required of the task. The task definition is also responsible for setting up the classpath for the task. In this case, we have the necessary XDoclet JAR files (see table 2.1) in the XDoclet lib directory. The property `xdoclet.lib.dir` should be defined earlier in the build.xml file containing this target.

② Next, the `<ejbdoclet/>` tag is started by specifying the source directory, the generated files destination directory, and the EJB specification version that the build.xml file should use. After starting the task, the next section defines the set of source files the build.xml file should examine for possible source-generation tags. Using the `<fileset/>` tag, not only can you specify which files to include, but you can also exclude files. For instance, the sample shows a file set of Java source files that end with *Bean.java*.

③ Before closing the `<ejbdoclet/>` task, you can specify subtasks that actually perform the source examination and generation of code. The declaration in this sample generates the remote, home, local home, and local interfaces for bean classes with the appropriate XDoclet tags.

XDoclet provides many more features than shown in this simple example. This chapter contains recipes that examine the most useful or commonly used features of XDoclet. We highlight the XDoclet JavaDoc tags in bold to distinguish them from the remaining code. In addition, we show generated code where appropriate.

We hope this chapter will encourage you to look further into XDoclet for your EJB development. Refer to the XDoclet website at http://XDoclet.sourceforge.net for downloads, examples, and more documentation. In addition, you can refer to the Ant website (http://jakarta.apache.org) to learn more about using Ant or creating build.xml files. For more information about creating an Ant task, or using existing tasks, check the Ant documentation at http://jakarta.apache.org/ant/manual/index.html, or check out the excellent book *Java Development with Ant*, from Manning Publications by Erik Hatcher and Steve Loughran.

2.1 Generating home, remote, local, and local home interfaces

◆ **Problem**

You want to generate the EJB home and remote interfaces.

◆ **Background**

While developing bean classes and interfaces, you must spend too much time keeping your interface file in synch with the implementation class. After developing the bean class, you would like to generate all the necessary interfaces for deployment. This includes the remote, home, local, and local home interfaces.

Likewise, after any modifications to the bean class, you want the interfaces to be updated similarly, and in the correct way for the specific interface.

◆ *Recipe*

To generate the interfaces (home, local home, remote, and local), you must do two things. You need to add the appropriate XDoclet tags to the bean implementation class, and then add the correct subtasks to the `<ejbdoclet/>` task in your build.xml file. This recipe covers adding create and business methods to the correct interfaces. Other methods, such as finder methods, are covered in later recipes.

A session bean example

The session bean example in listing 2.1 illustrates how to document a bean class in order to generate both remote and local interfaces. The XDoclet tags are shown in bold. Notice that assigned values for the tags always use double quotes.

Listing 2.1 UserBean.java

```
package ch2;

import javax.ejb.*;

/**
 * @ejb.bean type="Stateful"          Declares the
 *           view-type="both"         bean attributes
 */
public class UserBean implements SessionBean
{
  private String name = null;

  public UserBean(){}
  public void setSessionContext( SessionContext context) {}

  /**
   * @ejb.create-method          ◁
   */
  public void create(){}
  public void ejbCreate() {}
  public void ejbRemove() {}         Indicates
  public void ejbLoad() {}           which type of
  public void ejbStore() {}          methods to
  public void ejbActivate() {}       generate
  public void ejbPassivate() {}

  /**
   * @ejb.interface-method          ◁
   */
  public void setName( String value )
  {
    this.name = value;
```

```
}
/**
 * @ejb.interface-method
 */
public String getName()
{
   return name;
}
}
```

An entity bean example

The entity bean example in listing 2.2 illustrates the same tags as the previous session bean example.

Listing 2.2   DataBean.java

```
package ch2;

import javax.ejb.*;
/**
 * @ejb.bean type="CMP"              Declares the bean
 *           view-type="both"        attributes
 */
public abstract class DataBean implements EntityBean
{
     public void setEntityContext( EntityContext context) {}
     public void unsetEntityContext( ) {}

     public void ejbRemove() {}
     public void ejbLoad() {}
     public void ejbStore() {}
     public void ejbActivate() {}
     public void ejbPassivate() {}

     /**
      * @ejb.create-method
      *
      */
     public void ejbCreateData( String data1, String data2 )    Indicates
     {                                                           which type of
       setBigData(data1);                                        methods to
       setSmallData(data2);                                      generate
     }

     /**
      * @ejb.interface-method
      *
      */
     public void getAllData()
     {
```

```
      return getBigData() + " " + getSmallData();
   }

   /**
    * @ejb.interface-method
    */
   public abstract String getBigData();

   /**
    * @ejb.interface-method
    */
   public abstract String getSmallData();

   /**
    * @ejb.interface-method
    */
   public abstract void setBigData( String data );

   /**
    * @ejb.interface-method
    */
   public abstract void setSmallData( String data );
}
```

Modifying the build.xml

As shown in listing 2.3, you add the <ejbdoclet/> Ant task in your build.xml file
with the appropriate subtasks that will actually perform the code generation.

Listing 2.3   Sample Build.xml

```
<target name="ejbdoclet" depends="init">
  <taskdef name="ejbdoclet" classname="xdoclet.modules.ejb.EjbDocletTask">
    <classpath>
        <fileset dir="${xdoclet.lib.dir}" includes="*.jar"/>
    </classpath>
  </taskdef>

  <ejbdoclet  destdir="${src}" ejbspec="2.0" >

    <fileset dir="${src}">
       <include name="**/*Bean.java" />
    </fileset>

    <remoteinterface pattern="{0}Remote"/>
    <homeinterface/>                          Add subtasks for
    <localinterface/>                         code generation
    <localhomeinterface/>

  </ejbdoclet>
</target>
```

Notice that this target is only part of a larger build.xml file. In your build.xml, you need to configure the ${src} and ${xdoclet.lib.dir} properties for the task to work.

◆ *Discussion*

Examining each bean source, you should first notice the class-level JavaDoc comments. The class-level JavaDoc contains the XDoclet tags that describe the bean and specifies the interfaces that should be generated. The @ejb.bean tag describes the EJB defined in the source file. It contains two properties—type and view-type—that are involved in the interface generation. The type property describes the type of this EJB; it can be Stateful, Stateless, CMP, or BMP. The code generator needs this information in order to properly provide super interfaces for the generated interfaces. The second property, view-type, indicates which interfaces should be generated. Its possible values are local, remote, or both. By specifying both, you ensure that all four interfaces will be produced.

However, these two properties only help XDoclet to generate the interface declaration; you still must describe the methods that go into each interface. To do this, you need to make use of the @ejb.interface-method and @ejb.create-method XDoclet tags. As shown in the source, these tags are used to mark bean methods for declaration in the appropriate interfaces. Create methods are routed to the home interfaces, and interface methods are declared in the remote and local interfaces. Table 2.2 summarizes the tags that generate methods into the interfaces.

Table 2.2   Other tags used to specify methods for EJB interfaces

Tag	Description
@ejb.interface-method	Declares a method to be a business method
@ejb.create-method	Declares a method to be an ejbCreate method
@ejb.home-method	Declares a method to be a home method
@ejb.finder	Used to define a finder method for the home and local home interfaces
@ejb.select	Declares a method to be an ejbSelect method
@ejb.pk-field	When used properly, creates a findByPrimaryKey method in the home interface (see recipe 2.5)

Two method types noticeably absent from this discussion are finder and select methods for entity beans. We show these two method types in greater detail in later recipes in this chapter.

Finally, the additional subtasks must be specified in the `<ejbdoclet/>` task itself. As you can see in the recipe, we add tasks to generate all four interfaces for the beans. Indeed, all four will be generated because we also specified the view-type as both.

In addition, by default XDoclet will add a component name and JNDI name for both the local home and home interfaces as a `public final static` member variable. You can use the variable to make your client code more maintainable. By default, the names correspond to the fully qualified name of the bean class (using / instead of .).

Rather than show all four generated interfaces for each bean, we just show the local interfaces for each. For the session bean, the `getName()` and `setName()` methods will be in the local and remote interfaces. The session bean's home and local home interfaces will contain a `create()` method. Listing 2.4 contains the session bean's generated entire remote interface (comments and all).

Listing 2.4   Generated by XDoclet, User.java

```
/*
 * Generated by XDoclet - Do not edit!
 */
package ch2;

/**
 * Remote interface for ch2.User.
 */
public interface User
    extends javax.ejb.EJBObject
{

    public java.lang.String getName(  )
       throws java.rmi.RemoteException;

    public void setName( java.lang.String value )
       throws java.rmi.RemoteException;

}
```

The entity bean's home and local home interfaces will contain a `findByPrimaryKey()` method. Its remote and local interface will contain `getFirstName()`, `setFirstName()`, `getLastName()`, `setLastName()`, and `getName()`. Listing 2.5 contains the entity bean's generated remote interface

Listing 2.5   Generated by XDoclet, Data.java

```
/*
 * Generated by XDoclet - Do not edit!
 */
package ch2;

/**
 * Remote interface for ch2.Data.
 */
public interface Data
    extends javax.ejb.EJBObject
{
    public void getAllData( )
        throws java.rmi.RemoteException;

    public java.lang.String getBigData( )
        throws java.rmi.RemoteException;

    public java.lang.String getSmallData( )
        throws java.rmi.RemoteException;

    public void setBigData( java.lang.String data )
        throws java.rmi.RemoteException;

    public void setSmallData( java.lang.String data )
        throws java.rmi.RemoteException;
}
```

◆ **See also**

2.2—Adding and customizing the JNDI name for the home interface

2.5—Generating a primary key class

2.11—Generating finder methods for entity home interfaces

2.2 Adding and customizing the JNDI name for the home interface

◆ **Problem**

You want a good way to store the JNDI name of a bean for easy retrieval to aid in bean lookup.

◆ *Background*

You can use XDoclet to add a `public static final` member variable to the home interfaces that it generates to store the JNDI name of the bean. Without customization, it provides a default value for this name. By specifying the JNDI name in the home interface, you can modify it without changing your bean lookup code.

◆ *Recipe*

Use the recipe shown in recipe 2.1 (listing 2.4) to generate the home interface. However, change the class-level JavaDoc to look like the following and specify the JNDI name (the changes are shown in bold):

```
/**
 * @ejb.bean type="Stateful"
 *           jndi-name="ejb/UserBean"
 *           local-jndi-name="ejb/UserBeanLocal"
 *           view-type="both"
 */
public class UserBean implements SessionBean
{
```

No changes need to be made to the build.xml file from the target shown in recipe 2.1.

◆ *Discussion*

By including the JNDI lookup name as a `public static final` member variable in the home interface, you give your code a permanent, safe way of discovering the JNDI name for EJB lookup. Using this method, you don't have to hardcode a name in the lookup implementation. The resulting home interface has the following lines added to it:

```
public static final String
                COMP_NAME="comp/env/ejb/ch2/User";
public static final String JNDI_NAME="ejb/UserBean";
```

The resulting local home interface contains a different name (as specified in the bean source):

```
public static final String
                COMP_NAME="java:comp/env/ejb/ch2/UserLocal";
public static final String JNDI_NAME="ejb/UserBeanLocal";
```

Without customization, XDoclet will enter names using the package name of the bean class. For instance, the UserBean JNDI name would have been ch2/UserBean.

When looking up an EJB home interface via JNDI, you normally would use code similar to the following:

```
InitialContext ctx = new InitialContext();
UserHome home = (UserHome) ctx.lookup( "ejb/UserBean" );
```

By adding the JNDI name to the home interface, your code can change to something like this:

```
InitialContext ctx = new InitialContext();
UserHome home = (UserHome) ctx.lookup( UserHome.JNDI_NAME );
```

◆ See also

2.1—Generating home, remote, local, and local home interfaces

2.3 Keeping your EJB deployment descriptor current

◆ Problem

You want to generate the EJB deployment descriptor and update it as the EJB source files change.

◆ Background

When developing EJBs, you have a multitude of changes to the bean class that affect the final deployment descriptor of the bean. Even if you generate the deployment descriptor once, you may have to change it each time you alter a bean class, interface, or persistent feature. In addition, changes to security roles, method permissions, and EJB relationships require you to modify the XML descriptor. Generating the deployment XML is only part of an important task. XDoclet will help you maintain this file by updating it as your beans change and develop.

◆ Recipe

To have XDoclet generate your deployment descriptor, add the `<deploymentde-scriptor/>` subtask to your `<ejbdoclet/>` task in the build.xml file. (See the section "An XDoclet appetizer" at the beginning of this chapter for information about XDoclet setup and the build.xml file.) The `<ejbdoclet/>` task shown in listing 2.6 uses the descriptor subtask.

Listing 2.6   Sample Build.xml

```
<target name="ejbdoclet" depends="init">
 <taskdef name="ejbdoclet"
         classname="xdoclet.modules.ejb.EjbDocletTask">
   <classpath>
       <fileset dir="${xdoclet.lib.dir}" includes="*.jar"/>
   </classpath>
 </taskdef>

  <ejbdoclet  destdir="${src}" ejbspec="2.0" >

    <fileset dir="${src}">
       <include name="**/*Bean.java" />              Adds the subtask for
    </fileset>                                           XML generation

    <deploymentdescriptor destdir="${build}/ejb/META-INF" />   ◁──┘

  </ejbdoclet>
</target>
```

Let's examine the class declaration for a session bean (used from recipes 2.1 and 2.2). However, this time we also include the bean name (shown in bold):

```
/**
 * @ejb.bean type="Stateful"
 *        name="UserBean"
 *        jndi-name="ejb/UserBean"
 *        local-jndi-name="ejb/UserBeanLocal"
 *        view-type="both"
 */
public class UserBean implements SessionBean
```

XDoclet uses this information to build the basic deployment descriptor for each bean. The XML section shown in listing 2.7 is what XDoclet generated for this bean (we have shown only the portion of the XML that contains the UserBean).

Listing 2.7   Deployment descriptor generated by XDoclet

```
<?xml version="1.0" encoding="UTF-8"?>
<!DOCTYPE ejb-jar PUBLIC "-//Sun Microsystems, Inc.//DTD Enterprise
   JavaBeans 2.0//EN" "http://java.sun.com/dtd/ejb-jar_2_0.dtd">

<ejb-jar >

   <description><![CDATA[No Description.]]></description>
   <display-name>Generated by XDoclet</display-name>

   <enterprise-beans>

      <!-- Session Beans -->
      <session >
```

```
        <description><![CDATA[]]></description>

        <ejb-name>UserBean</ejb-name>

        <home>ch2.UserBeanHome</home>
        <remote>ch2.UserBean</remote>
        <local-home>ch2.UserBeanLocalHome</local-home>
        <local>ch2.UserBeanLocal</local>
        <ejb-class>ch2.UserBean</ejb-class>
        <session-type>Stateful</session-type>
        <transaction-type>Container</transaction-type>

     </session>

  </enterprise-beans>
```

◆ *Discussion*

The `<deploymentdescriptor/>` subtask tells XDoclet to generate the deployment descriptor for the beans it has examined from the file set described in the `<fileset/>` tag. XDoclet will also take care of including any other additions in the descriptor along with the actual bean description. As long as you keep this subtask in your `<ejbdoclet/>` task, XDoclet will generate or regenerate the XML deployment descriptor for each modified bean class in the file set. As you can tell, all you need to provide is the destination directory for the XML file.

XDoclet can also generate the numerous other pieces of the ejb-jar.xml file for your beans. This includes security roles, method permission, and related EJBs. As you add more XDoclet JavaDoc comments to your bean source files, more generated XML will appear. Many of the additional tags are covered in other recipes.

◆ *See also*

2.8—Generating vendor-specific deployment descriptors

2.4 *Creating value objects for your entity beans*

◆ *Problem*

You want to generate a value object for your entity beans.

◆ *Background*

An accepted practice for improving EJB application performance and for separating client, business, and data layers is to make use of value objects for entity beans.

Value objects create a decoupled view of entity beans and also shield clients from
back-end code changes. This class can represent the bean in every way and be
passed back to the client for a read-only snapshot of the entity data.

Creating value objects for entity beans adds one more file to the list of multiple
files that developers must create for each bean. As with other generated files,
XDoclet will help you maintain this file with changes as your beans change.

◆ Recipe

Use the `@ejb.value-object` tag in the class-level JavaDoc for entity beans needing
a value object. For example, the section of the entity bean `ItemBean` source shown
in listing 2.8 uses this tag. The new tag is shown in bold; reference the previous
recipes for information about the others. Don't worry about the tags `@ejb.pk-
field` and `@ejb.persistence` for now; we cover those in the next recipe.

Listing 2.8   ItemBean.java

```java
package ch2;

import javax.ejb.*;
/**
 * @ejb.bean type="CMP"
 *          name="ItemBean"
 *          jndi-name="ejb/ItemBean"
 *          view-type="both"
 *
 * @ejb.value-object
 *
 */
public abstract class ItemBean implements EntityBean
{
    public void setEntityContext( EntityContext context) {}
    public void unsetEntityContext( ) {}

    public void ejbRemove() {}
    public void ejbLoad() {}
    public void ejbStore() {}
    public void ejbActivate() {}
    public void ejbPassivate() {}

    /**
     * @ejb.create-method
     */
    public void ejbCreate( String id )
    {
     setID( id );
    }

    /**
```

```
   * @ejb.interface-method
   * @ejb.persistence
   * @ejb.pk-field
   */
  public abstract String getID();

 /**
  * @ejb.interface-method
  */
  public abstract String getType();

 /**
  * @ejb.interface-method
  */
  public abstract String setType();
}
```

In addition, you need to add the subtask `<valueobject/>` to your build.xml file in order for XDoclet to know it should generate the new class.

◆ *Discussion*

Listing 2.9 contains the generated value object class (including comments), reformatted for this chapter.

Listing 2.9   ItemBeanValue.java

```
/*
 * Generated file - Do not edit!
 */
package ch2;

import java.util.*;

/**
 * Value object for ItemBean.
 *
 */
public class ItemBeanValue extends java.lang.Object
                implements java.io.Serializable
{
   private java.lang.String iD;
   private boolean iDHasBeenSet = false;
   private java.lang.String type;
   private boolean typeHasBeenSet = false;

   private ch2.ItemBeanPK pk;

   public ItemBeanValue()
   {
        pk = new ch2.ItemBeanPK();
```

```
    }

    public ItemBeanValue( java.lang.String iD,
                          java.lang.String type )
    {
        this.iD = iD;
        iDHasBeenSet = true;
        this.type = type;
        typeHasBeenSet = true;
        pk = new ch2.ItemBeanPK(this.getID());
    }

    //TODO Cloneable is better than this !
    public ItemBeanValue( ItemBeanValue otherValue )
    {
        this.iD = otherValue.iD;
        iDHasBeenSet = true;
        this.type = otherValue.type;
        typeHasBeenSet = true;

        pk = new ch2.ItemBeanPK(this.getID());
    }

    public ch2.ItemBeanPK getPrimaryKey()
    {
        return pk;
    }

    public void setPrimaryKey( ch2.ItemBeanPK pk )
    {
        // it's also nice to update PK object - just in case
        // somebody would ask for it later...
        this.pk = pk;
    }

    public java.lang.String getID()
    {
        return this.iD;
    }

    public java.lang.String getType()
    {
        return this.type;
    }

    public String toString()
    {
        StringBuffer str = new StringBuffer("{");

        str.append("iD=" + getID() + " " + "type=" + getType());
        str.append('}');

        return(str.toString());
    }
```

Initializes the value object with data

Provides read-only access

```
/**
 *  A Value object has an identity if its
 *  attributes making its Primary Key
 *  have all been set.  One object without identity
 *  is never equal to any
 *  other object.
 *
 *  @return true if this instance have an identity.
 */
protected boolean hasIdentity()
{
    boolean ret = true;
    ret = ret && iDHasBeenSet;
    return ret;
}
public boolean equals(Object other)
{
    if ( ! hasIdentity() ) return false;
    if (other instanceof ItemBeanValue)
    {
        ItemBeanValue that = (ItemBeanValue) other;
        if ( ! that.hasIdentity() ) return false;
        boolean lEquals = true;
        if( this.iD == null )
        {
            lEquals = lEquals && ( that.iD == null );
        }
        else
        {
            lEquals = lEquals && this.iD.equals( that.iD );
        }

        lEquals = lEquals && isIdentical(that);

        return lEquals;
    }
    else
    {
    return false;
    }
}

public boolean isIdentical(Object other)
{
    if (other instanceof ItemBeanValue)
    {
        ItemBeanValue that = (ItemBeanValue) other;
        boolean lEquals = true;
        if( this.type == null )
        {
         lEquals = lEquals && ( that.type == null );
```

Implements equality testing

```
            }
            else
            {
             lEquals = lEquals && this.type.equals( that.type );
            }

            return lEquals;
        }
        else
        {
            return false;
        }
    }
    public int hashCode(){
        int result = 17;
      result = 37*result +
                ((this.iD != null) ? this.iD.hashCode() : 0);

      result = 37*result +
           ((this.type != null) ? this.type.hashCode() : 0);

        return result;
    }

}
```

The combination of the XDoclet tags and the `<ejbdoclet/>` subtask will cause
XDoclet to generate the value object for the entity bean. The generated class will
contain getters for all the data fields of the bean, as well as the primary key. When
used by a bean, the generated value object is a read-only snapshot of the entity
bean. It can therefore be passed to clients as a lightweight representation of the
bean. Value objects can also be used to separate a client's view to the data persistence model being used.

◆ *See also*

2.1—Generating home, remote, local, and local home interfaces

2.2—Adding and customizing the JNDI name for the home interface

2.5—Generating a primary key class

2.5 Generating a primary key class

◆ **Problem**

You want to generate a primary key class for your entity beans during development.

◆ **Background**

As you develop more and more entity beans, you find yourself also having to create the primary key class. As we emphasized in this chapter, having to code one more class just adds to the time it takes to develop a bean and increases your chances for having source files out of synch.

◆ **Recipe**

To have XDoclet generate a primary key class, use the `@ejb.pk` tag in your bean source file, use the `@ejb.pk-field` tag to denote an accessor for the primary key, and modify your `<ejbdoclet/>` task to include the `<entitypk/>` subtask. For instance, examine the `ItemBean` class shown in listing 2.10. The XDoclet tags applicable to this recipe are shown in bold; the others can be found in earlier recipes.

Listing 2.10   ItemBean.java

```
package ch2;

import javax.ejb.*;
/**
  * @ejb.bean type="CMP"
  *           name="ItemBean"
  *           jndi-name="ejb/ItemBean"
  *           view-type="both"
  *           primkey-field="ID";          ◁──┐  Identifies the
  * @ejb.pk          ◁──┐ Adds the primary key tag   primary key field
  */
public abstract class ItemBean implements EntityBean
{
     public void setEntityContext( EntityContext context) {}
     public void unsetEntityContext( ) {}

     public void ejbRemove() {}
     public void ejbLoad() {}
     public void ejbStore() {}
     public void ejbActivate() {}
     public void ejbPassivate() {}

     /**
      * @ejb.create-method
      */
```

```
   public void ejbCreate( String id )
   {
    setID( id );
   }
  /**
   * @ejb.interface-method
   * @ejb.persistence
   * @ejb.pk-field
   */
   public abstract String getID();
}
```

> Identifies the primary
> key getter method

Notice in addition to the placement of the specified tags that we included the
primkey-field attribute in the @ejb.bean tag at the class declaration level. Note
that you must also use the @ejb.persistence tag in combination with the
@ejb.pk-field tag.

◆ **Discussion**

The result of using these tags is a source file named ItemBeanPK.java (containing
the ItemBeanPK class). Listing 2.11 shows the generated code for this class.

Listing 2.11   ItemBeanPK.java

```
/*
 * Generated by XDoclet - Do not edit!
 */
package ch2;

/**
 * Primary key for ItemBean.
 */
public class ItemBeanPK extends java.lang.Object
   implements java.io.Serializable
{
   private int _hashCode = Integer.MIN_VALUE;
   private StringBuffer _toStringValue = null;

   public java.lang.String iD;

   public ItemBeanPK()
   {
   }

   public ItemBeanPK( java.lang.String iD )
   {
      this.iD = iD;
   }
```

```java
public java.lang.String getID()
{
    return iD;
}

public void setID(java.lang.String iD)
{
    this.iD = iD;
    _hashCode = Integer.MIN_VALUE;
}

public int hashCode()
{
    if( _hashCode == Integer.MIN_VALUE )
    {
        if (this.iD != null) _hashCode += this.iD.hashCode();
    }

    return _hashCode;
}

public boolean equals(Object obj)
{
    if( !(obj instanceof ch2.ItemBeanPK) )
        return false;

    ch2.ItemBeanPK pk = (ch2.ItemBeanPK)obj;
    boolean eq = true;

    if( obj == null )
    {
        eq = false;
    }
    else
    {
        if( this.iD == null &&
            ((ch2.ItemBeanPK)obj).getID() == null )
        {
            eq = true;
        }
        else
        {
            if( this.iD == null ||
                ((ch2.ItemBeanPK)obj).getID() == null )
            {
                eq = false;
            }
            else
            {
                eq = eq && this.iD.equals( pk.iD );
            }
        }
    }
}
```

```
        return eq;
    }
    /** @return String representation of
        this pk in the form of [.field1.field2.field3]. */
    public String toString()
    {
        if( _toStringValue == null )
        {
            _toStringValue = new StringBuffer("[.");
            _toStringValue.append(this.iD).append('.');
            _toStringValue.append(']');
        }

        return _toStringValue.toString();
    }

}
```

The generated primary key class contains a default constructor, an initialization constructor that accepts a `String ID` parameter, a getter method, a setter method, `hashcode()` and `equals()` methods, and a `toString()` method.

If you use the `@ejb.pk` tag without using the `@ejb.pk-field` tag, you generate a primary key file without the getter, setter, and initialization constructor.

◆ See also

2.1—Generating home, remote, local, and local home interfaces

2.6 *Avoiding hardcoded XDoclet tag values*

◆ Problem

You would like to centralize values in one place and not have to modify source files in order to update the values.

◆ Background

XDoclet is a great tool for generating necessary EJB files. In addition, it lets you specify values for the XML deployment descriptor and JNDI names for your beans. Using XDoclet with your development lets you automate and generate almost everything you need. However, as you add more XDoclet JavaDoc tags to your source files, you are specifying more values in code for things like JNDI names and bean names. Now you have many values spread out across many bean source files.

◆ *Recipe*

Use Ant properties in your XDoclet tags. Examine listing 2.12, which contains a subsection from a build.xml file. This subsection defines a property and the <ejbdoclet/> task.

Listing 2.12 Sample Build.xml

```xml
<property name="user.bean.jndi"
          value="ejb/session/UserBean"/>
```
Creates an Ant property

```xml
  <target name="ejbdoclet" depends="init">
   <taskdef name="ejbdoclet"
       classname="xdoclet.modules.ejb.EjbDocletTask">
       <classpath>
           <fileset dir="${xdoclet.lib.dir}" includes="*.jar"/>
       </classpath>

    </taskdef>

    <ejbdoclet  destdir="${src}" ejbspec="2.0" >

      <fileset dir="${src}">
        <include name="**/*Bean.java" />

      </fileset>

      <remoteinterface pattern="{0}Remote"/>
      <homeinterface/>
      <localhomeinterface/>
      <homeinterface/>

      <entitypk/>

      <deploymentdescriptor destdir="${build}/ejb/META-INF" />

    </ejbdoclet>
  </target>
```
Completes the remaining task

Notice the property `user.bean.jndi` at the top of the file. Now examine the class declaration for the UserBean; it uses the Ant property in the JNDI attribute of the @ejb.bean tag:

```java
/**
 * @ejb.bean type="Stateful"
 *        view-type="both"
 *        jndi-name="${user.bean.jndi}"
 *
 */
public class UserBean implements SessionBean{
```

◆ *Discussion*

When XDoclet attempts to generate the home interface for this bean, it will see that for the JNDI name it should use the value specified in the Ant property `user.bean.jndi`. Ant replaces the named property in the source file with the value contained in the build.xml file. Using this system, you can replace every hard-coded value in your source XDoclet JavaDoc tags with Ant property names. The advantage of this system is that it centralizes all of your property values into your build.xml file, and you no longer have to alter source code to change a value.

XDoclet allows you to specify everything about a bean in its source file. Not everything is included in this chapter, but the list includes security roles, EJB relationships, method permission, transactions, and more. By moving all the values of these various elements into Ant properties in the build.xml file, you create a centralized control of the various values that can be changed at build time in a single file.

◆ *See also*

2.1—Generating home, remote, local, and local home interfaces

2.2—Adding and customizing the JNDI name for the home interface

2.3—Keeping your EJB deployment descriptor current

2.7 *Facilitating bean lookup with a utility object*

◆ *Problem*

You want to generate a utility object to help with looking up the home interface of an EJB.

◆ *Background*

Two often-repeated tasks in an EJB application are the lookup of a bean's home interface and the subsequent creation of the bean. Developers sometimes handle these tasks by creating a static method that contains the lookup code for a particular bean. However, it is possible that this code also must change as a bean changes. The generated class will encapsulate all the code necessary for looking up the home interface of its parent EJB.

◆ *Recipe*

To generate a utility object, use the `@ejb.util` tag in the class-level JavaDoc of your bean and modify your `<ejbdoclet/>` task to include the `<utilityobject/>` subtask. This works for both entity and session beans. For example, examine the class declaration of the `UserBean`:

```
package ch2;

import javax.ejb.*;

/**
 * @ejb.bean type="Stateful"
 *         view-type="both"
 *
 * @ejb.util
 *
 */
public class UserBean implements SessionBean{
```

Listing 2.13 contains the build.xml used to generate the utility object.

Listing 2.13   Sample Build.xml

```
<target name="ejbdoclet" depends="init">
 <taskdef name="ejbdoclet" classname="xdoclet.modules.ejb.EjbDocletTask"  >
    <classpath>
        <fileset dir="${xdoclet.lib.dir}" includes="*.jar"/>
    </classpath>
 </taskdef>

  <ejbdoclet  destdir="${src}" ejbspec="2.0"  >

    <fileset dir="${src}">
        <include name="**/*Bean.java" />
    </fileset>

    <utilobject cacheHomes="true" />     ❶ Adds the utility
                                            object subtask
  </ejbdoclet>
</target>
```

❶ The `<utilobject/>` subtask tells XDoclet to search for source files containing the `@ejb.util` class-level JavaDoc tag and generate a utility object. Notice the subtask specifies an attribute `cacheHomes` equal to true. This attribute tells XDoclet to generate a utility object that caches the home object after the first lookup in order to improve performance. Listing 2.14 shows the generated utility class for this example (reformatted for this chapter).

Listing 2.14   UserUtil.java, generated by XDoclet

```java
/*
 * Generated by XDoclet - Do not edit!
 */
package ch2;

import javax.rmi.PortableRemoteObject;
import javax.naming.NamingException;
import javax.naming.InitialContext;

import java.util.Hashtable;

/**
 * Utility class for ch2.User.
 */
public class UserUtil
{
    /** Cached remote home (EJBHome). Uses lazy loading to obtain
    its value (loaded by getHome() methods). */
    private static ch2.UserHome cachedRemoteHome = null;

    /** Cached local home (EJBLocalHome). Uses lazy loading to obtain
    its value (loaded by getLocalHome() methods). */
    private static ch2.UserLocalHome cachedLocalHome = null;

    // Home interface lookup methods

    /**
     * Obtain remote home interface from default initial context
     * @return Home interface for ch2.User. Lookup using COMP_NAME
     */
    public static ch2.UserHome getHome() throws NamingException
    {
        if (cachedRemoteHome == null) {
            // Obtain initial context
            InitialContext initialContext = new InitialContext();
            try {
                java.lang.Object objRef =
                        initialContext.lookup(ch2.UserHome.COMP_NAME);
                cachedRemoteHome = (ch2.UserHome)
                    PortableRemoteObject.narrow(objRef,
                            ch2.UserHome.class);
            } finally {
                initialContext.close();
            }
        }
        return cachedRemoteHome;
    }

/**
 * Obtain remote home interface from parameterised initial context
 * @param environment Parameters to use for creating initial context
 * @return Home interface for ch2.User. Lookup using COMP_NAME
```

```
*/
   public static ch2.UserHome getHome( Hashtable environment )
                              throws NamingException
   {
      // Obtain initial context
      InitialContext initialContext =
                new InitialContext(environment);
      try {
         java.lang.Object objRef =
                initialContext.lookup(ch2.UserHome.COMP_NAME);
         return (ch2.UserHome)
            PortableRemoteObject.narrow(objRef, ch2.UserHome.class);
      } finally {
         initialContext.close();
      }
   }

/**
* Obtain local home interface from default initial context
* @return Local home interface for ch2.User. Lookup using COMP_NAME
*/
   public static ch2.UserLocalHome getLocalHome()
                              throws NamingException
   {
      // Local homes shouldn't be narrowed,
      //         as there is no RMI involved.
      if (cachedLocalHome == null) {
         // Obtain initial context
         InitialContext initialContext = new InitialContext();
         try {
            cachedLocalHome = (ch2.UserLocalHome)
                initialContext.lookup(ch2.UserLocalHome.COMP_NAME);
         } finally {
            initialContext.close();
         }
      }
      return cachedLocalHome;
   }

}
```

Looks up and stores the home interface

Looks up and stores the local home interface

◆ *Discussion*

In addition to the cacheHomes attribute, you could add the generate attribute to the @ejb.util tag to specify whether the generated utility class should use the JNDI name or the component name from the home interface to perform a lookup (see recipe 2.2). The default behavior for the utility object is to use the JNDI name, but the possible values are false, logical, or physical. Keep in mind that

XDoclet uses every piece of information it has on a bean to generate applicable files. The generated utility object uses the names declared in the `public static final` member variables of the home and local home interfaces to perform lookups, making your code more stable.

◆ **See also**

2.1—Generating home, remote, local, and local home interfaces

2.2—Adding and customizing the JNDI name for the home interface

2.8 Generating vendor-specific deployment descriptors

◆ **Problem**

You would like to generate a vendor-specific XML file along with the standard XML descriptor.

◆ **Background**

One of the great reasons to use J2EE is that its API is a published standard. This means that EJB applications should be portable across different vendors' application servers. Vendors maintain the specified functionality from the J2EE specification, but usually ask that developers deploy EJBs with an additional deployment XML file that is specific to the application server. This vendor-specific XML file allows the application server to correctly map EJB functionality to its EJB container.

◆ **Recipe**

Use the appropriate subtask in the `<ejbdoclet/>` task of your build.xml file. Table 2.3 lists the subtasks that XDoclet uses to generate the vendor-specific XML descriptors.

Table 2.3 These subtasks can be added to your `<ejbdoclet/>` task to generate the vendor-specific deployment XML for your EJBs. Along with each subtask are associated JavaDoc comments in order to help XDoclet completely generate the XML. Refer to the XDoclet documentation for more information about each of these tasks.

Application Server	Subtask	Comments
Weblogic	<weblogic/>	Generates descriptors for versions 6.0 and 6.1
JBoss	<jboss/>	Generates the jboss-xml and jaws.xml files

(continued on next page)

Table 2.3 These subtasks can be added to your `<ejbdoclet/>` task to generate the vendor-specific deployment XML for your EJBs. Along with each subtask are associated JavaDoc comments in order to help XDoclet completely generate the XML. Refer to the XDoclet documentation for more information about each of these tasks. *(continued)*

Application Server	Subtask	Comments
JonAS	<jonas/>	
JRun	<jrun/>	
Orion	<orion/>	Generates the orion-ejb-jar.xml
Websphere	<websphere/>	
Pramati	<pramati/>	
Resin	<resin-ejb-xml/>	Generates the resin-ejb xml
HPAS	<hpas/>	
EAServer	<easerver/>	Generates XML for EAServer 4.1

◆ *Discussion*

These subtasks have many common attributes, but also contain a set of subtask-specific attributes. Consult the XDoclet documentation for the details specific to your application server. In addition, many of the subtasks have XDoclet tags that you can include in your bean source file to make the XML generation more complete.

◆ *See also*

2.3—Keeping your EJB deployment descriptor current

2.9 *Specifying security roles in the bean source*

◆ *Problem*

You want to generate security roles directly into the EJB deployment descriptor. You do not want to edit the XML file manually.

◆ *Background*

Rather than updating the XML deployment descriptor for a bean with security information after development, you would like it generated along with the other XML parts of the descriptor. Creating security roles in the XML can be tedious and error prone when you edit by hand.

◆ **Recipe**

Listing 2.15 contains the UserBean from recipe 2.6 with additional JavaDoc comments (shown in bold) to create security constraints in the generated XML deployment descriptor.

Listing 2.15   Declaring security roles in the source code

```
/**
 * @ejb.bean type="Stateful"
 *       view-type="both"
 *       jndi-name="${user.bean.jndi}"
 *
 * @ejb.security-role-ref
 *       role-name="ADMIN"
 *       role-link="administrator"
 *
 */
public class UserBean implements SessionBean{
```

You must also be sure that your <ejbdoclet/> task in the build.xml file includes the correct subtask to generate the deployment XML file (see recipe 2.3).

◆ **Discussion**

As you can see, there is nothing too complicated about specifying security roles. In addition, you can use the @ejb.security-identity tag to declare the bean to assume a role when it acts as a client to another bean. This tag has the attributes user-caller-identity and run-as, which correspond to the XML elements you should recognize.

◆ **See also**

2.3—Keeping your EJB deployment descriptor current

2.8—Generating vendor-specific deployment descriptors

2.10—Generating and maintaining method permissions

2.10 *Generating and maintaining method permissions*

◆ **Problem**

You would like to automate the permission-creation method in the deployment XML. You also want the XML to change as your EJB methods and security roles change.

◆ ***Background***

In addition to needing security roles in the EJB deployment XML, EJB applications usually need method permissions based on those roles in order to provide access control to various EJB methods. As EJBs change, and as new EJBs are created, the method permissions created in the deployment descriptor must also change. In addition, as you create new methods (or new security roles), you will have to add method permissions in the XML.

◆ ***Recipe***

Use the `@ejb.permission` tag in the method-level JavaDoc comments to specify method permissions for specific methods. This tag must be used in combination with `@ejb.create-method` or `@ejb.interface-method`. Refer to recipe 2.1 for more information on those tags. The `UserBean` source subsection in listing 2.16 shows a single method declaring method permissions (highlighted in bold).

Listing 2.16   UserBean.java

```
package ch2;

import javax.ejb.*;

/**
  * @ejb.bean type="Stateful"
  *        view-type="both"
  *        jndi-name="${user.bean.jndi}"
  *
  */
public class UserBean implements SessionBean{

  private String name = null;

  /**
    * @ejb.interface-method
    * @ejb.permission
    *        unchecked="true";
    */
  public void setUserName( String name )
  {
    this.name = name;
  }
}
```

◆ ***Discussion***

When using the `@ejb.permission` tag, you can use the `role-name` attribute to specify a specific role for the method permission or the `unchecked` attribute to indicate universal access. The `role-name` attribute can have a single role name value, or it can be a comma-separated list of role names that can access the method. The use of the `@ejb.permission` tag, along with others in this chapter, helps you to more completely generate your ejb-jar.xml for deploying your EJBs. This tag must be used with `@ejb.create-method` or `@ejb.interface-method` so that XDoclet knows with which method the permission is associated. To that end, you must include the subtask `<deploymentdescriptor/>` in your build.xml file in order to generate any new XML.

The generated XML will differ depending on which EJB interfaces you are generating. If you generate both, you should see XML for the method permission generated for both view types.

◆ **See also**

2.1—Generating home, remote, local, and local home interfaces

2.3—Keeping your EJB deployment descriptor current

2.8—Generating vendor-specific deployment descriptors

2.9—Specifying security roles in the bean source

2.11 Generating finder methods for entity home interfaces

◆ **Problem**

You want to generate the finder method declaration as part of the home interface generation process.

◆ **Background**

Recipe 2.1 shows how to generate home (and other) interfaces for session and entity beans. In that recipe, we add creation methods to the home interface. In the case of entity beans, home interfaces often need to include finder methods. Adding these finder methods requires time-consuming changes to the interface and may cause file synchronization problems, as described in recipe 2.1.

◆ **Recipe**

To generate the finder method declaration, use the `@ejb.finder` tag in the class-level JavaDoc of your bean source. For example, the following class section of code from the `ItemBean` generates a finder method for the bean's home and local home interface:

```
package ch2;

import javax.ejb.*;
/**
 * @ejb.bean type="CMP"
 *           name="ItemBean"
 *           jndi-name="ejb/ItemBean"
 *           view-type="both"
 *
 * @ejb.finder signature="java.util.Collection findAll()"
 */
public abstract class ItemBean implements EntityBean
{
```

◆ *Discussion*

The result of this tag is the declaration of the finder method into the home and local home interface of the EJB. As long as you are generating the home or local home interface, you don't need to make any changes to the build.xml file.

◆ *See also*

2.1—Generating home, remote, local, and local home interfaces

2.12 *Generating the ejbSelect method XML*

◆ *Problem*

You want to use XDoclet to generate the XML for the select methods of a bean.

◆ *Background*

Entity beans often must declare specific select methods allowing you to select collections or specific entities from the persistent store. Select methods must be described in the deployment XML for a bean. As with all manual tasks, editing the XML descriptor is error prone and tedious.

◆ *Recipe*

To generate the XML for select methods, declare the abstract select methods in your bean class and identify them with the `@ejb.select` tag in their JavaDoc comments. Use the tag attribute query to specify the EJB-QL statement for the method. For instance, examine the `ItemBean` in listing 2.17.

Listing 2.17   ItemBean.java

```java
package ch2;

import javax.ejb.*;
/**
  * @ejb.bean type="CMP"
  *          name="ItemBean"
  *          jndi-name="ejb/ItemBean"
  *          view-type="both"
  */
public abstract class ItemBean implements EntityBean
{
  //various bean methods...

  //ejbSelect methods

    /**
    * @ejb.select query="SELECT OBJECT( i ) FROM Item AS i"
    */
    public abstract java.util.Collection ejbSelectAll();
}
```

Also, you must specify the `<deploymentdescriptor/>` subtask in your build.xml file.

◆ *Discussion*

Select methods are not generated into a particular interface—the only result you should see is in the XML deployment descriptor. The descriptor will contain the EJB-QL and proper declarations for the method. Keep in mind that `ejbSelect` methods run under the transaction context of the invoker.

◆ *See also*

2.3—Keeping your EJB deployment descriptor current

2.13 *Adding a home method to generated home interfaces*

◆ *Problem*

You want to add home methods to your generated home or local home interface.

◆ ***Background***

Occasionally you need to compute a value that encompasses all bean instances, such as the sum of all account balances over all `Account` entity beans. Since these methods are independent of any particular bean instance, they need to be defined on the home interface. As long as XDoclet is generating your home interface (see recipe 2.1), you should add any home methods to that generation. Please read recipe 2.1 before following this recipe.

◆ ***Recipe***

To add home methods to either/both of your home and local home interfaces, you simply need to add a method-level JavaDoc tag to the method in the bean source. For example, the following method from an entity bean illustrates the necessary JavaDoc:

```
/**
 * @ejb.home-method
 *       view-type="both"
 */
 public void addDataToAll()
 {
   //method implementation here
 }
```

◆ ***Discussion***

Adding a home method to your home interfaces (home and local home) is no different than adding a regular business interface method—except that the JavaDoc tag routes the method to the home interface. The `@ejb.home-method` JavaDoc tag has an optional attribute, `view-type`, which you can use to specify the home interfaces you want to add this method. The possible values are `remote`, `local`, and `both`. This recipe once again illustrates how XDoclet provides the easiest way to keep your interface synchronized with your EJB source. If you later add methods, such as a home method, to your bean source, another trip through the Ant build process will entirely regenerate your interfaces and keep them up to date.

◆ ***See also***

2.1—Generating home, remote, local, and local home interfaces

2.14 Adding entity relation XML
to the deployment descriptor

◆ **Problem**

You want to generate the deployment XML for an entity bean relationship.

◆ **Background**

A new feature for EJB 2.0 applications is the ability to relate entity beans using *relationships*. This is similar to what you would find in any relational database. With EJB 2.0, you can create one-to-one, one-to-many, and many-to-many data relationships. The only drawback is that creating relationships requires large additions to the ejb-jar.xml file. Please read recipes 2.1 and 2.3 before using this recipe.

◆ **Recipe**

The following source shows a method that indicates a relationship between two entity beans. This method comes from the `OwnerBean` entity bean. Each `OwnerBean` entity bean is related unidirectly to a `DataBean` entity bean.

```
/**
 * @ejb.interface-method
 * @ejb.relation
            name="OwnerToData"
            relation-role="Owner"
            target-ejb="ch2.DataBean"
 */
public abstract Data getData();
```

◆ **Discussion**

Using the method-level `@ejb-relation` tag shown in the recipe generates the following XML in the assembly descriptor section of the ejb-jar.xml file:

```
<relationships >
   <ejb-relation >
      <ejb-relation-name>OwnerToData</ejb-relation-name>

      <ejb-relationship-role >
         <multiplicity>One</multiplicity>
         <relationship-role-source >
            <ejb-name>ch2.Owner</ejb-name>
         </relationship-role-source>
         <cmr-field >
            <cmr-field-name>data</cmr-field-name>
         </cmr-field>
```

```
    </ejb-relationship-role>

    <ejb-relationship-role >
        <multiplicity>One</multiplicity>
        <relationship-role-source >
            <ejb-name>ch2.DataBean</ejb-name>
        </relationship-role-source>
    </ejb-relationship-role>

  </ejb-relation>
</relationships>
```

The JavaDoc tag is used to specify a data accessor that indicates the entity data
relationship. In this case, the `OwnerBean` entity data is related to the `DataBean`
entity bean. The three attributes shown with the tag are the mandatory properties
that must be set when using this tag.

◆ **See also**

> 2.3—Keeping your EJB deployment descriptor current
>
> 3.7— Modeling one-to-one entity data relationships

2.15 *Adding the destination type*
to a message-driven bean deployment descriptor

◆ **Problem**

You want to generate the XML for the JMS message destination type while generating the deployment descriptor for a message-driven bean.

◆ **Background**

Message-driven beans must declare their destination type in their deployment
descriptor from which they will be receiving JMS messages. Recipe 2.3 showed how
to use XDoclet to generate the deployment descriptor for EJBs. Additionally, you
can specify the destination type for a message-driven bean in its class source and
add it to the generated XML. Please read recipe 2.3 before using this one.

◆ **Recipe**

To generate the XML for the message destination type, add the `destination-type`
attribute to the class-level `@ejb.bean` XDoclet tag for your message-driven bean
class. The following code does this for the `MessageBean` class:

```
/**
 * @ejb.bean
 *     name="MessageBean"
 *     type="MDB"
 *     destination-type="javax.jms.Queue"
 */
public class MessageBean
                    implements MessageDrivenBean, MessageListener {
```

Notice also the change in the `type` attribute for this example. Instead of `session` or `entity`, its value is `MDB`, indicating that this class is a message-driven EJB.

◆ *Discussion*

Using the `destination-type` attribute with the `@ejb.bean` tag generates the additional XML (shown in bold):

```
<ejb-jar>
 <enterprise-beans>

  <message-driven>
    <ejb-name>MDB</ejb-name>
    <ejb-class>MessageBean</ejb-class>
    <transaction-type>Container</transaction-type>
    <message-driven-destination>
      <destination-type>javax.jms.Topic</destination-type>
    </message-driven-destination>
  </message-driven>

 </enterprise-beans>
<ejb-jar>
```

The other possible value would be `javax.jms.Topic`, which would add a Topic destination instead of a Queue. If you are using a Topic, then you can optionally specify whether the topic should be `Durable` or `NonDurable` by using an additional attribute, `subscription-durability`.

◆ *See also*

2.3—Keeping your EJB deployment descriptor current

2.16—Adding message selectors to a message-driven bean deployment descriptor

Chapter 6, "Messaging"

2.16 Adding message selectors to a message-driven bean deployment descriptor

◆ **Problem**

You want to generate the XML for a message selector while generating the deployment descriptor for a message-driven bean.

◆ **Background**

Message-driven beans have the ability to filter incoming messages by using message selectors. Each message selector for a message-driven bean must be specified in its deployment XML. Recipe 2.3 showed how to use XDoclet to generate the deployment descriptor for EJBs. You can also use XDoclet to add a message selector to generated deployment XML for a message-driven bean. Please read recipe 2.3 before using this one.

◆ **Recipe**

To generate the XML for a message selector, add the `message-selector` attribute to the class-level `@ejb.bean` XDoclet tag for your message-driven bean class. The following code does this for the `MessageBean` class:

```
/**
 * @ejb.bean
 *      name="MessageBean"
 *      type="MDB"
 *      message-selector="<![CDATA messageType = 'buyerRequest']]>"
 */
public class MessageBean
                implements MessageDrivenBean, MessageListener {
```

Notice also the change in the `type` attribute for this example. Instead of `session` or `entity`, its value is `MDB`, indicating that this class is a message-driven EJB.

◆ **Discussion**

Using the `message-selector` attribute with the `@ejb.bean` tag generates the following XML:

```
<ejb-jar>
  <enterprise-beans>
```

```
<message-driven>
  <ejb-name>MDB</ejb-name>
  <ejb-class>MessageBean</ejb-class>
  <transaction-type>Container</transaction-type>
  <message-selector>
        <![CDATA[ messageType = 'buyerRequest' ]]>
  </message-selector>
</message-driven>

</enterprise-beans>
<ejb-jar>
```

Notice the use of the CDATA brackets when specifying the message selector value. Because message selectors can use special characters like > and <, you must use the CDATA brackets so that the XML file can be correctly parsed.

◆ *See also*

> 2.3—Keeping your EJB deployment descriptor current
>
> 2.15—Adding the destination type to a message-driven bean deployment descriptor
>
> Chapter 6, "Messaging"

Part 2

Main courses

Part 2 encompasses the majority of this book. Here you will find chapters covering the major functional areas of Enterprise JavaBeans (EJB). These areas include working with data, transactions, security, messaging, and other important EJB activities.

Chapter 3, "Working with data," covers many of the problems encountered when EJBs interact with databases. The recipes presented in this chapter do more than just cover entity beans.

Chapter 4, "EJB activities," covers topics encountered by developers across a wide range of EJB topics. These recipes do not fall into the area of security, data, or transactions. In this chapter, you will find topics ranging from sending email to making EJB web service endpoints.

Chapter 5, "Transactions," solves many of the problems you'll encounter when developing with transactions. In this chapter we explain and demonstrate solutions for both bean-managed and container-managed EJBs.

Chapter 6, "Messaging," presents topics that deal with EJBs and the Java Message Service (JMS). Specifically, this chapter thoroughly covers message-driven EJB problems. In addition to learning about the message-driven bean, you will find topics that demonstrate solutions to JMS-specific problems.

Chapter 7, "Security," provides solutions to security-related problems; the solutions focus on good design and the EJB API. Many of the recipes use the declarative security model provided by the EJB container.

Working with data

3

"And I'm President of the United States and I'm not going to eat any more broccoli."

—*President George Bush*

EJB components were designed to provide a portable, reliable, and scalable persistence layer for enterprise applications. Accessing a data source is one of the most common tasks for EJBs. Whether you use entity beans or session beans with data access objects, this chapter should provide you with solutions for your data access problems. The topics we cover here range from using CMP persistence, to modeling entity bean relationships, to developing custom finder methods. In this chapter, you will learn about the following topics:

- Using data sources on a per-user basis
- Creating EJB 2.0 CMP entity beans
- Generating primary key values
- Finding a collection of entity beans
- Creating one-to-one entity relationships
- Creating one-to-many entity relationships
- Using a cascading delete
- Creating read-only entity beans
- Making use of a stored procedure
- Using EJB-QL
- Creating entity beans across table joins
- Tracking data changes
- Encapsulating entity bean access
- Discovering information about entity beans
- Reducing the number of calls to entity beans
- Managing large result sets

3.1 *Using a data source*

◆ *Problem*

You want your EJB to access a Java Database Connectivity (JDBC) data source.

◆ *Background*

Connecting to a database via JDBC is essential in many applications. For instance, a session bean needs to access data to complete a business function, and entity beans with bean-managed persistence require access to a JDBC connection to load and store data. The application server running the EJB application provides data sources as specified by the deployer.

◆ **Recipe**

To retrieve the `javax.sql.DataSource` object from the application server, you must complete two steps. First, you must configure the deployment descriptor for the bean that will need access to the `DataSource` object. Listing 3.1 shows the partial XML from a deployment descriptor file for the `SampleDataSourceBean` bean.

Listing 3.1   Deployment descriptor

```xml
<ejb-jar>
 <enterprise-beans>
  <session>
    <ejb-name>SampleDataSourceBean</ejb-name>
    <home>sample.SampleDataSourceHome</home>
    <remote>sample.SampleDataSource</remote>
    <ejb-class>sample.SampleDataSourceBean</ejb-class>
    <session-type>Stateless</session-type>
    <resource-ref>
      <res-ref-name>ejbBookDataSource</res-ref-name>
      <res-type>javax.sql.DataSource</res-type>
      <res-auth>Container</res-auth>
    </resource-ref>
  </session>
 </enterprise-beans>
 <assembly-descriptor>
 </assembly-descriptor>
</ejb-jar>
```

Describes the
data source

Second, acquire the `DataSource` reference by performing a JNDI lookup. Examine the partial source from the `SampleDAtaSourceBean` session EJB, shown in listing 3.2. This code contains a `getConnection()` method that returns a JDBC `Connection` object from a `DataSource` reference.

Listing 3.2   SampleDataSourceBean.java

```java
import javax.ejb.SessionBean;
import javax.naming.InitialContext;
import javax.sql.DataSource;
import java.sql.*;

public class SampleDataSourceBean implements SessionBean
{
 // Other bean methods left out intentionally
```

```
public Connection getConnection()
{
    DataSource ds = null;
    try
    {
        InitialContext ctx = new InitialContext();      Creates and uses the
        ds = ( javax.sql.DataSource )                   JNDI initial context
                ctx.lookup( "java:comp/env/ejbBookDataSource" );

        return ds.getConnection();     ◁─┐  Returns a JDBC
    }                                     │  connection
    catch(Exception e)
    {
        e.printStackTrace();
    }
    return null;
}
}
```

◆ *Discussion*

This recipe shows the best way to acquire the connection. Data sources allow you to use connection pooling and optimize database access. To use a data source from the application server, you must perform two steps:

1 Set up the EJB's deployment descriptor so that the implementation can find a JDBC data source.

2 From inside the EJB, look up the DataSource via a JNDI name and acquire a JDBC connection.

For the first step, you need to add a <resource-ref> tag to declare a DataSource resource for the EJB (and map it to a particular JNDI name). Resources available to an EJB include JDBC DataSource, JavaMail, and the Java Message Service (JMS). In this case, the name ejbBookDataSource is mapped to a JDBC DataSource instance provided by the EJB container. The JNDI name and DataSource mapping are configured by the application server in a vendor-specific manner. For more details about your application server, refer to your vendor's documentation.

The final step in creating the JDBC connection requires the EJB to look up the declared resource. To look up an object using JNDI, you first need to obtain the InitialContext provided to your bean from the EJB container. To do this, you simply have to construct a new InitialContext object with its default constructor. Once you have the context, you need only call its lookup() method, passing in the

JNDI value referenced in the deployment descriptor of your bean. Notice that the JNDI name is always relative to the standard JNDI context name, `java:comp/env`.

NOTE   It is generally accepted as best practice to open a connection from a `DataSource` object retrieved from the application server. This allows your EJB to have the maximum portability when it comes to JDBC connections. However, if you have strong motivation for not wanting to use a `DataSource`, you can load a JDBC driver and open the connection manually. You will most likely need values for a database URL, username, and password—all of which can be hardcoded or also looked up through JNDI.

◆ **See also**

4.1—Retrieving an environment variable

3.2 Creating EJB 2.0 container-managed persistence

◆ **Problem**

You want to set up your EJBs to use container-managed persistence (CMP).

◆ **Background**

Many developers are still looking to move previously developed CMP and bean-managed persistence (BMP) entity beans to the EJB 2.0 CMP model, which offers numerous advantages and functionality. For example, CMP beans allow you to use container-managed relationships (CMR) and perform optimizations such as entity caching and lazy loading. When you're creating entity beans, CMP beans should be your first choice.

◆ **Recipe**

To set up a CMP bean, first write the source code of the entity bean. Listing 3.3 contains an example of the `EquityBean` source code.

Listing 3.3   EquityBean.java

```
import java.util.*;
import java.rmi.RemoteException;
import javax.ejb.*;
import javax.naming.InitialContext;
```

```
import javax.naming.NamingException;

abstract public class EquityBean implements EntityBean      ◁─┐  Declares the
{                                                              │  class abstract
  private EntityContext ctx;

  public void setEntityContext( EntityContext ctx ) {
    this.ctx = ctx;
  }

  public void unsetEntityContext() {
    this.ctx = null;
  }

  /*
   Data access methods below
  */
  abstract public String getSymbol();
  abstract public void setSymbol(String symbol);

  abstract public String getDescription();
  abstract public void setDescription(String description);

  abstract public double getLastTrade();
  abstract public void setLastTrade(double lastTrade);

  abstract public double getChange();                          Declares
  abstract public void setChange(double change);               abstract
                                                                   data
  abstract public int getVolume();                            accessors
  abstract public void setVolume(int volume);

  abstract public double getMarketCap();
  abstract public void setMarketCap(double marketCap);

  abstract public double getPe();
  abstract public void setPe(double pe);

  abstract public int getAvgVolume();
  abstract public void setAvgVolume(int avgVolume);

  /*
   bean methods below (NOT ALL SHOWN)
  */
  public void ejbLoad() {
    System.out.println ( "EquityBean.ejbLoad (" + id() +  ")" );
  }

  public void ejbStore() {
    System.out.println( "EquityBean.ejbStore (" + id() + ")" );
  }

  public String ejbCreate( String symbol, String description )
    throws CreateException
  {
    setSymbol(symbol);
```

```
      setDescription(description);

      return null;
   }
   /* Application defined methods below (NOT SHOWN)
   */
}
```

After you've written the source code of the entity bean, the remaining changes need to take place in the deployment descriptor of the bean. The partial XML shown in listing 3.4 is the deployment descriptor for the EquityBean entity EJB.

Listing 3.4   Deployment descriptor

```
<ejb-jar>
 <enterprise-beans>

  <!-- ========[ ContainerManaged Bean ]======== -->
  <entity>
     <ejb-name>containerManaged</ejb-name>
     <home>containerManaged.EquityHome</home>
     <remote>containerManaged.Equity</remote>
     <ejb-class>containerManaged.EquityBean</ejb-class>
     <persistence-type>Container</persistence-type>
     <prim-key-class>java.lang.String</prim-key-class>
     <reentrant>False</reentrant>
     <cmp-version>2.x</cmp-version>
     <abstract-schema-name>EquityBean</abstract-schema-name>
     <cmp-field>
        <field-name>symbol</field-name>
     </cmp-field>
     <cmp-field>
        <field-name>description</field-name>
     </cmp-field>
     <cmp-field>
        <field-name>lastTrade</field-name>
     </cmp-field>
     <cmp-field>
        <field-name>change</field-name>
     </cmp-field>
     <cmp-field>
        <field-name>volume</field-name>
     </cmp-field>
     <cmp-field>
        <field-name>marketCap</field-name>
     </cmp-field>
     <cmp-field>
        <field-name>pe</field-name>
```

Declares the EJB that will use container-managed persistence

Declares the persistent fields of the bean

Indicates the use of the 2.0 specification and declares the schema name

```
      </cmp-field>
      <cmp-field>
        <field-name>avgVolume</field-name>
      </cmp-field>
      <primkey-field>symbol</primkey-field>      ◁──┐  Declares the primary
    </entity>                                          key field of the bean
    <!-- =========[ ContainerManaged Bean ]======== -->
  </enterprise-beans>
  <assembly-descriptor>
  </assembly-descriptor>
</ejb-jar>
```

◆ *Discussion*

As you can see in the EquityBean example, the source for a CMP bean is noticeably different from that of a BMP bean. First of all, the methods will not contain
any persistence code, like JDBC connections or SQL statements. Also, a CMP
entity bean has a much more descriptive deployment descriptor than a BMP
entity bean. However, like a BMP bean, it must declare its persistence type. In this
case, it should be declared Container. Similarly, the deployment descriptor
should also tell the container to use the EJB 2.0 specification (which is what this
recipe describes).

After declaring the bean to be a 2.0 CMP entity bean, you should describe the
persistent fields and schema used by the bean. Indicate each field that will be persisted with a <cmp-field/> tag. The EJB container will generate a concrete subclass
of your abstract bean that implements the abstract methods to actually perform
the persistence and loading of the bean data as needed.

The schema and persistent fields are mapped to an actual database table in a
vendor-specific manner, usually with a vendor deployment descriptor for the
bean. Check your vendor's documentation for more information on what you
need to do. Typically, application servers require you to provide an additional
XML descriptor file. For example, Weblogic requires you to build two files:
weblogic-ejb-jar.xml and weblogic-cmp-rdbms-jar.xml. Lastly, you should declare
which persistent field is the primary key for this entity bean.

When using entity beans in your application, you should always encapsulate
access to them through a session bean. Not only does this separate your clients
from the data layer, but it lets you provide better security, transaction management, and performance. For instance, when you access your entity beans through
a session facade (see recipe 3.15), your entity beans need only implement local

interfaces. This prevents any remote client from finding your entity data without first passing through the session bean layer and being validated.

◆ **See also**

2.3—Keeping your EJB deployment descriptor current

3.4—Using a database sequence to generate primary key values for entity beans

3.5—Using a compound primary key for your entity beans

3.3 *Using different data sources for different users*

◆ *Problem*

Within an EJB, you would like to provide different data sources to different user sessions.

◆ *Background*

In your application, you need the ability to provide a different database view (or database) depending on the current user. This is one way to prevent unauthorized users from updating restricted data. Since the EJB security model provides for the discovery of the invoking client, you can easily determine a user's identity and assigned roles. Programmatically restricting data access to specific users can make your code less flexible and maintainable.

◆ *Recipe*

In order to switch data sources for a particular user, you must first determine which user is calling an EJB method. Inside the UserSpecificDBBean session bean shown in listing 3.5, the getConnection() method determines the invoking user and returns a JDBC connection based on the retrieved value.

Listing 3.5   UserSpecificDBBean.java

```
public class UserSpecificDBBean implements SessionBean
{
  private SessionContext ctx;

  public void setSessionContext(SessionContext ctx) {
    this.ctx = ctx;
  }

  public Connection getConnection() throws SQLException{
    String          srcName = null;
```

```
InitialContext initCtx = null;

try {
  Principal p = this.ctx.getCallerPrincipal();          Finds the user
  String    username = p.getName();                     calling the bean

  initCtx = new InitialContext();
  System.out.println( "User Requesting Connection:" + username );

  srcName = "java:comp/env/"+userName+"BookDataSource" ;
  System.out.println("User Requesting DataSource:"+srcName);

  return ( (javax.sql.DataSource)
              initCtx.lookup( srcName ) ).getConnection();
}
catch(NamingException ne) {                        Looks up the data source
  ne.printStackTrace();                               by the username
  throw new EJBException( ne );
}
finally{
  try{
    if(initCtx != null) initCtx.close();
  }
  catch(NamingException ne) {
    throw new EJBException(ne);
  }
} //finally
}//method

}
```

The data source must be defined in the ejb-jar.xml deployment descriptor for
each of the users. The name of the data source must correspond to that of the
generated data source name. For this example, we created two data source references (for users "guest" and "markw"). Listing 3.6 shows the partial XML descriptor file for this bean.

Listing 3.6   Deployment descriptor

```
<ejb-jar>
  <enterprise-beans>

    <!-- =========[ UserSpecificDB Session Bean ]======== -->
    <session>
      <ejb-name>userSpecificDB</ejb-name>
      <home>userspecificdb.UserSpecificDBHome</home>
      <remote>userspecificdb.UserSpecificDB</remote>
      <ejb-class>userspecificdb.UserSpecificDBBean</ejb-class>
      <session-type>Stateless</session-type>
      <transaction-type>Container</transaction-type>
```

```
    <resource-ref>
      <res-ref-name>markwBookDataSource</res-ref-name>
      <res-type>javax.sql.DataSource</res-type>
      <res-auth>Container</res-auth>
    </resource-ref>

    <resource-ref>
      <res-ref-name>guestBookDataSource</res-ref-name>
      <res-type>javax.sql.DataSource</res-type>
      <res-auth>Container</res-auth>
    </resource-ref>

  </session>
  <!-- =========[ UserSpecificDB Session Bean ]======== -->

</enterprise-beans>
</ejb-jar>
```

**Describes
an available
data source**

◆ *Discussion*

In this example, we are including the user's login ID as part of the JNDI name used to look up the data source. The JNDI name is constructed by concatenating the user ID with a base `String` value. This is only an example implementation for switching data sources; you could easily have an if-else statement or some other switching logic. You will actually create the data sources using the application server console or configuration file, so check your vendor's documentation for more information. However, using the `ejb-jar.xml` deployment file of your beans, you should add a resource description of the data sources you will want your beans to access. In our recipe, we included two data sources, each with a user ID as part of the JNDI name (the `<resource-ref-name/>` element) for looking up the resource.

Many similar ways to implement a solution such as this one exist, but doing something like this will free you from having to code detailed data-access restrictions. Instead of using the username to build the data source name, you could easily use a role name—allowing for a larger group of users to be assigned to a single data source.

◆ *See also*

3.1—Using a data source

7.1—Finding the identity and role of the caller inside an EJB method

3.4 Using a database sequence to generate primary key values for entity beans

◆ Problem

You want to use a database sequence to generate primary keys for your CMP and BMP entity beans.

◆ Background

When creating entity data such as user profiles or product descriptions, you can easily make a primary key the username or some unique field contained in the data. However, many times you want to use a unique field generated solely for the purpose of identifying the entity data, not a piece of the actual data. In these cases, you don't want to programmatically create the key when creating the bean. Using a database sequence provides you with a reliable source of primary keys for your entity beans.

Another reason to use a database sequence to provide a numeric primary key for your entity beans is performance. Since shorter primary key fields perform better than longer ones, using a database sequence to generate your primary key values should actually improve the efficiency of your entity beans. Using a sequence requires you to link your entity bean with the database sequence, either in code or through the use of the container. The actual generation (via database sequence) of the key is specific to a particular database, but the end results are the same.

◆ Recipe

Using a database sequence to generate primary key values can be done in both BMP and CMP entity beans. No changes need to be made to the sequence in order for it to be used by a BMP or CMP entity bean. For this recipe, we chose an Oracle database as an example. We used the following SQL to create the sequence:

```
CREATE SEQUENCE test_sequence INCREMENT BY 1;
```

We will reference the test_sequence for generating primary keys for both types of entity beans shown in this example.

BMP recipe

Since BMP beans manage everything concerning their persistence, a BMP bean can easily access any value it needs for a primary key. The EJB accesses the test_sequence sequence to set the value of its primary key. Listing 3.7, which contains the partial source from the SequenceBean BMP entity bean, illustrates acquiring a primary key value in the ejbCreate() method.

Listing 3.7 SequenceBean.java

```
public class SequenceBean implements EntityBean {

  public Integer ejbCreate( String name ) throws CreateException{
    PreparedStatement ps = null;
    Connection        con = null;
    ResultSet         rs = null;

    this.name = name;

    try {
      String query = "select test_sequence.nextval from dual";
      con = getConnection();
      ps  = con.prepareStatement( query );
      ps.executeQuery();

      rs = ps.getResultSet();

      if( rs.next() )
      {
        sequenceId = rs.getInt(1);
      }
      else {
        String error = "ejbCreate: Sequence error creating";
        System.out.println(error);
        throw new CreateException (error);
      }

      ps.close();
      rs.close();

      query = "insert into ejbSequence( sequenceId, name ) "
              + values (?,?)";
      ps = con.prepareStatement(query);
      ps.setInt(1, sequenceId);
      ps.setString(2, name);

      if ( !(ps.executeUpdate() > 0) ) {
        String error = "ejbCreate: SequenceBean ("
                       + name + ") not created";
        System.out.println(error);
        throw new NoSuchEntityException (error);
      }

      ps.close();

    }
    catch(SQLException sqe) {
      throw new EJBException (sqe);
    }
```

Builds and
executes the
sequence query

Retrieves a
value from the
result set

Creates the
entity data

```
      finally {
        try{
          if(ps!=null) ps.close();
          if(rs!=null) rs.close();
          if(con!=null) con.close();
        }
        catch(SQLException e){}
      }
      return new Integer( sequenceId );            ◁─┐ Returns the
                                                       primary key
    }
  }
```

CMP recipe

For CMP entity beans, the solution is much simpler. Rewriting the SequenceBean, we need to add only a couple of data methods instead of including all the necessary JDBC code in the bean source:

```
abstract public class SequenceBean implements EntityBean {

  abstract public Integer getSequenceId();
  abstract public void setSequenceId(Integer val);

}
```

Next, we need to declare the deployment descriptor for the entity bean that signifies its primary key value and type (see listing 3.8).

Listing 3.8   Deployment descriptor

```
<ejb-jar>
  <enterprise-beans>
    <entity>
      <ejb-name>oracleSequence</ejb-name>
      <home>CMPsequence.SequenceHome</home>
      <remote>CMPsequence.Sequence</remote>
      <ejb-class>CMPsequence.SequenceBean</ejb-class>
      <persistence-type>Container</persistence-type>
      <prim-key-class>java.lang.Integer</prim-key-class>        ◁─┐
      <reentrant>False</reentrant>                                 Specifies the primary key type
      <cmp-version>2.x</cmp-version>
      <abstract-schema-name>SequenceBean</abstract-schema-name>  ◁─┘
      <cmp-field>
        <field-name>sequenceId</field-name>          Describes
      </cmp-field>                                    the
      <cmp-field>                                     persistent
        <field-name>name</field-name>                fields
      </cmp-field>
                                                       Identifies the
      <primkey-field>sequenceId</primkey-field>    ◁─┘ primary key field
```

```
    </entity>
  </enterprise-beans>
  <assembly-descriptor>
    <container-transaction>
      <method>
        <ejb-name>oracleSequence</ejb-name>
      <method-name>*</method-name>
      </method>
      <trans-attribute>Required</trans-attribute>
    </container-transaction>
  </assembly-descriptor>
</ejb-jar>
```

◆ *Discussion*

In the case of the BMP bean, acquiring a primary key value from a sequence is just a matter of completing an additional JDBC call. And after retrieving a primary key value, the BMP bean goes on to insert the new entity data into the database (because this is an `ejbCreate()` method).

The CMP bean relies on the EJB container to provide the value of the primary key. In this case, we simply set up the bean and its deployment descriptor in the normal CMP entity bean way. However, in the vendor-specific descriptor, we indicate how the primary key value is acquired (and we also set up the schema mapping of the bean). For instance, we used a Weblogic container for this example. One of the vendor files, weblogic-cmp-rdbms-jar.xml, contains a snippet of XML specifying a database sequence for generating our primary key:

```
<automatic-key-generation>
  <generator-type>ORACLE</generator-type>
  <generator-name>test_sequence</generator-name>
  <key-cache-size>10</key-cache-size>
</automatic-key-generation>
```

Check your vendor's documentation for your specific setup.

◆ *See also*

2.5—Generating a primary key class

3.1—Using a data source

3.2—Creating EJB 2.0 container-managed persistence

3.5—Using a compound primary key for your entity beans

3.5 *Using a compound primary key for your entity beans*

◆ *Problem*

You want to use a combination of column values for a primary key for an entity bean.

◆ *Background*

Typically, primary key values are more complex than a single column. Compound primary keys are an excellent way to drill down to specific data. Using a compound primary key is more complex for both CMP and BMP entity beans. For both types of beans, you must create a primary key class that follows specific rules, and also configure your entity bean to properly use an instance of the class.

◆ *Recipe*

To provide a compound primary key for an entity bean, you must create a primary key class. In this recipe, we define a complex key for a portfolio holdings table. This key consists of a `String` for the portfolio name as well as a `String` for the symbol of an equity in the portfolio holding. Listing 3.9 shows a primary key class that meets the EJB 2.0 rules for primary key classes (and models the equity situation described).

Listing 3.9   HoldingKey.java

```
public class HoldingKey implements Serializable   ◁────────┐  Implements the
{                                                           │  Serializable interface
  public String  portfolioName = null;  │ Declares public CMP
  public String  symbol = null;         │ field variables

    public HoldingKey(){}   ◁────────  Defines a default constructor

  public HoldingKey( String symbol, String portfolioName )
  {
     this.symbol = symbol;
     this.portfolioName = portfolioName;
  }                                      │ Implements an
  public boolean equals(Object obj){  ◁──┘ equals() method

    if( obj == null || !( obj instanceof HoldingKey ) )
      return false;

    HoldingKey key = ( HoldingKey ) obj;

    if( ( key.portfolioName.equals(portfolioName) )&&
                   ( key.symbol.equals(symbol) )   )
    {
      return true;
```

```
      }
      else{
        return false;
      }
    }
    public int hashCode(){          Implements a
                                    hashCode() method
      return portfolioName.hashCode() + symbol.hashCode();
    }

    public String toString()
    {
      return portfolioName + " " + symbol;
    }
  }
```

When an entity bean uses a primary key class, the entity bean source must be altered to meet certain requirements. Listing 3.10 shows the PortfolioHolding-Bean entity bean that uses a HoldingKey instance for a primary key.

Listing 3.10   PortfolioHoldingBean.java

```
public abstract class PortfolioHoldingBean implements EntityBean
{
    public HoldingKey ejbCreate( String symbol, String portfolioName )
                               throws CreateException{          Defines a create
        setSymbol( symbol );                                   method to accept
        setPortfolioName( portfolioName );                     pk fields
        return null;     ◁
    }                          Returns null

    abstract public String getPortfolioName();
    abstract public void setPortfolioName( String portfolioName );

    abstract public String getSymbol();
    abstract public void setSymbol( String Symbol );

    //other bean methods not shown
}
```

In the bean deployment descriptor (see listing 3.11), you must declare the primary key classname and its persistent fields.

Listing 3.11   Deployment descriptor

```
<ejb-jar>
  <enterprise-beans>

    <!-- ========[ PortfolioHolding Bean ]======== -->
```

```
<entity>
  <ejb-name>portfolioHoldingBean</ejb-name>
  <home>compoundKey.PortfolioHoldingHome</home>
  <remote>compoundKey.PortfolioHolding</remote>
  <ejb-class>compoundKey.PortfolioHoldingBean</ejb-class>
  <persistence-type>Container</persistence-type>
  <prim-key-class>compoundKey.HoldingKey</prim-key-class>      <—┐  Declares
  <reentrant>False</reentrant>                                        the primary
                                                                      key
  <cmp-field>                                                         classname
    <field-name>symbol</field-name>
  </cmp-field>
  <cmp-field>
    <field-name>portfolioName</field-name>
  </cmp-field>
</entity>
<!-- =========[ PortfolioHolding Bean ]======== -->

  </enterprise-beans>
</ejb-jar>
```

◆ *Discussion*

A primary key class must meet four requirements:

- It must implement the `java.io.Serializable` interface.

- It should declare public method variables that are a subset of the persistent fields of the entity bean. The names of these primary key fields and entity fields should be exactly the same.

- It should define a default constructor.

- It should define the `hashCode()` and `equals()` methods.

The EJB container uses these requirements, along with reflection, to create and populate an instance of the primary key class as needed. The `equals()` and `hashCode()` methods of the primary key class allow instances of the class to be properly used in collections.

The `PortfolioHolding` CMP entity bean returns null from its `ejbCreate()` method because the EJB container is going to instantiate and populate an instance of the `HoldingKey` class and return it to the EJB client as the primary key. A default constructor must exist in the primary key class for this to work successfully. Inside the `ejbCreate()` method, the bean must set the values passed in using the abstract methods in order for the EJB container to properly construct a primary key instance. The container will use the abstract getter methods to retrieve the appropriate values for the primary key instance. In addition, the `findByPrimary-Key()` method declared in the entity bean home interface should pass in an instance of the primary key class.

If you are using a BMP entity bean, you must manually create the primary key instance and return it from the `ejbCreate()` method instead of returning null (as a CMP bean does). BMP beans must do everything manually whereas the CMP bean relies on the container.

◆ **See also**

2.5—Generating a primary key class

3.1—Using a data source

3.2—Creating EJB 2.0 container-managed persistence

3.4—Using a database sequence to generate primary key values for entity beans

3.6 *Retrieving multiple entity beans in a single step*

◆ **Problem**

You want to retrieve multiple entity beans without performing multiple JNDI lookup calls.

◆ **Background**

In many of the recipes in this chapter, we've described a stock portfolio application. Consider the situation when we need to retrieve all of the `EquityBean` entity instances in a user's portfolio. Each bean must be looked up by its primary key (its symbol), resulting in many JNDI calls and database access calls. It would be better if we could streamline this into a single call.

◆ **Recipe**

Returning a collection of data requires you to add some specific helper methods to the EJB home interface. In the home interface of a bean, define a finder method that returns a `java.util.Collection` instance instead of a single instance of an entity bean. The following is the home interface of the `PortfolioHolding` EJB. This EJB represents a particular stock held in a user's portfolio:

```
public interface PortfolioHoldingHome extends EJBHome
{
  public PortfolioHolding create(PortfolioHoldingVO holding)
```

```
    throws CreateException, RemoteException;

  public PortfolioHolding findByPrimaryKey(HoldingKey primaryKey)
    throws FinderException, RemoteException;

  public Collection findByPortfolioName(String portfolioName)
    throws FinderException, RemoteException;
}
```

The last method declared in the interface, findByPortfolioName(), tells the container to return a set of PortfolioHolding instances. Listing 3.12 contains the partial bean implementation class showing the implementation of this method. Notice that we are populating a Collection with the primary keys for EJB instances and not the actual data. The EJB container will take care of instantiating and returning the actual EJBs to the calling program. The implemented method is renamed ejbFindByPortfolioName(), indicating to the container that this method is from the home interface.

Listing 3.12   PortfolioHoldingBean.java

```
public class PortfolioHoldingBean implements EntityBean
{
  public Collection ejbFindByPortfolioName( String portfolioName )
                      throws ObjectNotFoundException
  {
    ArrayList        array = new ArrayList();
    PreparedStatement ps = null;
    Connection       con = null;
    HoldingKey       key = null;

    try {

        String query = "select portfolioName,symbol "
              + "from ejbPortfolioHolding where portfolioName=?";

        con = getConnection();                          Sets up
        ps  = con.prepareStatement(query);              the query

        ps.setString(1, portfolioName);
        ps.executeQuery();

        ResultSet rs = ps.getResultSet();

        while( rs.next() ) {                            Executes the
          key = new HoldingKey();                       statement and
          key.portfolioName = rs.getString(1);          retrieves the
          key.symbol = rs.getString(2);                 results
          array.add(key);
        }
    }
    catch (SQLException sqe) {
```

```
      throw new EJBException (sqe);
    }
    finally {
      try{
        if(ps!=null) ps.close();
        if(con!=null) con.close();
      }
      catch(SQLException e){}
    }

    return array;
  }
}
```

◆ **Discussion**

Finder methods are easily added to EJB home interfaces. However, it is important to remember how useful a carefully crafted finder method is to your application. Finder methods should be used to improve your code, replacing EJB lookups when possible. For example, instead of looking up entity beans one at a time, you can write a finder method to return a collection of beans.

In the case of a BMP bean, the finder method returns a `Collection` instance full of the primary keys for the entity bean matching the query represented by the method. The container will replace each primary key with the entity bean instance it represents. We will cover the creation of finder methods without using SQL later in the chapter.

◆ **See also**

3.1—Using a data source

3.12—Using EJB-QL to create custom finder methods

3.7 *Modeling one-to-one entity data relationships*

◆ **Problem**

You want to model a one-to-one data relationship using entity beans.

◆ **Background**

As you model more of your data with entity beans, you will eventually want to model some of the data relationships with entity beans as well. For instance, a stock purchase application contains a one-to-one relationship between owner data and address data. With the EJB 2.0 specification release, entity beans can model one-to-one data relationships. Creating entity relationships requires you to follow specific configuration and coding rules detailed by the EJB specification.

◆ *Recipe*

To create a one-to-one relationship, you must define two entity beans that contain methods for setting/getting an instance of the other bean. For this recipe, we will use the OwnerBean and AddressBean entity beans. For example, the OwnerBean declares setAddress() and getAddress() as methods, and the AddressBean declares setOwner() and getOwner() as methods. These methods create the one-to-one relationship of these beans.

Listing 3.13 contains the source for the OwnerBean EJB. Listing 3.14 shows the source for the AddressBean.

Listing 3.13   OwnerBean.java

```
public abstract class OwnerBean implements EntityBean
{
  abstract public java.lang.String getOwnerName();
  abstract public void setOwnerName(java.lang.String val);
  abstract public java.sql.Date getLastAccess();
  abstract public void setLastAccess(java.sql.Date val);
  abstract public Address getAddress();
  abstract public void setAddress(Address address);    ◁── Relates the
                                                            owner to the
  //bean methods not shown                                 address
}
```

Listing 3.14   AddressBean.java

```
public abstract class AddressBean implements EntityBean
{
  abstract public String getAddressField();
  abstract public void    setAddressField(String val);
  abstract public Owner   getOwner();                   Relates the address
  abstract public void    setOwner(Owner owner);    ◁── to the owner

  //bean methods not shown
}
```

Finally, you must describe in the assembly descriptor of the ejb-jar.xml file the entity relationship between the OwnerBean and the AddressBean (see listing 3.15).

Listing 3.15   Deployment descriptor

```
<ejb-jar>
 <enterprise-beans>
  <entity>
    <ejb-name>OwnerEJB</ejb-name>
    <local-home>one2oneRelation.OwnerHome</local-home>
    <local>one2oneRelation.Owner</local>
    <ejb-class>one2oneRelation.OwnerBean</ejb-class>
    <persistence-type>Container</persistence-type>
    <prim-key-class>java.lang.String</prim-key-class>
    <reentrant>False</reentrant>
    <cmp-version>2.x</cmp-version>
    <abstract-schema-name>OwnerBean</abstract-schema-name>
    <cmp-field>
      <field-name>ownerName</field-name>              Lists persistent
    </cmp-field>                                        fields of the
    <cmp-field>                                         OwnerBean
      <field-name>lastAccess</field-name>
    </cmp-field>
    <primkey-field>ownerName</primkey-field>
  </entity>

  <entity>
    <ejb-name>AddressEJB</ejb-name>
    <local-home>one2oneRelation.AddressHome</local-home>
    <local>one2oneRelation.Address</local>
    <ejb-class>one2oneRelation.AddressBean</ejb-class>
    <persistence-type>Container</persistence-type>
    <prim-key-class>java.lang.String</prim-key-class>
    <reentrant>False</reentrant>
    <cmp-version>2.x</cmp-version>
    <abstract-schema-name>AddressBean</abstract-schema-name>
    <cmp-field>
      <field-name>addressField</field-name>           Lists persistent fields
    </cmp-field>                                        of the AddressBean
    <primkey-field>addressField</primkey-field>
  </entity>
 </enterprise-beans>
<assembly-descriptor>
 <relationships>
  <ejb-relation>
    <ejb-relation-name>Owner-Address</ejb-relation-name>
      <ejb-relationship-role>
        <ejb-relationship-role-name>
           Owner-Has-Address                           Describes the
        </ejb-relationship-role-name>                  roles of the
        <multiplicity>one</multiplicity>               beans in the
        <relationship-role-source>                     relationship
          <ejb-name>OwnerEJB</ejb-name>
        </relationship-role-source>
```

```
            <cmr-field>
              <cmr-field-name>address</cmr-field-name>
            </cmr-field>
          </ejb-relationship-role>

          <ejb-relationship-role>
            <ejb-relationship-role-name>
                Address-Belongs-To-Owner
            </ejb-relationship-role-name>
            <multiplicity>one</multiplicity>

            <relationship-role-source>
              <ejb-name>AddressEJB</ejb-name>
            </relationship-role-source>
            <cmr-field>
              <cmr-field-name>owner</cmr-field-name>
            </cmr-field>
          </ejb-relationship-role>

      </ejb-relation>

    </relationships>
  </assembly-descriptor>
  <ejb-jar>
```

Indicates which field establishes the relationship

◆ *Discussion*

As with any other CMP beans, we must describe which fields of the bean are persistent fields. Both the OwnerBean and AddressBean declare persistent fields, but also notice the absence of the one field from each bean. The OwnerBean does not declare its address field, nor does the AddressBean declare its owner field persistent. Fields used to create the relationship are moved to the <relationship/> section.

Each bean participating in a relationship has a role in that relationship. The entire relationship is described in the <relationships/> section of the ejb-jar.xml. Inside that tag, you can add <ejb-relation/> elements that describe the roles played by each bean in a relationship. In this case, we describe each role with a name, a multiplicity, and the field that establishes the link to the other bean (address and owner).

The container uses these relationship descriptions to enforce the relations between beans. For example, if you attempt to set an instance of the OwnerBean into two or more AddressBean instances, the container will stop you.

◆ *See also*

2.14—Adding entity relation XML to the deployment descriptor

3.2—Creating EJB 2.0 container-managed persistence

3.8—Creating a one-to-many relationship for entity beans

3.9—Using entity relationships to create a cascading delete

3.10—Developing noncreatable, read-only entity beans

3.8 Creating a one-to-many relationship for entity beans

◆ **Problem**

You want to model a one-to-many data relationship in a database using entity beans.

◆ **Background**

As you model more of your data with entity beans, you will start to model certain data relationships as well. For example, owner entity data can be related to a set of portfolio entity data. With the EJB 2.0 specification release, entity beans can now handle one-to-many data relationships. Creating entity relationships lets you model table joins in the database and avoid implementing code to create and manage the relationships.

◆ **Recipe**

To create a one-to-many relationship, you must define two entity beans. For this recipe, we will again use the `OwnerBean` EJB and the `PortfolioBean` EJB (both CMP entity beans), as in recipe 3.7. Both beans contain methods for setting/getting an instance of the other bean. For example, the `OwnerBean` declares `setPortfolio()` and `getPortfolio()` as methods. And the `PortfolioBean` declares `setOwner()` and `getOwner()` as methods. These methods create the one-to-many relationship of these beans.

Listing 3.16 shows the source for the `OwnerBean` EJB. Listing 3.17 contains the definition of the `PortfolioBean` EJB.

Listing 3.16   OwnerBean.java

```
public abstract class OwnerBean implements EntityBean
{
  abstract public java.lang.String getOwnerName();
  abstract public void setOwnerName(java.lang.String val);
  abstract public java.sql.Date getLastAccess();
  abstract public void setLastAccess(java.sql.Date val);
  abstract public Collection getPortfolios();
```

```
abstract public void setPortfolios(Collection portfolios);
```
Relates the owner to the portfolios

```
//bean methods not shown
}
```

Listing 3.17   PortfolioBean.java

```
public abstract class PortfolioBean implements EntityBean
{
   abstract public String getPortfolioName();
   abstract public void   setPortfolioName(String val);
   abstract public double getCashValue();
   abstract public void   setCashValue(double val);
   abstract public Owner  getOwner();
   abstract public void   setOwner(Owner owner);
```
Relates the portfolio to the owner

```
   //bean methods not shown
}
```

Finally, you must describe the entity relationship between the `OwnerBean` and `AddressBean` in the assembly descriptor of the ejb-jar.xml file (see listing 3.18). Notice that the bean deployment descriptors are normal CMP entity bean sections, except for missing one persistent field. The missing field is the one used to create the entity relationship.

Listing 3.18   Deployment descriptor

```
<ejb-jar>
   <enterprise-beans>
    <entity>
      <ejb-name>OwnerEJB</ejb-name>
      <local-home>cascadeDelete.OwnerHome</local-home>
      <local>cascadeDelete.Owner</local>
      <ejb-class>cascadeDelete.OwnerBean</ejb-class>
      <persistence-type>Container</persistence-type>
      <prim-key-class>java.lang.String</prim-key-class>
      <reentrant>False</reentrant>
      <cmp-version>2.x</cmp-version>
      <abstract-schema-name>OwnerBean</abstract-schema-name>
      <cmp-field>
         <field-name>ownerName</field-name>
      </cmp-field>
      <cmp-field>
         <field-name>lastAccess</field-name>
      </cmp-field>
```
Lists persistent fields of the OwnerBean

```
    <primkey-field>ownerName</primkey-field>
  </entity>

  <entity>
    <ejb-name>PortfolioEJB</ejb-name>
    <local-home>cascadeDelete.PortfolioHome</local-home>
    <local>cascadeDelete.Portfolio</local>
    <ejb-class>cascadeDelete.PortfolioBean</ejb-class>
    <persistence-type>Container</persistence-type>
    <prim-key-class>java.lang.String</prim-key-class>
    <reentrant>False</reentrant>
    <cmp-version>2.x</cmp-version>
    <abstract-schema-name>PortfolioBean</abstract-schema-name>
    <cmp-field>
      <field-name>portfolioName</field-name>
    </cmp-field>
    <cmp-field>
      <field-name>cashValue</field-name>
    </cmp-field>
    <primkey-field>portfolioName</primkey-field>
  </entity>
</enterprise-beans>

<assembly-descriptor>
<relationships>
  <ejb-relation>
    <ejb-relation-name>Owner-Portfolio</ejb-relation-name>
    <ejb-relationship-role>
      <ejb-relationship-role-name>
        Owner-Has-Portfolios
      </ejb-relationship-role-name>
      <multiplicity>one</multiplicity>
      <relationship-role-source>
        <ejb-name>OwnerEJB</ejb-name>
      </relationship-role-source>
      <cmr-field>
        <cmr-field-name>portfolios</cmr-field-name>
       <cmr-field-type>java.util.Collection</cmr-field-type>
      </cmr-field>
    </ejb-relationship-role>
    <ejb-relationship-role>
      <ejb-relationship-role-name>
        Portfolio-Has-Owner
      </ejb-relationship-role-name>
      <multiplicity>many</multiplicity>
      <cascade-delete/>
      <relationship-role-source>
        <ejb-name>PortfolioEJB</ejb-name>
      </relationship-role-source>
      <cmr-field>
        <cmr-field-name>owner</cmr-field-name>
```

Lists persistent fields of the PortfolioBean

Describes the roles of the beans in the relationship

Indicates which field establishes the relationship

```
        </cmr-field>
        </ejb-relationship-role>
      </ejb-relation>
    </relationships>
   </assembly-descriptor>
  </ejb-jar>
```

◆ *Discussion*

As with any other CMP beans, you must describe which fields of the bean are persistent fields. Both the OwnerBean and PortfolioBean declare fields persistent, but also notice the absence of the one field from each bean. The Owner-Bean does not declare its portfolios field, nor does the PortfolioBean declare its owner field persistent. Fields used to create the relationship are moved to the <relationship/> section.

Each bean participating in a relationship has a role in that relationship. The entire relationship is described in the <relationships/> section of the ejb-jar.xml. Inside that tag, you can add <ejb-relation/> elements that describe the roles played by each bean in a relationship. In this case, we describe each role with a name, a multiplicity, and the field that establishes the link to the other bean (portfolios and owner). In the case of the owner, the <cmr-field/> must indicate a type of java.util.Collection (because this is a one-to-many relationship).

◆ *See also*

2.14—Adding entity relation XML to the deployment descriptor

3.7—Modeling one-to-one entity data relationships

3.9—Using entity relationships to create a cascading delete

3.10—Developing noncreatable, read-only entity beans

3.9 *Using entity relationships to create a cascading delete*

◆ *Problem*

After modeling data relationships with entity beans, you want to add the ability to perform a cascading delete.

◆ Background

Relational databases have the ability to constrain related data to the point where, if one part of a relationship is deleted, the other part will also be deleted (called a *cascading delete*). Cascading deletes are a valuable timesaving tool when you're working with data. In addition, they are an essential part of maintaining the referential integrity of your data within the database. Now that entity beans can model data relationships, you should also create entity beans to handle cascading deletes. Be sure to read recipe 3.7 before using this recipe.

◆ Recipe

To create a cascading delete, you first need a relationship between two entity beans. For this example, we are examining a relationship between an Owner entity EJB (the one) and its potentially many Portfolio entity beans (the many). Listing 3.19 contains a partial source for the OwnerBean class. The OwnerBean models the data of an owner of several equity portfolios.

Listing 3.19   OwnerBean.java

```java
public abstract class OwnerBean implements EntityBean
{
  abstract public java.lang.String getOwnerName();
  abstract public void setOwnerName(java.lang.String val);
  abstract public java.sql.Date getLastAccess();
  abstract public void setLastAccess(java.sql.Date val);
  abstract public Collection getPortfolios();
  abstract public void setPortfolios(Collection portfolios);   ◁────┐

  //bean methods not shown                      Relates the owner
}                                                 to portfolios
```

Listing 3.20 contains the partial source of the PortfolioBean class. The PortfolioBean EJB models a set of data that makes up a portfolio owned by an owner.

Listing 3.20   PortfolioBean.java

```java
public abstract class PortfolioBean implements EntityBean
{
  abstract public String getPortfolioName();
  abstract public void    setPortfolioName(String val);
  abstract public double getCashValue();
  abstract public void    setCashValue(double val);
  abstract public Owner  getOwner();
```

```
abstract public void    setOwner(Owner owner);    ◁────┐
                                           Relates the portfolio
//bean methods not shown                       to the owner
}
```

Since the relationship has already been modeled in recipe 3.8, we need only add the cascade delete tag, `<cascade-delete/>`, to the deployment descriptor, as shown in listing 3.21.

Listing 3.21   Deployment descriptor

```
<ejb-jar>
   <enterprise-beans>
   . . . . . .
   </enterprise-beans>

<assembly-descriptor>

  <relationships>
    <ejb-relation>
      <ejb-relation-name>Owner-Portfolio</ejb-relation-name>
      <ejb-relationship-role>
        <ejb-relationship-role-name>
          Owner-Has-Portfolios
        </ejb-relationship-role-name>
        <multiplicity>one</multiplicity>
        <relationship-role-source>
          <ejb-name>OwnerEJB</ejb-name>
        </relationship-role-source>
        <cmr-field>
          <cmr-field-name>portfolios</cmr-field-name>
          <cmr-field-type>java.util.Collection</cmr-field-type>
        </cmr-field>
      </ejb-relationship-role>
      <ejb-relationship-role>
        <ejb-relationship-role-name>
          Portfolio-Has-Owner
        </ejb-relationship-role-name>          Indicates the
        <multiplicity>many</multiplicity>      relationship supports
        <cascade-delete/>    ◁────┐            cascade deletes
        <relationship-role-source>
          <ejb-name>PortfolioEJB</ejb-name>
        </relationship-role-source>
        <cmr-field>
          <cmr-field-name>owner</cmr-field-name>
        </cmr-field>
      </ejb-relationship-role>
    </ejb-relation>
```

```
            </relationships>
          </assembly-descriptor>
        </ejb-jar>
```

◆ *Discussion*

A cascading delete is created by adding the element `<cascade-delete/>` to the relationship role describing an EJB relationship in the deployment descriptor. A cascading delete can be used only with one-to-one or one-to-many relationships, not with many-to-many relationships. When the EJB container removes an EJB participating in an EJB relationship marked with a cascade delete tag, it will automatically remove the data represented in the relation. For example, when an `OwnerBean` entity bean is removed from the database, all related `PortfolioBean` data will also be removed.

You do not have to set up your persistent tables to support cascading deletes (in the database)—the container will manage everything. Combining cascading deletes with entity relationships is an excellent way to maintain referential integrity in your database. You can be sure that no data is left without its related counterparts.

◆ *See also*

3.2—Creating EJB 2.0 container-managed persistence

3.10—Developing noncreatable, read-only entity beans

3.10 *Developing noncreatable, read-only entity beans*

◆ *Problem*

You want to create an entity bean that is read only and that cannot be created by any method.

◆ *Background*

Entity beans represent a data model existing in a data store. However, in some situations, you may want to present the data model as read-only and noncreatable. For example, suppose you want an application to compare passwords entered by users for validation against those stored in the database, but you don't want to allow updates to those passwords. In a case like this, you need an entity bean that could not be created by a user and that only allows the user to look up existing

instances. To accomplish this, you must create an entity bean that cannot be
created by any program code whatsoever. In addition, you need a way to keep the
entity bean from being removed, even with CMP beans.

◆ *Recipe*

To complete this recipe, you have to create a home interface without any create
methods for the EJB. In addition, the EJB class file should throw an exception
from its `ejbRemove()` method. The following is the home interface for the `Pass-`
`wordBean` EJB. This EJB contains a username and password combination corre-
sponding to an application user. Notice that the home interface does not contain
a create method. Without a create method, a client cannot create this type of
bean; it can only look up an instance of the bean.

```
import java.rmi.RemoteException;
import javax.ejb.*;

public interface Password extends EJBObject {
  public boolean isValid(String password)throws RemoteException;
}
```

Listing 3.22 shows the partial source of the `PasswordBean` EJB. The bean class
implements everything that a normal entity bean would need. However, in the
`ejbRemove()` method, the bean throws an exception, preventing the entity data
from being removed.

Listing 3.22   PasswordBean.java

```
public class PasswordBean implements EntityBean {

  public void ejbStore() {
  }

  public void ejbLoad(){
  }

  abstract public String getOwnerName();          Declares
  abstract public void setOwnerName(String ownerName);   data
                                                   accessors
  abstract public String getPassword();
  abstract public void setPassword(String password);

  public void ejbRemove()throws RemoveException{
    throw new RemoveException("Remove Method Not allowed");   ◁
  }                                                  Prevents
  public boolean isValid( String inPassword ){    data removal
    return (this.password.equals(password));
  }
}
```

Finally, the remote interface (or the local interface if you need it) declares the isValid() method only available to clients of this EJB. This effectively prevents any of the entity data from being updated by the client. The following is the remote interface for this bean:

```
import java.rmi.RemoteException;
import javax.ejb.*;

public interface Password extends EJBObject {
    public boolean isValid( String password )throws RemoteException;
}
```

◆ Discussion

The following two items make the PasswordBean read only:

- The home interface does not declare a create method.

- The remote interface does not declare any methods that update entity data.

With these measures in place, the only way to create entity data for these beans is to manually add data to the database. In the case of the application, a user management system takes care of adding users and passwords to the application. Using a read-only EJB like this one is a good way to secure sensitive data from the remaining part of the application. This solution will work equally well for both container-managed and bean-managed entity beans.

◆ See also

3.2—Creating EJB 2.0 container-managed persistence

3.7—Modeling one-to-one entity data relationships

3.8—Creating a one-to-many relationship for entity beans

7.6—Preventing access to entity data

3.11 Invoking a stored procedure from an EJB

◆ Problem

You want to invoke a stored procedure from an EJB.

◆ Background

Stored procedures are a good way to improve the performance of an enterprise application. The stored procedure can encapsulate database work that is more easily performed by the database, rather than your application (through JDBC).

◆ *Recipe*

Invoking a stored procedure requires you to use a BMP bean and to know how to use the stored procedure through JDBC programming. For example, examine the partial source of the `PricingBean` session bean shown in listing 3.23. It uses a stored procedure to determine the price of a particular equity.

Listing 3.23   PricingBean.java

```java
public class PricingBean implements SessionBean
{
  //other bean methods and attributes not shown

  public double getStoredProcPrice( String symbol ){

    Connection          conn  = null;
    CallableStatement cstmt = null;
    double              price = 0;

    try{
      conn = getConnection();
      cstmt = conn.prepareCall ("{ call getEquityPrice (?,?)}");

      cstmt.setString(1, symbol);
      cstmt.registerOutParameter(2, Types.DOUBLE);

      cstmt.execute();

      price = cstmt.getDouble(2);

      System.out.println("The Price is: " + price);

      cstmt.close();
      conn.close();
    }
    catch(Exception e){
      e.printStackTrace();
    }
    finally {
      try{
        if(cstmt!=null) cstmt.close();
        if(conn!=null) conn.close();
      }
      catch(SQLException e){}
    }
    return price;
  }
}
```

Sets up the call to the stored procedure

Executes the call and retrieves a value

◆ *Discussion*

To execute a stored procedure, you have to first set up a JDBC `CallableStatement` object. After acquiring a connection, build a `CallableStatement` instance using the `prepareCall()` method, passing in a `String` describing the statement and procedure. With the example statement in hand, you need to pass in a single input parameter (the equity symbol) and also register an output parameter (a double indicating the price returned).

   Input parameters are populated in the same manner as using a `PreparedStatement` instance. For output parameters, you must use the `registerOutParameter()` method, which lets you declare the type of the return value as well. After setup, all you need to do is call the `CallableStatement`'s `execute()` method and retrieve the result using the `getDouble()` method (the type of our output parameter).

◆ *See also*

   3.1—Using a data source

3.12 *Using EJB-QL to create custom finder methods*

◆ *Problem*

When writing entity bean create and finder methods, you want the container to manage the SQL queries and data access.

◆ *Background*

Every entity bean home interface has a mandatory `findByPrimaryKey()` method. The EJB specification has always allowed you to specify custom finder methods in the home interface for more specific and different lookups. However, in EJB 1.1 the custom finder relied on vendor-specific implementations for CMP beans. This reduced the portability of your EJBs and the power of custom finder methods. In EJB 2.0, the specification added a standard EJB query language (EJ-BQL). Using EJ-BQL to replace the implementation of a finder method does not in any way affect the source of an entity bean.

◆ *Recipe*

To add finder methods to a CMP entity bean, you need to use EJ-BQL. For this recipe, we are going to add some customer finder methods to the `EquityBean` CMP entity bean that we have used in other recipes in this chapter. The home interface is shown in listing 3.24.

Listing 3.24   EquityHome.java

```
public interface EquityHome extends EJBHome
{
  public Equity create(String symbol, String description)
    throws CreateException, RemoteException;

  public Equity findByPrimaryKey(String primaryKey)
    throws FinderException, RemoteException;

  public Collection findHighPriced( double minPrice )          Adds custom
    throws FinderException, RemoteException;                   finder methods

  public Collection findHighPricedLowPE(double minPrice,double PE)
    throws FinderException, RemoteException;
}
```

The finder methods specified in the home interface will not appear in the bean class. In fact, the bean source remains unchanged, specifying only its abstract data getters and setters. The real changes for finder methods take place in the entity bean deployment descriptor, as shown in listing 3.25.

Listing 3.25   Deployment descriptor

```
<entity>
  <ejb-name>EBQL</ejb-name>
  <home>EBQL.EquityHome</home>
  <remote>EBQL.Equity</remote>
  <ejb-class>EBQL.EquityBean</ejb-class>           Declares the
  <persistence-type>Container</persistence-type>   bean CMP
  <prim-key-class>java.lang.String</prim-key-class>
  <reentrant>False</reentrant>
  <cmp-version>2.x</cmp-version>     Declares the EJB 2.x compliant
  <abstract-schema-name>EquityBean</abstract-schema-name>
  <cmp-field>
    <field-name>symbol</field-name>
  </cmp-field>
  <cmp-field>
    <field-name>description</field-name>
  </cmp-field>
  <cmp-field>
    <field-name>lastTrade</field-name>
  </cmp-field>
  <cmp-field>
    <field-name>change</field-name>
```

```
      </cmp-field>
      <cmp-field>
        <field-name>volume</field-name>
      </cmp-field>
      <cmp-field>
        <field-name>marketCap</field-name>
      </cmp-field>
      <cmp-field>
        <field-name>pe</field-name>
      </cmp-field>
      <cmp-field>
        <field-name>avgVolume</field-name>
      </cmp-field>
      <primkey-field>symbol</primkey-field>
      <query>
        <query-method>
          <method-name>findHighPriced</method-name>
          <method-params>
            <method-param>double</method-param>
          </method-params>
        </query-method>
        <ejb-ql>
          <![CDATA[SELECT OBJECT(a) FROM EquityBean AS a
                          WHERE a.lastTrade > ?1]]>
        </ejb-ql>
      </query>
      <query>
        <query-method>
         <method-name>findHighPricedLowPE</method-name>
          <method-params>
            <method-param>double</method-param>
            <method-param>double</method-param>
          </method-params>
        </query-method>
        <ejb-ql>
          <![CDATA[SELECT OBJECT(a) FROM EquityBean AS
              a WHERE a.lastTrade > ?1 and a.pe < ?2]]>
        </ejb-ql>
      </query>
  </entity>
```

Describes the
findHighPriced()
method

Describes the
findHighPricedLowPE()
method

♦ **Discussion**

Since the 2.0 release of the EJB specification, EJBs can make use of EJB-QL. This query language is an SQL-like syntax that allows you to describe a query to the EJB container for finder and create methods. Using EJB-QL lets the container perform the actual database query to retrieve entity data, which is usually more efficient and portable. Let's examine a query method description from the deployment descriptor more closely:

```
<query>
  <query-method>
    <method-name>findHighPriced</method-name>
    <method-params>
      <method-param>double</method-param>
    </method-params>
  </query-method>
  <ejb-ql>
  <![CDATA[SELECT OBJECT(a) FROM EquityBean AS a WHERE a.lastTrade > ?1]]>
  </ejb-ql>
</query>
```

Each custom finder method should be described by a `<query/>` block in the deployment descriptor for each bean. In the `<query/>` tag, you specify the method name and its parameter types (in the order that they appear in the method). Lastly, you specify the EJB-QL string that represents the entity bean query that the method should execute to return an entity bean or beans to the EJB client.

An EJB-QL string resembles a JDBC prepared statement in that arguments are represented by a question mark (?). However, in EJB-QL you also add a number next to the ? that specifies which argument it represents (first, second, third, and so forth). EJB-QL is not hard to use, but it also does not encompass as many features as SQL. Examining our statements, you can see they have three parts:

- The SELECT clause can return any EJB object, CMP, or CMR field. When returning an EJB, the statement must use the OBJECT() operator to surround the return type. If returning a field, you can simply state the field, like SELECT a.symbol. In the SELECT part, you can also make use of the DISTINCT keyword, as in SELECT DISTINCT OBJECT(a). This will cause each returned value to be unique, with no duplicates.

- The FROM clause allows you to select the scope to pull data from. For instance, in our queries we are extracting data from the EquityBean EJBs. The AS keyword lets you rename the bean with an identifier. The identifier cannot be a name that is already used for an EJB name or abstract schema name (and the identifier is not case sensitive).

- The WHERE clause lets you drill down to specific data by setting up conditions. The data returned from the statement must meet the conditions in this clause. In our example, the lastTrade field of an EquityBean EJB should be greater than our input parameter.

For more information on EJB-QL, go to http://www.javasoft.com.

◆ **See also**

2.11—Generating finder methods for entity home interfaces

3.2—Creating EJB 2.0 container-managed persistence

3.13 *Persisting entity data into a database view*

◆ **Problem**

You want to use a database view to represent the table in which entity beans load and store data.

◆ **Background**

In some situations, entity data crosses over multiple tables. When using a CMP entity bean, you cannot persist into more than one table or load from a table join. However, using a database view and a BMP bean, you can model data from multiple tables with a single entity bean. To do this requires you to correctly configure your BMP bean and interact with the database view through JDBC calls.

◆ **Recipe**

To represent data from multiple tables (like a table join) with a single entity bean, create a database view and use it to create entity beans. The following is the SQL that creates a sample view for this recipe:

```
DROP VIEW equityPriceView;
create view equityPriceView as select symbol,Description,LastTrade from
    equities;
```

We define our CMP bean exactly as we would if the bean were working with a normal table. The bean class will still define the abstract methods to define the data elements for the bean:

```
public abstract class EquityBean implements EntityBean
{
  abstract public String getSymbol();
  abstract public void setSymbol(String symbol);

  abstract public String getDescription();
  abstract public void setDescription(String description);

  abstract public double getLastTrade();
  abstract public void setLastTrade(double lastTrade);
}
```

Listing 3.26 shows the deployment descriptor for the bean. Note that there is no change from a normal CMP deployment.

Listing 3.26   Deployment descriptor

```
<entity>
  <ejb-name>cmpViewEquity</ejb-name>
  <home>CMPView.EquityHome</home>
  <remote>CMPView.Equity</remote>
  <ejb-class>CMPView.EquityBean</ejb-class>
  <persistence-type>Container</persistence-type>
  <prim-key-class>java.lang.String</prim-key-class>
  <reentrant>False</reentrant>
  <cmp-version>2.x</cmp-version>
  <abstract-schema-name>EquityBean</abstract-schema-name>
  <cmp-field>
    <field-name>symbol</field-name>
  </cmp-field>
  <cmp-field>
    <field-name>description</field-name>
  </cmp-field>
  <cmp-field>
    <field-name>lastTrade</field-name>
  </cmp-field>
  <primkey-field>symbol</primkey-field>
</entity>
```

The only difference comes in the container deployment. Using the vendor-specific method, you normally bind the abstract schema name from the deployment descriptor to a physical table. However, in this case you bind the bean to your database view. You also do not want the container to try to create the table, because it is really a view. When setting up the vendor descriptor, be sure to:

- Use the column names from the view, not the tables (if they are different).
- Tell the EJB container not to create the table; the view has already been constructed in the database.

♦ *Discussion*

Because CMP entity beans cannot persist into multiple tables (like a join), EJB developers are stuck sometimes creating an unnecessary extra entity bean or compromising their data model. One way around this problem is to construct a database view in which to persist the beans. Developing a bean to use a database view is no different than developing a normal CMP entity bean. The main difference lies in the vendor-specific deployment descriptor that tells the container how to map an entity bean to a physical database schema. When persisting to a view, you need to map to its *columns*, not the *tables*, and also inform the container not to create the tables (the view should be constructed before deployment of any beans).

◆ **See also**

> 3.2—Creating EJB 2.0 container-managed persistence

3.14 *Sending notifications upon entity data changes*

◆ **Problem**

You want your enterprise beans to notify certain listeners when data changes.

◆ **Background**

Many enterprise applications are dependent on other systems for completing a workflow. Actually, enterprise applications many times represent steps within an enterprise workflow. In these situations, data represented by your entity beans may also be shared by (or be important to) other applications. These outside applications might need to know when the data is changed in order to begin their steps in the workflow. Sending notifications is best accomplished using a JMS implementation accessed from the application server running your EJB container.

◆ **Recipe**

To notify outside listeners of entity changes, you will use a JMS publisher. Before looking at the bean source, let's examine the object used to publish messages into a JMS system (listing 3.27). It publishes provided messages to a particular JMS topic created in the application server (see your vendor's documentation for setting up JMS topics in your application server). This publisher provides access to a JMS topic in a Weblogic application server.

Listing 3.27 JMSPublisher.java

```
public class JMSPublisher
{
    private TopicConnection          topicConnection = null;
    private TopicSession             topicSession = null;
    private TopicPublisher           topicPublisher = null;
    private Topic                    topic = null;
    private TopicConnectionFactory   topicFactory = null;
    private String                   url="t3://localhost:7001";

    private Context getInitialContext() throws NamingException {
```

```
    try {
      // Get an InitialContext
      Properties props = new Properties();
      props.put( Context.INITIAL_CONTEXT_FACTORY,
                      "weblogic.jndi.WLInitialContextFactory" );
      props.put(Context.PROVIDER_URL, url);

      return new InitialContext(props);              Builds an
    }                                          InitialContext instance
    catch (NamingException ne) {
       System.out.println( "Could not connect "
                   + "to the application server" );
       throw ne;
    }
  }

 public JMSPublisher( String factoryJNDI, String topicJNDI )
                 throws JMSException, NamingException {

    // Get the initial context
    Context context = getInitialContext();

    // Get the connection factory
    topicFactory = (TopicConnectionFactory)
                             context.lookup(factoryJNDI);

    // Create the connection
    topicConnection = topicFactory.createTopicConnection();

    // Create the session
    TopicSession = topicConnection.createTopicSession(false,
                               Session.AUTO_ACKNOWLEDGE);
    // Look up the destination
    topic = (Topic)context.lookup(topicJNDI);        Establishes a
                                                    connection to
    // Create a publisher                              the topic
    topicPublisher = topicSession.createPublisher(topic);
  }

 public void publish(String msg) throws JMSException {

    // Create a text message
    TextMessage message = topicSession.createTextMessage();
    message.setText(msg);

    // Publish the message                      Publishes a message
    topicPublisher.publish(message);               to the topic
  }

 public void close() throws JMSException {
    topicSession.close();
    topicConnection.close();
  }

}
```

With an object available to use for sending JMS messages, you can add calls to its `publish()` method whenever you want to indicate a change has occurred in an entity bean. For example, the `EquityBean` entity bean in listing 3.28 sends messages upon data change. The bean also implements a `publishMessage()` method to encapsulate calls to the `JMSPublisher` instance.

Listing 3.28   EquityBean.java

```
public class EquityBean implements EntityBean {

  private JMSPublisher publisher = null;

  private void publishMessage( String msg )       ◁─┐ Encapsulates
  {                                                   │ calls to the
    try{                                              │ publisher
      if( publisher=null )
        publisher = new JMSPublisher("BookJMSFactory","BookJMSTopic");

      System.out.println( "Publishing message: "+msg );
      publisher.publish(msg);
      publisher.close();
    }
    catch(Exception e){

      e.printStackTrace();
    }
  }

  public void ejbRemove()throws RemoveException{
    //implementation not shown
    publishMessage("Removed Equity from Database:"+symbol);    ◁─┐
  }

  public String ejbCreate(String symbol, String description)
                                    throws CreateException
  {
    //implementation not shown

    publishMessage("Inserted Equity into Database:"+symbol);   ◁─  Sends a
  }                                                                 message

  public void setEquity( EquityVO equity ){

    //implementation not shown
    publishMessage("Changed the Equity in the Database:"+symbol); ◁┘
  }
 }
```

◆ **Discussion**

Now that you have an EJB that publishes JMS messages, any JMS clients you have will be able to pick up the entity messages as needed. You can use a solution like this one to provide notification of data changes, and even to track the state of data. However, you should not use a system like this one to compute the end result of several data updates unless you add functionality to guarantee the correct ordering of messages. If the JMS client is allowed to receive messages in any order, the final state of the data on the client may not match the actual state of the data.

This example shows simple JMS code that will get the job done. For more information about JMS, visit the JMS site at http://www.javasoft.com.

◆ See also

Chapter 6, "Messaging"

3.15 *Creating an interface to your entity data*

◆ Problem

You don't want to expose your entity data directly to the client layer.

◆ Background

For security and ease of use, a session bean should always wrap your entity beans. This allows you to implement security in the session bean, as well as provide a local interface only to your entity beans (ensuring that no unauthorized remote access can occur). Using a session facade also helps shield your client application from data model changes and provide the most appropriate transactional support for accessing your entity data.

◆ Recipe

For this recipe, we will use the common session facade design pattern. This pattern wraps all entity bean access with a session bean. Wrapping your entity beans lets you develop only a local interface for the entity beans, preventing any remote access to them. For example, the following is the local interface for the Password-Bean EJB, a bean that manages a username and password combination:

```
public interface Password extends EJBLocalObject
{
  public boolean isPasswordValid(String password);
}
```

The entity bean source is the normal CMP entity bean. No changes need to be made to accommodate the local interface:

```
public abstract class PasswordBean implements EntityBean
{
  private EntityContext  ctx;

  abstract public java.lang.String getUserName();
  abstract public void setUserName(java.lang.String val);
  abstract public java.lang.String getPassword();
  abstract public void setPassword(java.lang.String val);
  abstract public java.sql.Date getLastAccess();
  abstract public void setLastAccess(java.sql.Date val);

  public boolean isPasswordValid( String password )
  {
    String passwd = getPassword();
    return password.equals( passwd );
  }
}
```

In order for clients to access this entity data to do a password comparison, they must go through a session bean. (Actually, if the client were in the local JVM, it could look up the entity bean, but you should enforce otherwise.) We developed a session bean, `HelperBean`, that provides a `login()` method for clients to use to access the entity data for password comparison. Here is the `HelperBean` EJB partial source:

```
public class HelperBean implements SessionBean
{

  private SessionContext  ctx;
  private PasswordLocalHome  passwordHome;

  public boolean login(String userName, String password)
         throws RemoteException {

    Password passwd = null;

    try{

      //use the previously looked up PasswordBean localHome interface
      passwd = passwordHome.findByPrimaryKey(userName);
      return passwd.isPasswordValid(password);
    }
    catch(Exception e){
      throw new RemoteException("Finding Password object failed");
    }

  }
  //other bean methods not shown
}
```

◆ *Discussion*

The `PasswordBean` entity EJB in the recipe implements only a local and a local home interface. Using only the local interface prevents any remote creation or lookup of the entity bean. In order for remote clients to access the entity data, they need access through a wrapper session bean. The session bean can then manage user session data, transactions, and more. The session facade pattern is widely accepted by the enterprise development community, and you should use it for all of your entity bean access.

◆ **See also**

3.2—Creating EJB 2.0 container-managed persistence

7.6—Preventing access to entity data

3.16 *Retrieving information about entity data sets*

◆ *Problem*

You want to query your persistent system for information about entity data without creating entity beans or using JDBC.

◆ *Background*

When using entity beans, one of the common problems you'll encounter is retrieving information about the data that entity beans represent. For example, you want to know how many rows of data exist of a certain type. Using multiple entity bean lookups (either directly or through finder methods) will certainly provide you with your desired information but will cost you dearly in performance as your data set grows. The EJB 2.0 specification details a new solution to this problem. It allows you to declare methods in the home interface of an EJB (called home methods) that return information about the entity data without returning an EJB instance.

◆ *Recipe*

To find information about entity data sets, add an EJB home method to the entity bean. For example, the following `EquityHome` home interface (to the `EquityBean`) declares a method, `getCountOfSymbols()`, as a home method:

```
public interface EquityHome extends EJBHome
{
  public Equity create(String symbol, String description)
    throws CreateException, RemoteException;

  public Equity findByPrimaryKey(String primaryKey)
    throws FinderException, RemoteException;
```

```
    //home method
    public int getCountOfSymbols() throws RemoteException;
}
```

Listing 3.29 contains the EquityBean EJB source, showing the implementation of the home method. For this recipe, the EquityBean EJB is a BMP bean. Notice that the home method is prefixed with ejbHome. This indicates to the container that this is a home method and can be executed directly from the home object. The remaining source would remain unchanged and is not shown.

Listing 3.29   EquityBean.java

```java
public class EquityBean implements EntityBean
{
  //other bean methods not shown

  public int ejbHomeGetCountOfSymbols()
  {
    System.out.println("Executing Home Method: getCountOfSymbols");

    PreparedStatement ps = null;
    Connection        con=null;
    int               count=0;

    try {

      String query="select count(*) from EQUITIES";
      con = getConnection();
      ps  = con.prepareStatement(query);
      ps.executeQuery();

      ResultSet rs = ps.getResultSet();
      if( rs.next() )
      {
        count = rs.getInt(1);
      }
    }
    catch (SQLException sqe) {
      throw new EJBException (sqe);
    } finally {
      try{
        if(ps != null) ps.close();
        if(con != null) con.close();
      }
      catch(SQLException e){}
    }
    return count;
  }
}
```

◆ *Discussion*

Home methods let clients retrieve information about entity data without return-ing an instance of the entity bean. When declaring home methods in the home interface, keep in mind that the name of the method must not start with *create*, *remove*, or *find*. Home methods are designed to operate over the entire set of entity data represented by the bean class. As opposed to returning information about the number of symbols (`getCountOfSymbols()`), you could apply a change to the entire set of data. For example, an entire set of bank account data could be credited with an amount of data. Home methods are meant to be convenience methods used in place of retrieving the entire set of data to make changes across the whole set.

3.17 *Decreasing the number of calls to an entity bean*

◆ *Problem*

You want to increase the performance of your clients that access fields of entity beans.

◆ *Background*

Entity beans are a good way to encapsulate database access and provide a main-tainable and flexible persistence layer. However, if used improperly, they can start to affect the performance of your application. For instance, after looking up an entity bean instance, you might have to invoke several getter methods to access all its data attribute values. Each of the getter invocations could take a hit to the data-base to retrieve the value. When using entity beans, you want to avoid having them become the performance bottleneck of your applications.

◆ *Recipe*

To improve your client's performance, instead of accessing entity bean methods one at a time to retrieve all of the entity data, implement a single bulk accessor method that returns a lightweight value object for the bean. The value object encapsulates all of the entity data in a single object that can be passed back to a client (session bean or client layer) with a single method call. For example, revisit-ing the `EquityBean` EJB used in other recipes in this chapter, the code in listing 3.30 lists its value object class.

Listing 3.30   EquityVO.java

```
public class EquityVO implements Serializable
{
  private String symbol = null;
  private String description = null;
  private double lastTrade = 0.0;

  public String getSymbol()
  {
    return symbol;
  }

  public String getDescription()
  {
    return description;
  }

  public double getLastTrade()
  {
    return lastTrade;
  }

  public void setSymbol( String value )
  {
    symbol = value;
  }

  public void setDescription( String value )
  {
    description = value;
  }

  public void setLastTrade( String value )
  {
    lastTrade = value;
  }
}
```

After creating the value object, add the bulk accessor method to the entity bean class. For example, the source in listing 3.31 lists the new EquityBean EJB.

Listing 3.31   EquityBean.java

```
abstract public class EquityBean implements EntityBean {

  abstract public String getSymbol();
  abstract public void setSymbol(String symbol);

  abstract public String getDescription();
  abstract public void setDescription(String description);
```

```
abstract public double getLastTrade();
abstract public void setLastTrade(double lastTrade);
```

```
public EquityVO getAllData()
{
  EquityVO vo = new EquityVO();
  vo.setSymbol( getSymbol() );
  vo.setDescription( getDescription() );
  vo.setLastTrade( getLastTrade() );

  return vo;
}
}
```

> **Implements a bulk accessor method**

◆ Discussion

Using a value object for an entity bean is a quick and easy way to improve the performance of your EJB applications. For instance, for a large amount of data you can save several method calls to an entity bean.

Many developers create value objects by extending a Map class, allowing any number of future fields to be added to the class. Using a subclass of Map lets you add and retrieve key/value pairs to the value object as needed using the super class put() and get() methods.

3.18 *Paging through large result sets*

◆ Problem

A session bean uses a query that returns an enormous result set—too large to pass back to a client in one chunk. You would like to page through the data.

◆ Background

Using session beans to query databases via JDBC calls is an effective way to present data to an EJB client. However, if a query returns hundreds of rows, you cannot possibly expect your application to return all the data at one time to a client. Paging through data is an excellent way for clients to navigate through large result sets.

◆ *Recipe*

Creating a page-able session bean requires you to perform a little different JDBC connection setup. This recipe shows a generic mechanism that you can alter to fit your needs. The following session bean operates over an SQL statement that is passed to it by the client. Clients can then use the `next()` and `previous()` methods to return a manageable set of data as needed. Clients would use the bean in the following order:

1   Create the session bean.

2   Call `paginate()`, passing in an SQL statement to retrieve data and a statement that counts data.

3   Call `next()` or `previous()` as needed.

4   Call `cleanup()` when you're through with a particular statement.

Listing 3.32 contains the session bean class.

Listing 3.32   PaginationBean.java

```java
import java.sql.*;
import java.util.*;
import java.lang.reflect.*;
import javax.ejb.*;

public class PaginationBean implements SessionBean
{
    private int page = 10;              Stores the size of
    private ResultSet set = null;       a page of data
    private int total = 0;
    private Connection con = null;
    private Statement stmt = null;
    private int firstRowNumber = 1;

    /*******************************
    *other bean methods not shown *
    *******************************/

    public void paginate( String sql, String countSQL )
    {
        try
        {
            ResultSet temp = executeQuery( countSQL );      Executes the count SQL and
            total = temp.getInt( 1 );                       stores the total number of rows
            cleanup();
            set = executeQuery( sql );      Executes the query SQL
        }catch( Exception e ){              and stores the result set
                set = null;
                e.printStackTrace();
```

```
      }
    }
    public Object[] next()
    {
      if( total == 0 )
        return null;

      Object[] rvalue = null;

      int count = page;  //try to return a full page

      try
      {
        //see if we can return a total page,
        //    if not get as much as allowed
        if( (count + set.getRow() ) > total )
        {
          count = total - set.getRow() + 1;
        }

        //if count is zero, we are at the end of the set
        if( count == 0 )
          return null;

        //update the current page index
        current++;

        rvalue = new Object[ count ];

        for( int i = 0; i < count; i++ )
        {
          rvalue[ i ] = buildObject( set.next() );        <-- Builds an object
        }                                                     from a row of data

        //reset the first row number variable
        //          for previous() comparisons
        if (set.isAfterLast())
            firstRowNumber = total - count + 1;
        else
            firstRowNumber = set.getRow() - count;
      }
      catch( Exception e )
      {
        e.printStackTrace();
      }
      return rvalue;
    }
    public Object[] previous()        <-- Returns the
    {                                     previous page
      if( total == 0 )
        return null;

      int count = page; //try to return a full page
```

```
    Object[] rvalue = null;
    try
    {
      if( ( firstRowNumber - count ) < 0 )
      {
        count = count - firstRowNumber;
      }

      if( count <= 0 )
        return null;

      //decrement the current page index
      current--;

      //test to see if we should be at the beginning
      if( ( firstRowNumber - count) == 0 )
          set.absolute( firstRowNumber - count + 1 );
      else
          set.absolute( firstRowNumber - count );

      rvalue = new Object[ count ];
      for( int i = 0; i < count; i++ )
      {
        rvalue[ i ] = buildObject( set.next() );
      }

      firstRowNumber = set.getRow() - count;

    }
    catch( Exception e )
    {
      e.printStackTrace();
    }

    return rvalue;
}

public int getTotalPages()
{
    try
    {
        int mod = total % page;

        int result = total/page;

        if( mod != 0 )
            return result + 1 + "";
        else
            return result + "";
    }
    catch( Exception e )
    {
      e.printStackTrace();
    }
```

Returns the total number of pages

```
      return -1;
    }

    public void cleanup()
    {
      try{
        if( stmt != null ){
          stmt.close();
          stmt = null;
        }
        if( con != null && !con.isClosed())
        {
          con.close();
        }
      }catch( Exception ex ) { ex.printStackTrace(); }

    }

    public boolean canNext()
    {
      try{
        return !(set.isAfterLast());
      } catch( Exception e ){e.printStackTrace();}
      return false;
    }

    public boolean canPrevious()
    {
     try{
      if( firstRowNumber <= 1 )
        return false;
     }catch( Exception e ){

       e.printStackTrace();
       return false;
     }
      return true;;
    }

    private ResultSet executeQuery( String sql ) throws Exception
    {
      con = null;
      stmt= null;
      ResultSet rs = null;

        con = getConnection();
        stmt = con.createStatement(|#10
                ResultSet.TYPE_SCROLL_INSENSITIVE,
                ResultSet.CONCUR_UPDATABLE);    |#10
        rs = stmt.executeQuery( sql );
        rs.next();

        return rs;
    }
```

Annotations:
- **Cleans up the statement and connection** (points to `public void cleanup()`)
- **Tests to see if next() will return a value** (points to `public boolean canNext()`)
- **Tests to see if previous() will return a value** (points to `public boolean canPrevious()`)
- **Creates a scrollable result set** (points to `stmt = con.createStatement` block)

```
private Connection getConnection()
{
  //implementation not shown
}

private Object buildObject()
{
  //implementation not shown
}
}
```

◆ *Discussion*

While the code in the solution is lengthy, it is pretty straightforward. There are a couple of key points to make about this session bean. First, in order to predict the number of data pages, the session bean requires you to pass in an SQL statement that returns the row count of the query that will be paginated. Second, the result set created by executing the query must be scrollable. This is done by creating the Statement object with the following line of code:

```
stmt = con.createStatement(ResultSet.TYPE_SCROLL_INSENSITIVE,
                           ResultSet.CONCUR_UPDATABLE);
```

Once the actual result set is acquired, the next() and previous() methods just keep track of the database cursor as they scroll through the result set. The only tricky part is being careful with the beginning and end indexes of the result set. Both methods use the total number of rows, the page size constant, and the return value of the getRow() method to determine how much data to return. The getRow() method of the ResultSet object returns the index number of the current row selected.

Using a page-able mechanism like this one allows your clients to build page-able tables in their displays. Users can then navigate forward and backward through the result set as needed. Another convenience method you could easily add to this bean is a jump() method. A jump method could loop through successive calls of next() or previous() to reach a certain page of data. Since the bean knows the total number of pages, this would be a simple exercise.

EJB activities

4

"You know her, she knows you, but she wants to eat him,
and everyone's okay with this?"

—*Timon from "The Lion King"*

EJBs are hard workers that can perform many activities. In addition to working with data (covered in chapter 3), EJBs can be used to retrieve environment variables, access the file system, send email, and more. This chapter also covers two important improvements added to EJBs with the 2.1 specification: the EJB timer service, and the use of EJBs as web service endpoints.

You will find the following topics in this chapter:

- Using environment variables
- Describing EJBs
- Providing common methods declarations
- Reusing trivial implementations
- Sending synchronous email
- Using the new EJB 2.1 timer service
- Creating a web service endpoint
- Sending a JMS message
- Building asynchronous processes
- Using asynchronous processes without JMS
- Insulating EJB from service changes
- Creating batch processes

4.1 Retrieving an environment variable

◆ Problem

You want your EJBs to be able to access environment type variables at runtime.

◆ Background

Environment variables are useful for providing constant values to applications about their runtime environment. Using environment variables can increase the portability of your EJBs. EJBs that rely on environment entries can customize their behavior and decrease the need for hardcoded values. Because Java can execute on many different platforms, you must take special precautions when accessing the hosting environment of the application. Fortunately, the EJB container provides an excellent way to supply environment values to executing EJBs. EJBs have the ability to use environment variables that are specified in their deployment descriptors.

◆ Recipe

To specify an environment variable that you want your EJB to access, use the `<env-entry>` tag in the deployment descriptor. The following XML shows a sample session bean descriptor that declares an environment variable `CONTACT_URL`:

```
<ejb-jar>
 <enterprise-bean>
  <session>
   <!- - bean description not shown - ->
   <env-entry>
     <description>The url to contact</description>
     <env-entry-name>CONTACT_URL</env-entry-name>
     <env-entry-type>java.lang.String</env-entry-type>
     <env-entry-value>http://thehost/withpath</env-entry-value>
   <env-entry>
   </session>
 </enterprise-bean>
</ejb-jar>
```

To look up the value of an environment variable from inside the session bean, use the EJB's Java Naming and Directory Interface (JNDI) context. You could use the following code to find the value of the environment variable shown in the previous XML descriptor:

```
InitialContext context = new InitialContext();
String contactURL = ( String ) context.lookup(
                         "java:comp/env/CONTACT_URL" );
```

◆ Discussion

The example shown in the recipe retrieves the `CONTACT_URL` property. The bean might use the property in order to contact a remote process or other object. Each `<env-entry>` in the deployment descriptor must contain at least a name, type, and value—the description is optional. The type of an environment entry can be `String` or any of the primitive type wrapper objects (`Integer`, `Long`, `Double`, `Byte`, `Float`, `Boolean`, or `Short`).

To retrieve the value of an entry, you need only perform a simple lookup with the JNDI context contained by the EJB. Use the context's `lookup()` method, passing it the name of the environment entry you wish to find. Remember that JNDI names are relative to the standard `java:comp/env` root.

◆ See also

3.1—Using a data source

4.2 Implementing toString() functionality for an EJB

◆ **Problem**

You want to give your EJBs the ability to describe themselves with a `String` value
for debugging and logging purposes.

◆ **Background**

Adding `toString()` functionality to your EJBs is a quick way to provide an excellent logging and debugging tool for future development work and problem solving. However, you cannot expose a `toString()` method remotely, because you
would have to override the method and add a `RemoteException` (which cannot be
done when overriding a method). Therefore, you must create a new method with
the same functionality.

◆ **Recipe**

To implement `toString()` functionality for an EJB, define a method, `ejb-ToString()`, that describes the implementing EJB. The `ejbToString()` method can
be exposed on the remote or local interface to be used by EJB clients. The following entity bean remote interface declares the `ejbToString()` along with some
other attributes:

```
public interface Equity extends EJBObject{
    public void setEquity( EquityVO equity )throws RemoteException;
    public EquityVO getEquity()throws RemoteException;

     //other methods not shown....

    public String ejbToString()throws RemoteException;
}
```

The method implementation in listing 4.1 shows how the Equity entity bean
might use the `ejbToString()` method to describe its attribute values to a client. In
this case, the entity bean makes use of a value object to construct the return
`String` value.

Listing 4.1 The ejbToString() method

```
public String ejbToString(){
    StringBuffer buffer = new StringBuffer();
    EquityVO     equity = new EquityVO();

    equity.symbol = getSymbol();
```

```
equity.description = getDescription();
equity.lastTrade = getLastTrade();
equity.change = getChange();
equity.volume = getVolume();
equity.marketCap = getMarketCap();
equity.PE = getPe();
equity.avgVolume = getAvgVolume();

buffer.append("-------------[ Equity Entity Bean ]------------\n");
buffer.append("Entity ID:"+id()+"\n\n");
buffer.append( equity.toString()+"\n");
buffer.append("-------------[ Equity Entity Bean ]------------");

return buffer.toString();
}
```

◆ Discussion

EJB clients can choose to log the returned bean description, or even parse it. When developers are using a debugger to examine EJB data, they can use the `ejbToString()` method to quickly ascertain the state of the bean's attributes. For instance, the `ejbToString()` method in the recipe example describes an instance of the `EquityBean` entity bean by returning the value of all its attributes.

4.3 Providing common methods for all your EJBs

◆ Problem

You want your remote and/or local interface for all your EJBs to have common methods.

◆ Background

When developing complex enterprise applications, you should use good object-oriented practices to increase the maintainability and ease of understanding of your code. One way to do this is to use super classes and super interfaces to encapsulate common functionality or methods in a single location that can be inherited by other classes or interfaces. In the Enterprise JavaBean world, you can use a super interface to provide common methods across all business interfaces of your EJBs. By including a super interface, your EJB clients can always expect certain methods to be present in the EJB interfaces.

◆ *Recipe*

In order to provide common methods for all your EJBs, you need to create a base interface. For this example, we want all of our EJBs to implement the method we describe in recipe 4.2, `ejbToString()`. First, create a base interface like the following:

```
public interface UtilInterface extends EJBObject{
  public String ejbToString() throws RemoteException;
}
```

With the base interface completed, all of the EJB remote (or local) interfaces just need to extend it instead of the EJBObject interface (or the EJBLocalObject interface if you use that instead):

```
public interface Equity extends UtilInterface{
  public void setEquity(EquityVO equity)throws RemoteException;
  public EquityVO getEquity()throws RemoteException;
}
```

The actual EJB class (listing 4.2) does not implement the base interface, but still must implement its methods since they are inherited into the remote (or local) interface of the EJB.

Listing 4.2   EquityBean.java

```
abstract public class EquityBean implements EntityBean {

  public String ejbToString(){
    StringBuffer buffer = new StringBuffer();
    EquityVO     equity = new EquityVO();

    equity.symbol=getSymbol();
    equity.description=getDescription();
    equity.lastTrade=getLastTrade();
    equity.change=getChange();
    equity.volume=getVolume();
    equity.marketCap=getMarketCap();
    equity.PE=getPe();
    equity.avgVolume=getAvgVolume();

    buffer.append("-------------[ Equity Entity Bean ]------------\n");
    buffer.append("Entity ID:"+id()+"\n\n");
    buffer.append(equity.toString()+"\n");
    buffer.append("-------------[ Equity Entity Bean ]------------");

    return buffer.toString();
  }

  //other bean methods not shown
}
```

◆ ***Discussion***

Using super interfaces is an excellent way to ensure that all your EJBs at least attempt to provide an implementation for a common method. By supplying the base interface, implementing EJBs are required to provide at least a trivial implementation of the methods (of the base interface) in order to compile. With each EJB interface inheriting a common super interface, EJB clients assume that EJBs will contain the common methods. In fact, with the super interface in place, your clients can make use of casting techniques to provide greater flexibility and perhaps create longer-lived code through more object-oriented coding practices.

◆ ***See also***

2.1—Generating home, remote, local, and local home interfaces

2.4—Creating value objects for your entity beans

3.17—Decreasing the number of calls to an entity bean

4.1—Retrieving an environment variable

4.4—Reducing the clutter of unimplemented bean methods

4.4 Reducing the clutter of unimplemented bean methods

◆ ***Problem***

In many cases, EJB methods such as `ejbPassivate()` and `ejbActivate()` are left with empty implementations. You would like to remove the clutter of unimplemented methods from your EJB classes.

◆ ***Background***

When you're developing EJBs, many times the numerous EJB lifecycle methods are left without meaningful implementation. This leaves beans with a more cluttered class file, with several empty methods. In addition, each time you develop a new bean, you could find yourself adding the empty methods via cut and paste. It would be nice to remove these methods from your bean class file and not have to add them for each new EJB.

◆ ***Recipe***

For each type of EJB, create an adapter super class that defines all of the standard methods required for that type. Your bean classes can subclass the correct adapter class and inherit the method definitions. Each derived class can choose to inherit the bean methods or provide an implementation by overriding methods.

Entity beans

The abstract class shown in listing 4.3 is the bean adapter class for entity beans. It provides a simple implementation for all the necessary methods needed for entity beans, and also includes a couple of convenience methods.

Listing 4.3   EntityBeanTemplate.java

```java
abstract public class EntityBeanTemplate implements EntityBean {
  protected EntityContext           eContext=null;;

  public EntityBeanTemplate() {};

  public void setEntityContext(EntityContext eContext) {
    log(this.getClass().getName()+".setEntityContext (" + id() + ")");
    this.eContext = eContext;
  }

  public void unsetEntityContext() {
    log(this.getClass().getName()
          +".unsetEntityContext (" + id() + ")");
    this.eContext = null;
  }

  protected String id() {
    return "" + System.identityHashCode(this) + ", PK = " +
      (String) ((eContext == null) ? "nulleContext"
                : ((eContext.getPrimaryKey() == null ?
                  "null" : eContext.getPrimaryKey().toString()))));
  }

  public void ejbActivate() {
    log(this.getClass().getName()+".ejbActivate (" + id() + ")");
  }

  public void ejbPassivate() {
    log(this.getClass().getName()+".ejbPassivate (" + id() + ")");
  }

  public void ejbLoad() {
    log(this.getClass().getName()+".ejbLoad (" + id() + ")");
  }

  public void ejbStore() {
    log(this.getClass().getName()+".ejbStore (" + id() + ")");
  }

  public void ejbRemove() throws RemoveException {
    log(this.getClass().getName()+".ejbRemove (" + id() + ")");
  }
```

```
protected void log(String s){
  System.out.println(this.getClass().getName()+"::"+s);
}
}
```

The `TestEntityBean` entity bean class (listing 4.4) extends the `EntityBeanTem-`
`plate` class in order to inherit all the bean methods. Notice that all the entity bean
does now is provide the getters and setters for data, as well as the `ejbCreate()` and
`ejbPostCreate()` methods.

Listing 4.4   TestEntityBean.java

```
abstract public class TestEntityBean extends EntityBeanTemplate {

  public TestEntityBean() {};

  abstract public int getStatus();
  abstract public void setStatus(int status);

  abstract public String getProcessId();
  abstract public void setProcessId(String processId);

  public String ejbCreate(String processId,int status)
    throws CreateException
  {
    log("TestEntityBean.ejbCreate( id = " +
        System.identityHashCode(this) +
        ", PK = " +
        processId + ", " + "Status =  " + status + ")");

    setProcessId(processId);
    setStatus(status);

    return null;  // See 9.4.2 of the EJB 1.1 specification
  }

  public void ejbPostCreate(String processId, int status)
  {
    log("TestEntityBean.ejbPostCreate (" + id() + ")");

}
```

Session beans

For the session bean, the bean adapter looks like the class shown in listing 4.5.

Listing 4.5   SessionBeanTemplate.java

```
public class SessionBeanTemplate implements SessionBean {
  protected SessionContext   sContext;
```

```
    public void ejbRemove() {
      log("ejbRemove called");
    }

    public void ejbPassivate() {
      log("ejbPassivate called");
    }

    public void setSessionContext(SessionContext ctx) {
      log("setSessionContext called");
      this.ctx = ctx;
    }

    public void ejbCreate () throws CreateException {
      log("ejbCreate called");
    }

    private void log(String s) {
      System.out.println(this.getClass().getName()+"::"+s);
    }

    public void ejbActivate() {
      log("ejbActivate called");
    }
  }
```

The following `TestSessionBean` session bean class makes use of the session bean adapter class:

```
public class TestSessionBean extends SessionBeanTemplate {

  public void doFunction(String message)
  {
    //implementation not shown
  }
}
```

As you can see, by using the adapter class, session beans now only contain their business methods. However, you could implement additional `create()` methods as needed.

Message-driven beans

Listing 4.6 contains the bean adapter class for message-driven beans.

Listing 4.6   MessageBeanTemplate.java

```
public class MessageBeanTemplate implements MessageDrivenBean,
  MessageListener {
  private MessageDrivenContext        mContext;

  public void ejbRemove() {
```

```
      log("ejbRemove called");
    }
    public void ejbPassivate() {
      log("ejbPassivate called");
    }
    public void setMessageDrivenContext(MessageDrivenContext ctx) {
      log("setMessageDrivenContext called");
      this.mContext = ctx;
    }
    public void ejbCreate () throws CreateException {
      log("ejbCreate called - This is called "
              + "by Container when deploying bean");
    }
    public void ejbActivate() {
      log("ejbActivate called");
    }
    public void log(String s) {
      System.out.println(this.getClass().getName()+"::"+s);
    }
    public void onMessage(Message msg) {
      log("onMessage called");
    }
  }
```

By extending the message-driven adapter class, the `MessageBean` message-driven
bean only needs to provide the `onMessage()` method implementation and any
other helper methods needed:

```
  public class MessageBean extends MessageBeanTemplate{
  
    public void onMessage(Message msg) {
      //implementation not shown
    }
  }
```

◆ *Discussion*

As you can tell from the three examples, using a bean adapter class greatly
reduces the size of the EJB class source file. By using adapter classes, you essentially factor out methods that are common to all EJBs of a certain type—those
methods that many of us just give trivial implementations. Each bean instance
inherits these methods, and can provide its own implementation of specific methods if needed.

◆ **See also**

4.3—Providing common methods for all your EJBs

4.5 *Sending an email from an EJB*

◆ *Problem*

You want to send an email from a session EJB.

◆ *Background*

In many enterprise situations, you will need to inform a user of specific events or notices by using an email message. Sending an email from a Java application has become a simple process now that developers can use the `javax.mail` package. The Java mail API is usually more than enough to satisfy the email needs of developers.

◆ *Recipe*

To provide the ability to send email from a session bean, we need a new method, `sendEmail()`. Listing 4.7 contains a simple stateless session bean that exposes the `sendEmail()` method in its remote interface (the interface is not shown).

Listing 4.7   SendEmailBean.java

```
import javax.mail.*;

public class SendEmailBean implements SessionBean
{

  //other bean methods not shown

  private void sendEmail(String recipient, String text)
  {
    Session mailSession = null;
    javax.mail.Message msg = null;

    try{
      System.out.println( "Sending Email to: " + rcpt );

      mailSession = (Session) ctx.lookup("BookMailSession");

      msg = new MimeMessage(mailSession);
      msg.setFrom();
      msg.setRecipients(Message.RecipientType.TO,
                    InternetAddress.parse( recipient , false));
      msg.setSubject("Important Message");
      msg.setText(text);
```

Looks up the mail session object

Creates and populates an email message

```
    Transport.send(msg);          <─────────────────────    Sends the
    System.out.println("Sent Email to: "+rcpt);            message
  }
  catch(Exception e){
    e.printStackTrace();
  }
 }
}
```

◆ ***Discussion***

For EJBs, the mail session object should be retrieved from the EJB container as a resource. After you've retrieved the email session object, it's just a matter of creating and populating a message instance before sending it using the `Transport` object. However, with large emails, you should be aware of the time clients may have to wait when invoking the `sendEmail()` method.

NOTE   If you are concerned about holding a lock on an object while waiting for the `sendEmail()` method to complete, you could always send the email asynchronously using a message-driven bean. For more about performing this and other tasks with message-driven beans, see chapter 6.

◆ ***See also***

6.11—Sending an email message asynchronously

4.6 *Using the EJB 2.1 timer service*

◆ ***Problem***

You want to execute business logic at specific instances in time.

◆ ***Background***

Enterprise applications often require certain business logic to run at specific times or at specific intervals that are triggered by time notifications. With the release of the EJB 2.1 specification, developers now have the ability to incorporate timers into their EJBs. Using the new timer service allows you to concentrate on the business logic instead of trying to develop a robust timing mechanism.

◆ *Recipe*

To demonstrate how to use the timer service, let's create a session bean that provides timers for its EJB client. The session bean must be stateful, since stateless beans cannot use the timer service. Here is the remote interface for the stateful session bean:

```
public interface TimerSession extends EJBObject {
  public void startTimer() throws RemoteException;
}
```

The remote interface `TimerSession` forces the session bean implementation class to provide the `startTimer()` method. In addition to implementing this method, the session bean must implement the `TimedObject` interface. The `TimedObject` interface provides the session bean with the `ejbTimeout()` method. Listing 4.8 shows the `TimerSessionBean` stateful session bean.

Listing 4.8 TimerSessionBean.java

```
public class TimerSessionBean implements SessionBean,TimedObject
{
  private SessionContext ctx;

  //other bean methods not shown

  public void startTimer()
  {
    TimerService timerService = ctx.getTimerService();      ← Retrieves the TimerService instance from the SessionContext object
    Timer timer =
      timerService.createTimer( 10000,                        Creates a timer that times out after 10 seconds
                       "EJBTimer1");
    Timer timer2 =
      timerService.createTimer( 2000,                         Creates a timer that times out after 2 seconds, and then every 5 seconds
                       5000, "EJBTimer2" );
  }

  public void ejbTimeout(Timer timer)
  {
    System.out.println( "*******ejbTimeout Called by Container" );
    System.out.println( "Next Timed Event:"
               + timer.getNextTimeout() );                    ← Prints the next timeout event for the timer
    System.out.println( "Timer Application Info:"
               + timer.getInfo() );                           ← Prints the value used in the creation of the timer
  }
}
```

◆ *Discussion*

The ejbTimeout() method of the TimedObject interface is a callback method that is invoked when a timer event occurs. A timer event is either a single expiration of the timer (as in the case of EJBTimer1 in the session bean) or a repeated event at an interval (as in the case of EJBTimer2). When the ejbTimeout() callback is invoked, the method receives the Timer instance that corresponds to the timeout. The session bean in the recipe uses the instance to print some information from the timer. Timer instances are created by specifying their interval times, and by passing in some user "info" that can be retrieved when the timer expires using the getInfo() method (it is optional and can be null).

Timers are cancelled in a few specific situations. In the case of the single event timer, it expires after invoking the ejbTimeout() method. If the timer was started in an entity bean instance and the bean is removed, the timer is also cancelled. Finally, if the cancel() method is invoked on the Timer instance, it is stopped.

Similar to EJB home objects, Timer objects contain a method, getHandle(), that allows you to store a handle object for a Timer instance. The TimerHandle object is serializable, which allows you to persist the object to storage. You can rebuild the TimerHandle object and use its getTimer() method to re-create a Timer instance.

Another important feature of the EJB timer service is its persistent nature. If the server crashes while timers are running, the application can assume they will still be running when the server restarts. If the interval of the timer expires while the server is down, the ejbTimeout() method will be invoked as soon as the server restarts.

Transactions also apply to the timer service. If you create a timer within a transaction that is rolled back, the timer creation will also be rolled back. Similarly, if you cancel a timer within a transaction that is rolled back, the cancellation will also be rolled back.

◆ *See also*

4.11—Insulating an EJB from service class implementations

4.7 *Sending a JMS message from an EJB*

◆ *Problem*

You want to send a JMS message from one of your EJBs.

◆ Background

JMS now provides Java enterprise applications with connectivity into other messaging platforms and applications. In addition, with the creation of message-driven beans, other EJBs have the ability to use JMS messages to create asynchronous processes. Using JMS requires developers to write some special code, as well as set up the environment in the application server.

◆ Recipe

The method shown in listing 4.9 illustrates how to send a JMS message from a session bean. You use this method to send a message to a JMS topic, and the session bean loads the JMS topic connection factory from the application server with a JNDI lookup.

Listing 4.9   The publish() method

```
private void publish(String subject, String content) {

    TopicConnection        topicConnection = null;
    TopicSession           topicSession = null;
    TopicPublisher         topicPublisher = null;
    Topic                  topic = null;
    TopicConnectionFactory topicFactory = null;
    try{

        topicFactory = ( TopicConnectionFactory )
                    context.lookup("TopicFactory");

        topicConnection =
            topicFactory.createTopicConnection();

        topicSession =
            topicConnection.createTopicSession( false,
                            Session.AUTO_ACKNOWLEDGE );

        topic =
            ( Topic ) context.lookup( "ProcessorJMSTopic" );
        topicPublisher =
            topicSession.createPublisher(topic);

        MapMessage message = topicSession.createMapMessage();
        message.setString("Subject", subject );
        message.setString("Content", content);
        topicPublisher.publish(message);
    }catch(Exception e){
        e.printStackTrace();
    }
}
```

Looks up the topic factory using the EJB's context object

Creates a topic connection and session

Finds the topic and builds a publisher

Builds and sends the message

◆ *Discussion*

The ability to create and send JMS messages gives EJBs the ability to contact enterprise systems and start asynchronous business processes using message-driven EJBs. All EJBs can send JMS messages, but only message-driven beans should accept messages. Message-driven beans are uniquely positioned to accept messages without blocking clients. Chapter 6 focuses on using message-driven beans.

This recipe only shows a JMS topic destination, but EJBs can also send messages to JMS queue destinations. The code for sending to a message queue is similar to that for sending to a topic; you need only change the classes to represent their queue counterparts.

◆ *See also*

Chapter 6, "Messaging"

4.8 *Using an EJB as a web service*

◆ *Problem*

You want to expose your session EJB as the business logic for a web service.

◆ *Background*

As web services become easier to implement, and more important to enterprise solutions, many developers would like to leverage their existing enterprise applications by reusing already developed business logic. With the release of the 2.1 EJB specification, EJBs can be created to serve as web service endpoints. For those who are new to web services, creating them is sometimes a daunting task.

◆ *Recipe*

Web service endpoints can be created using a stateless session bean; no other type of EJB may be used. The web service client will not know that a stateless session bean implements the web service. In order for the EJB to act as a web service, it must have a web service endpoint interface. The following shows a sample web service endpoint interface:

```
public interface EJBWebService extends Remote
{
  public void serviceMethod() throws RemoteException;
}
```

The EJB implementation class now needs to implement the method declared by the web service endpoint interface. The following sample session bean does this:

```
public class EJBWebServiceBean implements SessionBean
{
    //other bean methods not shown

     public void serviceMethod()
    {
       System.out.println( "Invoked by a web service client" );
    }
}
```

After compiling the two files (interface and bean implementation), you need to run the `wscompile` tool that comes with the Java 2 Platform Enterprise Edition (J2EE) JDK. Depending on your build environment, you should use something like the following:

```
wscompile -define config.xml
```

The `wscompile` tool reads the config.xml file, which describes the web service endpoint. The tool uses a .wsdl file for the service, packages everything into an ejb.jar file, and finally packages everything into an .ear file.

Here is a sample config.xml file used for this recipe:

```
<?xml version="1.0" encoding="UTF-8"?>
<configuration
  xmlns="http://java.sun.com/xml/ns/jax-rpc/ri/config">
  <service
      name="EJBWebService"
      targetNamespace="urn:Name"
      typeNamespace="urn:Name"
      packageName="ch4">
      <interface name="ch4.EJBWebService"/>
  </service>
</configuration>
```

◆ *Discussion*

This recipe only shows how to create the web service endpoint. For information about creating web service clients, go to http://java.sun.com. Creating web services allows you to expose previously developed business logic (that is encapsulated in an EJB) to platform-neutral web service clients. Doing this lets you reuse business logic and expose your application to a variety of clients. In addition, all the web service clients don't need to know the implementation platform or language of your application.

The example in the recipe provides a simple demonstration of exposing a business method as a web service. In this case, the example exposes the method `serviceMethod()`. The business logic to be shared as a web service should be placed in this method.

4.9 *Creating asynchronous behavior for an EJB client*

◆ *Problem*

You want to provide an EJB client with the ability to start an asynchronous business method without the client using the Java Message Service (JMS).

◆ *Background*

With the release of the 2.0 EJB specification, EJB applications have the ability to create asynchronous behavior using message-driven beans. However, if an EJB client wants to use a message-driven bean, it must be able to send a JMS message in order to trigger the business logic. To reduce the complexity of the client, you would like to provide asynchronous behavior without the need for the client to use JMS.

◆ *Recipe*

To provide asynchronous processing, use a message-driven bean, but also create a session bean to start the asynchronous process and check the status of that process. This recipe completes three tasks:

1 Develops a session facade to a message-driven bean. The facade gives an EJB client the capability to invoke the message-driven bean without using JMS from the client.

2 Develops an entity bean to represent the process ID and status of an asynchronous process.

3 Develops the message-driven bean to contain the business logic for the asynchronous process.

Listing 4.10 shows the implementation of the `AsyncProcessBean` session bean that starts an asynchronous process for an EJB client. The session bean exposes a method that stores a unique ID in a database and then starts a process with a message-driven bean. It exposes a second method that checks the status of the process by querying the database (which is updated by the message-driven bean).

Listing 4.10   AsyncProcessBean.java

```java
public class AsyncProcessBean implements SessionBean {

  private SessionContext ctx;

  //bean methods not shown

  public String startProcess(){              ◁─┐  Starts a new
    String processId = null;                      asynchronous
                                                   process
    processId = "" + System.currentTimeMillis();
    createStatus( processId );      │ Initializes the process status
    sendMessage( processId );       │ and sends the JMS message

    return processId;
  }

  private void createStatus( String processId ){
    int        status = 0;
    Context    ctx = null;
    StatusHome home = null;

    try {
      home = (StatusHome) ctx.lookup("statusHome");
      home=(StatusHome) PortableRemoteObject.narrow(home,
                  StatusHome.class);
      home.create(processId, status );
    }
    catch (Exception e) {
      e.printStackTrace();
    }
  }
  public int getStatus(String processId){    ◁─┐  Checks the status
    int        status = 0;                        of the process
    StatusHome home = null;
    Status     statusBean = null;

    try {
      home = (StatusHome) ctx.lookup("statusHome");
      home=(StatusHome) PortableRemoteObject.narrow(home,
                  StatusHome.class);
      statusBean = (Status) PortableRemoteObject.narrow(
                  home.findByPrimaryKey(processId), Status.class);
      status = statusBean.getStatus();
      ctx.close();
    }
    catch (Exception e) {
      e.printStackTrace();
    }
```

```
      return status;
   }

   private void sendMessage(String processId){
       TopicConnection           topicConnection=null;
       TopicSession              topicSession=null;
       TopicPublisher            topicPublisher=null;
       Topic                     topic=null;
       TopicConnectionFactory    topicFactory = null;

       try{
         topicFactory = (TopicConnectionFactory)
                              context.lookup("BookJMSFactory");
         topicConnection = topicFactory.createTopicConnection();
         topicSession = topicConnection.createTopicSession(false,
                              Session.AUTO_ACKNOWLEDGE);
         topic = (Topic)context.lookup("BookJMSTopic");
         topicPublisher = topicSession.createPublisher(topic);

         MapMessage message = topicSession.createMapMessage();
         message.setString("ProcessId",processId);
         topicPublisher.publish(message);
       }
       catch(Exception e){
         e.printStackTrace();
       }
   }
}
```

Listing 4.11 shows the StatusBean entity bean that is used to persist and update the status of the asynchronous process.

Listing 4.11   StatusBean.java

```
abstract public class StatusBean implements EntityBean {
  private EntityContext ctx;

  public StatusBean(){}

  public void setEntityContext(EntityContext ctx) {
    this.ctx = ctx;
  }

  public void unsetEntityContext() {
    this.ctx = null;
  }

  abstract public int getStatus();                       Accesses the status attribute
  abstract public void setStatus(int status);

  abstract public String getProcessId();                 Accesses the process ID
  abstract public void setProcessId(String processId);
```

```
public String ejbCreate(String processId,int status)
  throws CreateException
{
  setProcessId(processId);
  setStatus(status);

  return null;
}

//remaining bean methods not shown
}
```

Listing 4.12 shows the message-driven EJB that executes the asynchronous process. In an enterprise application, this bean would contain the business logic for execution. This EJB is also responsible for updating the status of the process in the database.

Listing 4.12   MessageBean.java

```
public class MessageBean implements MessageDrivenBean, MessageListener {

  private MessageDrivenContext ctx;

  public void onMessage(Message msg) {
    MapMessage map=(MapMessage)msg;

    try {
      String processId = map.getString("ProcessId");        ◁  Retrieves the
                                                                 new process ID

      //execute custom business logic (not shown)

      //update the status of the process
      updateStatus(processId);     ◁  Updates the process status
    }                                 after executing business logic
    catch(Exception ex) {
      ex.printStackTrace();
    }
  }

  private void updateStatus(String processId){
    int        status = 1;
    StatusHome home = null;
    Status     statusBean = null;

    try {
      home = (StatusHome) ctx.lookup("statusHome");               Uses the
      home = (StatusHome) PortableRemoteObject.narrow(home,  StatusBean entity
                         StatusHome.class);                    bean to set the
      statusBean = (Status) PortableRemoteObject.narrow(         new status
                 home.findByPrimaryKey(processId), Status.class );
      statusBean.setStatus(status);
```

```
    }
    catch (Exception e) {
      e.printStackTrace();
    }
  }

  //other bean methods not shown
}
```

Finally, the following pseudo-code shows how an EJB client can use the session facade to start an asynchronous process and check its progress as needed:

```
//lookup session facade
AsyncProcessRemote bean = lookupBean();
String processId = bean.startProcess();

//do something else for a while

int status = bean.checkStatus( processId );
```

◆ *Discussion*

To provide asynchronous processing, clients should still use a message-driven bean. However, to shield those clients that wish to make use of the message-driven functionality, you should create a session facade for the message-driven bean. When an EJB client invokes a particular session bean method, the session bean will send a JMS message to trigger business logic in a message-driven bean.

In the recipe, the AsyncProcessBean session bean acts as the session facade to the MessageBean message-driven bean. To give more power to the EJB client, the session bean will also provide a way for the client to check the status of the asynchronous process. To do this, each message will have a unique ID assigned to it. The recipe makes use of the StatusBean entity bean to store the status and the process ID for each asynchronous process. The message-driven bean will update the status of its process in the database according to the process ID from the original message. The session bean can check the status of the process by querying the database (either with or without an entity bean). Of course, it's up to the client how often, and if at all, it checks the status of the process.

Asynchronous behavior has been possible in EJB applications since the creation of the message-driven bean. However, to execute a message-driven bean, EJB clients must make use of JMS. If your client is using JMS only for invoking message-driven beans, it is really only adding more complexity for potentially little gain. It would be better to create asynchronous behavior without requiring EJB clients to use JMS.

◆ *See also*

4.7—Sending a JMS message from an EJB

4.10—Creating asynchronous behavior without message-driven beans

Chapter 6, "Messaging"

4.10 *Creating asynchronous behavior without message-driven beans*

◆ *Problem*

You want to execute some business logic asynchronously without the use of message-driven beans.

◆ *Background*

Asynchronous behavior is a valuable attribute of many enterprise applications. It became more feasible in EJB applications with the advent of the message-driven bean. The only drawback of message-driven beans is that your applications must make use of JMS. If your applications already use JMS, it's not so hard to start using message-driven beans. However, JMS may be more of an inconvenience if all you use it for is to contact a message-driven bean. You would like to create asynchronous processes without using JMS or message-driven beans. This recipe requires the use of a J2EE 1.4 feature, the EJB timer service (see recipe 4.6).

◆ *Recipe*

To create an asynchronous process, EJB clients can make use of a session bean that uses the EJB timer service. The session bean implementation class in listing 4.13 provides a single method, startProcess(), that creates a timer in order to trigger business logic.

Listing 4.13   AsynchBean.java

```
public class AsynchBean
                    implements SessionBean,TimedObject
{
  private SessionContext ctx;

  //other bean methods not shown

  public void startProcess( Serializable arguments )
  {
      TimerService timerService = ctx.getTimerService();   ◁⎯
```

**Acquires an
instance of the
TimerService**

```
        Timer timer  = timerService.createTimer( 1000, arguments );
    }
    public void ejbTimeout(Timer timer)
    {
        Serializable arguments = timer.getInfo();

        //perform business logic below (not shown)
    }
}
```

**Creates a timer to
expire in I second**

**Retrieves the
arguments from
the client**

◆ *Discussion*

Creating a session bean like this one allows a client to create a process to execute business logic without having to stick around and wait for it to complete. The client merely invokes the startProcess() method. The startProcess() method accepts a Serializable object as arguments to the business process. When the startProcess() method returns, the client simply continues with other work. The timer started by the startProcess() method will eventually time out; the recipe sets it for 1 second and invokes the callback method on the session bean. The ejbTimeout() callback method contains the actual business logic for execution. The session bean pulls out any arguments from the Timer instance and executes the business logic. Using the timer service in this way enables you to create asynchronous processes without the use of JMS and message-driven beans.

◆ *See also*

4.1—Retrieving an environment variable

4.5—Sending an email from an EJB

4.6—Using the EJB 2.1 timer service

4.11 *Insulating an EJB*
from service class implementations

◆ *Problem*

You want to insulate your EJBs from the implementation of classes that encapsulate the services of your application.

♦ *Background*

Many times EJBs make use of other objects to encapsulate business functions as services to the bean. Encapsulating business logic allows many EJBs to reuse the business logic. However, as your application grows, you may find that your service classes have subclasses that provide specialized implementations of the business logic. As your EJBs start to use the specialized subclasses of the service classes, they become less portable and more dependent on outside classes.

♦ *Recipe*

To insulate your EJB, create an interface for each service class and load the implementation class using reflection and environment variables. For instance, assume we have a service class that performs three important functions. Its interface would look like this:

```
public interface MyService
{
  public void performTaskOne();
  public void performTaskTwo();
  public void performTaskThree();
}
```

By using an interface, the EJB can store any implementation class in a member variable (of the interface type). The EJB method in listing 4.14 could be used to load a service implementation for use by an EJB.

Listing 4.14 The createServiceInstance() method

```
private MyService createServiceInstance(){
    MyService service = null;
    Class     c = null;                              Finds the
                                                     implementation
    try{                                             classname
      String classname = ( String )
              context.lookup( "java:comp/env/MY_SERVICE_CLASS" );
      c = Class.forName(classname);           Creates an instance of the class and
      service = (MyService) c.newInstance();   casts it to the interface type
    }
    catch(Exception e){
      e.printStackTrace();
    }
    return service;
}
```

◆ *Discussion*

The key to this recipe is the use of reflection, interface, and environment variables stored in a bean's deployment descriptor. This example loads the implementation classname from an environment variable in its deployment descriptor, and uses reflection to instantiate an instance of the class. For more information about using the deployment descriptor to store variables, see recipe 4.1.

◆ *See also*

4.1—Retrieving an environment variable

4.12 *Creating a batch process mechanism*

◆ *Problem*

You want to create an EJB mechanism to start and run batch processes.

◆ *Background*

Batch processing is a powerful tool in many enterprise applications. With a batch system, you can advance daytime orders through to the next step in a workflow during nighttime hours. This enables data to be ready for the next day's work, and allows the system to utilize resources that might be tied up during peak usage hours. Unfortunately, many times the batch processing system is not a part of the actual enterprise application. This separation sometimes creates problems because you now have applications to keep in synch (code wise) and maintain in production. This recipe requires the use of a J2EE 1.4 feature, the EJB timer service (see recipe 4.6). This recipe is a combination of an asynchronous process using an entity bean to report status (recipe 4.9) and an asynchronous process using a timer (recipe 4.6).

◆ *Recipe*

To create a batch process, use the EJB timer service to create an asynchronous process, and use an entity bean to create a status for the process. The stateful session bean in listing 4.15 should be used by EJB clients to create a batch process. It contains a single method that allows clients to schedule a process.

Listing 4.15 BatchProcessBean.java

```
public class BatchProcessBean implements SessionBean,TimedObject
{
  private SessionContext ctx;

  //other bean methods not shown

  public void createBatchProcess( String batchName, long timeFromNow )
  {
      TimerService timerService =          | Acquires an instance of
              ctx.getTimerService();       | the TimerService
      Timer timer  =
              timerService.createTimer( timeFromNow,    | Creates a timer to
                                        batchName );    | expire in 1 second

      //create an entity bean to update the status of this batch
      try {
        StatusHome home = (StatusHome) ctx.lookup("statusHome");
        home=(StatusHome) PortableRemoteObject.narrow(home,
                                  StatusHome.class);

        int status = 0;
        home.create( batchName, status );
      }
      catch (Exception e) {
        e.printStackTrace();
      }
  }
                                           | Executes when
  public void ejbTimeout(Timer timer)  <─┘ | the timer expires
  {
      String batchName = timer.getInfo();

      //perform business logic for batch process below (not shown)
      //update status as needed
  }
}
```

◆ *Discussion*

This solution creates a batch process that executes only once. You could, however, change the creation of the timer to execute repeatedly (instead of only once). See recipe 4.6 for the specifics of the EJB timer service. By timing the batch process to run at off-peak hours, you are safe from tying up resources that are needed by actual users. When you're developing a mechanism like this one, your business logic would be located in the ejbTimeout() method. This is the method that is executed when the timer expires. If you use a repeating timer, this method is also invoked repeatedly. Management consoles (or your client application) can look up the entity beans that represent the batch status using the batch name.

Another factor to consider when developing a batch system like this one is your ability to encapsulate business logic from the `ejbTimeout()` method. This way, when your batch business logic changes (its code), your batch system does not need to also change. Recipe 4.11 presents an example of insulating your EJBs from the business logic.

◆ *See also*

4.9—Creating asynchronous behavior for an EJB client

4.10—Creating asynchronous behavior without message-driven beans

4.11—Insulating an EJB from service class implementations

5 Transactions

"Never eat more than you can lift."

—*Miss Piggy*

Enterprise JavaBeans are well integrated into a transactional API provided by the Java 2 Enterprise Edition (J2EE) platform. Transactions control the permanence of the result from a section of code that creates new data or modifies existing data. Not all applications require transactions, but critical applications must have ways of ensuring that data is consistent for all data clients and that it exists in a predictable way. For example, transactions help remove data modifications made by a failed process.

The importance of transactions is clearly demonstrated by imagining what happens when you remove them from critical situations. Imagine a multistep process such as transferring money between two bank accounts—money is withdrawn from one account and deposited into a second. A single transaction should control this two-step process in a single event. If one half of the event cannot succeed, then none of it should. If the withdrawal of money succeeds but the deposit fails, then the withdrawal must be reversed (or *rolled back*).

Without transactions, an automated process is prone to self-corruption due to uncorrected errors. In the account example, someone could lose money if a deposit failed and the withdrawal were not reversed. Granted, this is an overly simplified example, but it does illustrate the value of transactions. Just as important, transactions protect data accessors from reading bad data. If a database update fails midway through, you need to remove the already updated data. For example, getting an account balance during a money transfer should reflect only those transfers that have completed successfully, not those in progress because they still might fail. Transactions provide the mechanism for ensuring that data changes and processes run correctly. This chapter contains recipes for EJB transactions and covers the following topics:

- Modifying the transaction control of your EJBs
- Creating bean-managed transactions
- Rolling back the current transaction
- Avoiding rollbacks by handling errors
- Forcing a rollback
- Imposing timeouts on transactions
- Updating more than one entity bean
- Managing state during a transaction
- Using multiple transactions
- Managing state after a rollback

- Throwing exceptions during a transaction
- Propagating transactions to other EJBs
- Propagating transactions to nonEJBs
- Starting transactions in the client layer
- Using transactions in JavaServer Pages
- Creating distributed transactions

A transaction appetizer

Transactions in the J2EE platform are ACID transactions—atomic, consistent, isolated, and durable. Being *atomic* means that a transaction must either complete entirely or not at all. If any part of the transaction fails, the entire process is reversed with a rollback. Transactions are *consistent* by guaranteeing that the process running within the transaction does not result in inconsistent data. For example, one database connection should not be able to read data that might not be completely updated by another transaction—or data that might get rolled back. *Isolated* transactions are those that operate without interference from other processes. Finally, *durable* transactions must commit data to a persistent storage so that it survives application crashes.

Transactions are best used when they span business rules, not just actual methods. For instance, using a transaction to cover each single entity bean attribute is not as useful as covering the entire insert of a data set. When developing EJB transactional behavior, it's easy to become too fine grained—using one transaction for each method. Be sure to take careful consideration and lay out your transactions across business logic and functions to create a more robust enterprise application.

Also, it is useful to have some background context for many of the recipes by discussing the two mechanisms for handling transactions in the Enterprise Java-Bean world:

- *Container-managed transactions (CMT)*—The most common way of managing transactions in your EJB applications is to use container-managed transactions. CMT beans rely on the EJB container to create, propagate, and commit transactions. By relying on the container, enterprise beans can concentrate more on business logic development without worrying about coordinating the transactional operations of an enterprise application. In the majority of cases, CMTs are the most secure, reliable, and efficient way to manage transactions.

■ *Bean-managed transactions (BMT)*—Developers should use bean-managed transactions in order to have a finer-grained control over their transactional system. For instance, with BMT beans, you can create more than one transaction per bean method (see recipe 5.9). A BMT bean is responsible for creating, propagating, committing, and rolling back its transactions. By not relying on the container, the bean developer must face the sometimes daunting task of coordinating a transactional system. EJB applications that use BMT beans can be every bit as secure and reliable as CMT applications, but there is a larger chance of developer-introduced transactional errors. In most cases, the EJB container is sufficient for enterprise applications' transaction management.

5.1 *Tuning the container transaction control for your EJB*

◆ *Problem*

You want to be able to control how the container manages the transactions of each of your EJBs.

◆ *Background*

Your enterprise beans are declared to use container-managed transactions. Container-managed transaction EJBs declare their transaction behavior in the deployment descriptor. When declaring a bean to use CMTs, you need to specify the transaction behavior for the methods using transactions. The EJB specification defines six levels of transaction support, each causing an EJB to behave in a different way.

◆ *Recipe*

A CMT bean declares the transaction level of each method in the assembly descriptor portion of the ejb-jar.xml file for the bean. To do this, you use the `<container-transaction/>` element. For example, the XML file shown in listing 5.1 is the deployment descriptor for the session bean `SampleBean`. It declares the transaction attribute for a single method (shown in bold).

Listing 5.1   Deployment descriptor

```
<ejb-jar >

  <description>Sample Deployment XML</description>
  <display-name>Sample XML</display-name>

  <enterprise-beans>
    <!—Beans described in this section -->
  </enterprise-beans>

  <assembly-descriptor>

   <container-transaction>
     <method>
        <ejb-name>SampleBean</ejb-name>
        <method-name>simpleBusinessMethod</method-name>
     </method>
     <trans-attribute>Mandatory</trans-attribute>
   </container-transaction>

  </assembly-descriptor>
</ejb-jar>
```

The `<trans-attribute/>` element value can be one of six values: `NotSupported`, `Supports`, `Required`, `RequiresNew`, `Never`, or `Mandatory`. The Discussion section describes each value. In addition, ensure that your bean is declaring itself a user of container-managed transactions. To do this, modify the `<transaction-type/>` element in the deployment descriptor for your bean. For example, the following is a sample descriptor for the session bean `UserBean`:

```
<session>
      <description>Example</description>
      <ejb-name>User</ejb-name>
      <home>UserHome</home>
      <remote>User</remote>
      <ejb-class>UserBean</ejb-class>
      <session-type>Stateful</session-type>
      <transaction-type>Container</transaction-type>
</session>
```

The two values for the `<transaction-type/>` element are `Container` and `Bean`, indicating CMT and BMT, respectively.

◆ Discussion

In the assembly descriptor section of the ejb-jar.xml file, you should set the transaction attribute for each EJB method. The `<container-transaction/>` element's

<ejb-name> value lists the name of the EJB that contains the named method in the <method-name> value. In addition, the <method-name> value can be an *, indicating that the transaction attribute applies to all the methods of an EJB. Each <container-transaction/> element can list several methods and must contain the <trans-attribute/> tag. This tag declares the transaction level for the specified method. Table 5.1 details the possible values for the transaction attribute tag.

Table 5.1   The <trans-attribute> tag value can be one of the following values. Each value sets a transaction level for an EJB.

Transaction Control Level	Description
NotSupported	No transaction can be propagated to a method with this attribute. The current transaction will be suspended until the method completes, and then will resume. This attribute is commonly used for a method that should never be used in a transaction.
Supports	Indicates that a method does not require a transaction but can be executed within the scope of a transaction. Methods with this attribute support operation with or without transactions.
Required	A transaction must be used when invoking a method with this attribute. If one cannot be propagated to it, the container will create a new transaction. This attribute should be used for methods that must always run inside a transaction. Required transaction methods are those that are usually critical business functions that must complete successfully to ensure data integrity or to complete a user process (and should be reversible upon failure).
RequiresNew	When a method with this transaction attribute is invoked, the EJB container will create a new transaction for it. Methods declared with this attribute should never run inside transactions that have already completed work.
Mandatory	The invoked method must always be part of a transaction. If a nontransactional method invokes it, the invocation will fail with a TransactionRequiredException (for remote clients) or RequiredLocalException (for local clients) exception being thrown.
Never	The method with this attribute must never be invoked inside a transaction; otherwise, it will fail with a RemoteException (for remote clients) or EJBException (for local clients) exception being thrown.

As the recipe states, you should also ensure that your EJB declares itself a CMT bean by specifying Container in the <transaction-type/> element of the deployment descriptor. A value of Bean indicates that the bean itself is handling its own transactions, in which case you do not need to specify the transaction attribute for methods.

5.2 Handling transaction management without the container

◆ **Problem**

You want to know how to develop your enterprise beans to manage transactions without the container.

◆ **Background**

In most situations, container-managed transactions will satisfy the needs of your EJB application. However, situations may arise where beans need more control over the transactions controlling their methods. For instance, with CMT beans you are limited to a single transaction per method. By managing transactions without the container you'll have finer-grained control of the transactions within a single method. Only session beans are allowed to manage their own transactions. Entity beans must always use container-managed transactions.

◆ **Recipe**

Use the `EJBContext` instance of your EJB to acquire the current `UserTransaction` instance from the container:

```
UserTransaction transaction = ejbContext.getUserTransaction();
```

After acquiring a transaction instance, you can use it to wrap a certain section of code (as described in the Discussion section). In addition, you can use the `EJBContext` to access more transactions as needed.

◆ **Discussion**

While you may invoke this method from any type of EJB, it will actually succeed only inside EJBs that can manage their own transactions—and only session beans and message-driven beans are free to manage their own transactions. If an entity bean makes a call to this method, it will result in a `java.lang.IllegalState-Exception`. Likewise, invocations by beans that have not declared their transaction type to be bean-managed will result in an exception. The following sample XML describes a BMT session bean. Use something similar for your own EJB.

```
<session>
    <description>Example</description>
    <ejb-name>User</ejb-name>
    <home>UserHome</home>
    <remote>User</remote>
```

```
      <ejb-class>UserBean</ejb-class>
      <session-type>Stateful</session-type>
      <transaction-type>Bean</transaction-type>
</session>
```

Use the `getUserTransaction()` method of the `EJBContext` class (as shown in the recipe) to acquire a transaction instance. Once you have an instance of `User-Transaction`, you can do the following:

```
transaction.begin();
    //perform operations inside a transaction
transaction.commit();
```

After committing a transaction, you can acquire another one in the same manner, allowing you to program fine-grained transaction control of your method implementation. (See recipe 5.9 for more information.) Generally, you should always use container-managed transactions because the EJB container is specifically designed to handle transactions properly to avoid problems associated with transactional systems. However, there certainly is a time and place for BMT beans, for instance when you need a finer-grained transactional method.

Instead of using your `EJBContext` object to get a transaction, acquire the transaction using JNDI. The following code demonstrates:

```
InitialContext context = new InitialContext();
UserTransaction transaction = ( UserTransaction )
        context.lookup( "java:comp/env/UserTransaction" );
```

After acquiring the `UserTransaction` instance, you can use it as illustrated in the discussion.

◆ **See also**

> 5.1—Tuning the container transaction control for your EJB

5.3 *Rolling back the current transaction*

◆ **Problem**

You want to know how to force the rollback of the current transaction.

◆ **Background**

Before the end of a transaction, you want to roll back the current transaction regardless of the outcome of the method. Your code has detected an error or a condition that will cause the code to fail, and you want to roll back the previously executed code within the transaction.

◆ *Recipe*

If you are using bean-managed transactions, you should use the methods in the `UserTransaction` class. Acquire the `UserTransaction` instance from the `EJBContext` set in your EJB (see recipe 5.2 for more information). From the `UserTransaction`, use one of the following methods:

```
transaction.rollback();
transaction.setRollbackOnly();
```

On the other hand, if your bean uses container-managed transactions, it must use the following method of the `EJBContext` :

```
ejbContext.setRollbackOnly();
```

◆ *Discussion*

For BMT beans, use one of the rollback methods in the `UserTransaction` object acquired from the container. The `rollback()` method tells the container to start a rollback immediately, while the `setRollbackOnly()` method only marks the transaction for rollback (which will occur after the EJB method completes). Ultimately, these methods will cause the current transaction to be rolled back and undo any updates that were performed. Collectively, they can throw three different exceptions:

- `SecurityException`—Thrown by the `rollback()` method if the thread using the `UserTransaction` is not allowed to perform a rollback

- `IllegalStateException`—Thrown if the current thread is not associated with a transaction

- `SystemException`—Thrown if an unexpected error occurs while the transaction is being rolled back

EJBs typically make use of the `rollback()` method after detecting an error in the processes contained in a transaction. For example, say an exception is thrown in the method implementation, and you want to immediately roll back the previous updates. Programmers can use the `getStatus()` method (from the `UserTransaction` class) to determine the state of the current transaction. This method returns an `int` value contained in the `javax.transaction.Status` class, such as `STATUS_ACTIVE`. You can use the `int` value to check if the current transaction has already been marked for a rollback.

For CMT beans, you must use the `setRollbackOnly()` method of the `EJBContext` class. It marks the current transaction for rollback regardless of the transaction's outcome. It can throw the following exceptions:

- `IllegalStateException`—Thrown if the current thread is not associated with a transaction
- `SystemException`—Thrown if an unexpected error occurs while the transaction is being rolled back

Combined with `getRollbackOnly()`, the `setRollbackOnly()` method should be used to successfully manage errors that may occur in a method implementation. For instance, if the EJB detects an error, it can test the transaction with the `getRollbackOnly()` method to see if the error causes the transaction to be marked for rollback. If not, it can attempt to correct the problem and complete the transaction, or mark the transaction for rollback if necessary.

◆ *See also*

5.4—Attempting error recovery to avoid a rollback

5.5—Forcing rollbacks before method completion

5.8—Managing EJB state at transaction boundaries

5.10—Managing EJB state after a rollback

5.4 Attempting error recovery to avoid a rollback

◆ *Problem*

You want your EJBs to attempt to recover from errors before causing a transaction rollback.

◆ *Background*

You would like a particular EJB method to have the highest possibility of success. To do this, you want to code a particular method to monitor the status of the executing code in order to detect errors or conditions that may cause a rollback to occur. If a rollback is necessary, you want your EJB to attempt to recover from the error before performing a rollback.

◆ *Recipe*

With both bean-managed and container-managed transaction EJBs, you can avoid causing a rollback by correctly handling errors.

For bean-managed transaction beans

Listing 5.2 contains a code section from a BMT bean business method that attempts to avoid a rollback.

Listing 5.2   Avoiding a rollback in a BMT bean

```
UserTransaction transaction = ejbContext.getUserTransaction();
transaction.begin();                      Acquires an instance of UserTransaction
try
{
    //perform business logic here
}
catch( Exception e )
{
  boolean errorFixed = false;
  boolean markedForRollback = transaction.getRollbackOnly();  Tests for a
                                                              potential rollback
  if( !markedForRollback ) //not marked for rollback
  {
     //discover actual error and attempt a fix
     errorFixed = fixError();      Attempts to fix
  }                                the error
  else return; //skip remaining method body

  if( !errorFixed )
  {
     transaction.rollback();       Rolls back the
  }                                transaction
}
transaction.commit();
```

For container-managed transaction beans

Listing 5.3 contains a code section from a CMT bean business method that attempts to avoid a rollback.

Listing 5.3   Avoiding a rollback in a CMT bean

```
Ltry
{
    //perform business logic here
}
catch( Exception e )
{
  boolean errorFixed = false;
  boolean markedForRollback = ejbContext.getRollbackOnly();
  if( !markedForRollback )              Tests for a potential rollback
  {
     //discover actual error and attempt a fix
```

```
      errorFixed = fixError();        ←┐ Attempts to fix the error
   }
   else return; //skip remaining method body

   if( !errorFixed )
   {
      ejbContext.setRollbackOnly();   ←┐ Marks the transaction
   }                                       for rollback
}
```

◆ *Discussion*

The recipe describes how to test for rollbacks for both BMT and CMT beans. Bean-managed transaction beans should use the methods from the `UserTransaction` instance being used, and container-managed transaction beans should use the methods of their `EJBContext` instance. The recipe demonstrates in both cases an attempt to recover from exceptions thrown within the current transaction. The ability to acquire the status of a transaction and to mark it for rollback gives you more control over your transactions in both BMT and CMT beans.

For BMT bean methods containing many steps, the transaction rollback control shown in the recipe allows you to test the transaction after each significant step in the method. After each step, you can attempt recovery or begin a rollback. For CMT beans, you have only one transaction per method, but you can mark the transaction for rollback without throwing an exception to the container. In both cases, testing the transaction allows you to skip the remaining code in a method if you plan to roll back the transaction. This can be important for improving performance.

In addition, BMT beans could use the `rollback()` method to immediately force a rollback of the current transaction.

◆ *See also*

5.2—Handling transaction management without the container

5.3—Rolling back the current transaction

5.8—Managing EJB state at transaction boundaries

5.10—Managing EJB state after a rollback

5.5 *Forcing rollbacks before method completion*

◆ *Problem*

You want the container to roll back the current transaction without waiting for the current method to complete execution.

◆ *Background*

In certain conditions, it is best to immediately roll back a transaction without attempting to complete the remaining code within the transaction. For instance, if attempts to acquire a database connection time out, trying to complete the method that uses the connection is pointless. For performance and application health reasons, it is simply best to roll back any previous changes without completing the method.

◆ *Recipe*

In order to force a rollback, you should throw an instance, or subclass, of the `javax.transaction.SystemException` exception class (see listing 5.4).

Listing 5.4 Sample business method throwing a SystemException

```
public void businessMethod() throws EJBException
{
    //perform important logic
    boolean returnValue = performBusinessFunction();
    try
    {
      //evaluate success of logic
      if( returnValue ){
        //do something else
      }
      else{
        //force immediate rollback
        throw new SystemException( "Condition failed, rolling back");
      }
    }catch( CustomException ce )
    {
      throw new EJBException( ce );
    }
}
```

◆ *Discussion*

Transactions are automatically rolled back if a system exception is thrown at any time during the transaction. System exceptions are the `RuntimeException` and any of its subclasses. Because system exceptions are runtime exceptions, they do not need to be declared in the method declaration.

If a system exception is thrown from within the method that started the transaction, the transaction is rolled back. If a client started the transaction, the client's transaction is marked for rollback.

Using system exceptions to force rollbacks does have certain, important side effects. When the container catches a system exception, it rolls back the transaction, logs the exception, and discards the EJB that originated the exception. For stateless session and entity beans, losing a bean instance is not that important, since a new one will be identical in every way for the client. However, losing a reference to a stateful bean will cause a client to lose the state it might have accumulated in that bean.

◆ *See also*

> 5.3—Rolling back the current transaction
>
> 5.8—Managing EJB state at transaction boundaries
>
> 5.10—Managing EJB state after a rollback

5.6 Imposing time limits on transactions

◆ *Problem*

You want to set a timeout value for your transactions.

◆ *Background*

A particular transaction appears to be taking longer than expected and you need to impose time limits on it. In other words, for a transaction to be considered successful, it must execute in a predefined time limit. Using time limits is a good way to discover performance-related errors. For example, even if your application transactions are completing successfully but they are unusually slow, they should be flagged as errors. If an executing transaction exceeds a certain time, it should be considered in an error state, and any completed work should be rolled back.

◆ *Recipe*

Bean-managed transaction EJBs can set a timeout value for a transaction using the `setTransactionTimeout()` method from the `UserTransaction` instance acquired from the `EJBContext` set in the bean. For example:

```
UserTransaction transaction = ejbContext.getUserTransaction();
transaction.begin();
transaction.setTransactionTimeout( 30 ); //set value to 30 seconds
   // invoke business functions here
transaction.commit();
```

The timeout value for container-managed transaction beans comes from the EJB container itself. Your vendor's documentation should explain how to set this value.

◆ *Discussion*

As you can see from the recipe, setting timeout values for transactions is simple. When a timeout occurs, the transaction will be rolled back because a `SystemException` will be thrown. An EJB can receive notification of the rollback by implementing the `SessionSynchronization` interface for session beans only. If an EJB client has a reference to the transaction, it can test the transaction using the `getRollbackOnly()` method from the `UserTransaction` instance.

◆ *See also*

5.2—Handling transaction management without the container

5.5—Forcing rollbacks before method completion

5.8—Managing EJB state at transaction boundaries

5.10—Managing EJB state after a rollback

5.7 *Combining entity updates into a single transaction*

◆ *Problem*

You want to update more than one entity bean in a single transaction.

◆ *Background*

You have two or more entity beans that represent data in a single step of a transaction. For example, from the account transfer example in the chapter introduction, you might have entity beans that represent each of the two accounts. In this case, you want to perform both updates in single transaction.

◆ *Recipe*

Develop a session bean that contains a business method that updates the entity beans within its transaction. In addition, each entity bean's transaction attribute should not be set to `RequiresNew`, `Never`, or `NotSupported`; you must set it to `Requires`, `Mandatory`, or `Supports`. The `SampleBean` session bean shown in listing 5.5 updates two entity beans in a single transaction.

Listing 5.5   SampleBean.java

```
public class SampleBean implements SessionBean
{
   private SampleEntityBean bean1;
   private SampleEntityBean bean2;

   /**
   * Sample business method executing in a single transaction.
   */
   public void commitMultipleEntities()
   {
      bean1.setMyAttribute( "abc" );
      bean2.setMyAttribute( "def" );
   }
   //session bean methods below
}
```

The transaction attribute for the session bean should be set to `Required`, `Mandatory`, or `RequiresNew`.

◆ *Discussion*

Using session beans to encapsulate access to entity beans is an accepted practice by all EJB developers. The session bean uses its transaction for the `commitMultipleEntities()` business method to contain the two updates of the entity beans. In order to keep the multiple entity bean updates within a single transaction, make sure that each entity bean's transaction attribute is not set to `RequiresNew`. If you use `RequiresNew`, the EJB container will create a separate transaction for each entity bean update, breaking the single-transaction requirement. By propagating the business method's transaction to the entity beans, all the updates can be rolled back together. This ensures that all entity beans are updated if and only if they all succeed in the update.

◆ **See also**

> 5.1—Tuning the container transaction control for your EJB
>
> 5.16—Updating multiple databases in one transaction

5.8 Managing EJB state at transaction boundaries

◆ **Problem**

In order to manage their state, you want your EJBs to know when a transaction starts, completes, and/or rolls back.

◆ **Background**

You don't want to use bean-managed transactions, but you do want to be notified when a transaction starts and when one completes. Being notified of transaction events allows your beans to manage their member state variables appropriately. For instance, when a transaction starts, you want to make sure the EJB has initialized its state variables. When the transaction completes, you want to make sure you are preparing state variables for the next transaction. This doesn't apply to stateless session beans, because they should not contain any state that needs to be managed at transaction boundaries.

◆ **Recipe**

To get information about transaction status for stateful session beans, implement the `javax.ejb.SessionSynchronization` interface. The example session bean in listing 5.6 receives a callback for the beginning, successful completion, and post-completion of a transaction.

Listing 5.6 SampleBean.java

```
public class SampleBean implements SessionBean, SessionSynchronization
{
    private Object stateVariable;

    public void afterBegin() throws RemoteException
    {
      //Transaction has started...
      stateVariable = initializeState();
    }

    public void beforeCompletion() throws RemoteException
    {
      //Transaction is about to complete
```

```
      saveState();
    }

    public void afterCompletion( boolean committed ) throws RemoteException
    {
      //test for rollback
      if( !committed )
         stateVariable = initializeState();
    }

    //implementation of the EJB below...
  }
```

For entity beans, the `ejbLoad()` and `ejbStore()` methods are the beginning and end of a transaction (also `ejbCreate()` and `ejbRemove()`—basically where data is loaded or stored). If a rollback occurs, `ejbLoad()` will be invoked to restore the bean's state.

◆ *Discussion*

The `SessionSynchronization` interface should be used to prepare a stateful session bean before specific transaction boundaries. It provides callback methods to the bean occurring after the transaction begins, before the transaction commits, and after the transaction completes. The `afterCompletion()` callback provides a `boolean` parameter indicating whether the transaction has been marked for a rollback. In addition, the `beforeCompletion()` callback will be invoked only if the transaction is about to perform a commit.

The container will invoke all the methods of this interface at the correct times. The first callback method, `afterBegin()`, should be used to prepare data for use inside a transaction. This process might include reading from a database. The second callback should be used to save the state of data that was created from the business method and needs to be preserved. The final method should be used to test for a rollback condition. If a rollback has occurred, use this method to restore the session bean's data to its original state before the transaction started.

◆ *See also*

5.2—Handling transaction management without the container

5.4—Attempting error recovery to avoid a rollback

5.5—Forcing rollbacks before method completion

5.10—Managing EJB state after a rollback

5.9 *Using more than one transaction in a method*

◆ **Problem**

In a single business method, you want to make use of more than one transaction.

◆ **Background**

With container-managed transaction beans, you are limited to a single transaction per method. You would like to group some important sections of code into a single method but use multiple transactions within the entire method. You need transaction control like this if you have a method that contains critical sections of code that cannot be broken into separate methods for CMT control. This enables you to roll back a small section of code and exit the method without executing the remaining method. This applies only to session beans, because entity beans must always use container-managed transactions.

◆ **Recipe**

Change your session bean to manage its own transactions by altering its XML descriptor. For example, the following code sets up a `UserBean` EJB for bean-managed transactions:

```xml
<session>
    <description>Example</description>
    <ejb-name>User</ejb-name>
    <home>UserHome</home>
    <remote>User</remote>
    <ejb-class>UserBean</ejb-class>
    <session-type>Stateful</session-type>
    <transaction-type>Bean</transaction-type>
</session>
```

Create transactions around your important code sections as needed. For example, the business method in listing 5.7 uses multiple transactions.

Listing 5.7 Sample business method

```java
public void businessMethod()
{
    UserTransaction transaction = null;
    try
    {
        transaction = ejbContext.getUserTransaction();
        transaction.begin();
            //perform important code
```

```
      transaction.commit();

  }catch( Exception e )
  {
    //need to rollback?
    if( transaction == null )
       transaction.rollback();
  }

   //start next section of important code
  try
  {
    transaction = ejbContext.getUserTransaction();
    transaction.begin();
       //perform important code
    transaction.commit();

  }catch( Exception e )
  {
    //need to rollback?
    if( transaction == null )
       transaction.rollback();
  }
}
```

◆ **Discussion**

At times, you need a finer-grained control of transactions than the single-transaction-per-business method provided by container-managed transactions. If this is the case, it makes sense to change your session beans to bean-managed transactions. By managing transactions on your own, you can create as many as you need within a single method. This gives you the ability to specify small rollbacks, attempt to recover from errors, and provide specific explanation of exceptions.

In a situation like this, you may even consider using nested transactions—starting one transaction while executing within another. Unfortunately, this type of transactional programming is not allowed. Possibly in the future we will see the EJB specification modified to handle this behavior. For clarification, an EJB that declares its transactional behavior with RequiresNew called within another transaction is not an example of nested transactions. The containing transaction is suspended while the new one executes, and resumes when the new transaction completes. The "inside" transaction does not affect the first transaction. For EJBs, transactions are either suspended or propagated.

◆ **See also**

5.1—Tuning the container transaction control for your EJB

5.12—Propagating a transaction to another EJB business method

5.13—Propagating a transaction to a nonEJB class

5.10 *Managing EJB state after a rollback*

◆ **Problem**

You want to make sure your EJBs have correct state variables after a rollback completes.

◆ **Background**

After a rollback has occurred, a stateful session EJB must reset its state to what it was before the rolled-back transaction began execution. The goal of a rollback is to restore an EJB state to the pre-transaction version, ensuring that new transactions can start with the correct state. You need your EJB to know when a transaction rollback has occurred within a method, and you want to restore the EJB state before a new transaction can start.

◆ **Recipe**

To reset the state for a session bean after a rollback, implement the `javax.ejb`
`.SessionSynchronization` interface shown in listing 5.8.

Listing 5.8   SampleBean.java

```
public class SampleBean implements SessionBean, SessionSynchronization
{
    public void afterBegin() throws RemoteException
    {
      //Transaction has started...
    }

    public void beforeCompletion() throws RemoteException
    {
      //Transaction is about to complete
    }

    public void afterCompletion( boolean committed )
                        throws RemoteException
    {
      //test for rollback
```

```
      if( !committed )
         restoreState(); //invoke bean method to restore state
   }

   //implementation of the EJB below…
}
```

For entity beans, don't do anything. The container will invoke ejbLoad() on the entity bean and restore it to its original state before the transaction.

◆ Discussion

Only session beans can implement the SessionSynchronization interface. It provides session beans with three callback methods that indicate the beginning, successful completion, and postcompletion of a transaction within the bean.

After the transaction has completed, the container invokes the afterCompletion() method, passing in a boolean parameter indicating whether the transaction was rolled back. If a rollback occurred, you should use this method to restore the original state of the bean before the business method invocation.

As you can see, the SessionSynchronization interface should be used with beans using container-managed transactions. If your bean is managing its own transactions, you won't need this interface to know about transaction boundaries because the bean itself manages those events.

Entity beans, on the other hand, do not need to be informed of transaction boundaries. Their ejbLoad() and ejbStore() methods are the indicators of transaction boundaries. If a rollback occurs on an entity bean, the container will invoke the ejbLoad() method to restore the bean's state.

5.11 Throwing exceptions without causing a rollback

◆ Problem

You want to throw exceptions from methods within a transaction without causing a rollback.

◆ Background

In a container-managed transaction session bean, you want to throw an exception that does not force a transaction rollback. In some of your business methods, you want to do some data validation before actually doing any work that might require a rollback. If the validation fails, you want to indicate as such by throwing an exception. However, the data validation would not require a rollback. For example, registering a user would require validation of user data before persisting it in a data store. You might want to throw an exception upon invalid data, and no rollback would be needed because no data has been persisted.

◆ *Recipe*

To avoid causing a rollback, throw an application exception from your business method. An application exception is any exception that does not subclass `RuntimeException` or `RemoteException`. Consider the `registerUser()` business method:

```
public void registerUser( String user, String password ) throws
        InvalidUserDataException
{
    if( user == null || password == null )
      throw new InvalidUserDataException();
}
```

◆ *Discussion*

Unlike system exceptions, application exceptions do not necessarily force a transaction to be rolled back. Application exceptions do not extend `RuntimeException` or `RemoteException`. Typically, they are used in validation situations, such as the one in the recipe. Application exceptions must be declared in the method declaration and are returned to the client without being wrapped in an `EJBException` or `RemoteException`. As you can see in the recipe, the `InvalidUserDataException` instance is thrown because either the user or the password was null. The application exception is thrown before any actual work is completed in the method, and therefore no rollback is needed.

Obviously, this works only if your method has not done something that needs a rollback. While developing such methods, you must be careful to force rollbacks when necessary.

◆ *See also*

5.5—Forcing rollbacks before method completion

5.12 *Propagating a transaction to another EJB business method*

◆ *Problem*

You want to propagate the current transaction to another EJB method.

◆ *Background*

You want a transaction to cross two or more business methods within a single EJB, or you need to contain two or more business methods from two or more separate EJBs. Propagating transactions across methods lets you break up a multistep process into many methods or beans and still contain it in a single transaction. Using propagation lets you keep the benefits of a single transaction—a single transaction and a single commit—while letting you break up large sections of code into multiple methods and beans.

◆ *Recipe*

Both CMT and BMT beans can propagate their current transaction to another EJB.

For container-managed transaction beans

For CMT beans you need to ensure that the methods being invoked from within a transaction do not use the RequiresNew, Never, or NotSupported transaction attributes. The deployment descriptor of each bean describes the transaction attributes for the business methods. For example, a CMT session bean SampleBean, with the business method simpleBusinessMethod(), might be described like this:

```
<container-transaction>
    <method>
        <ejb-name>SampleBean</ejb-name>
        <method-name>simpleBusinessMethod</method-name>
    </method>
    <trans-attribute>Mandatory</trans-attribute>
</container-transaction>
```

As long as each business method does not declare its transaction attribute to be RequiresNew (or NotSupported or Never), the current transaction will be propagated to it.

For bean-managed transaction beans

In this situation, a BMT bean wants to pass along its transaction to another business method. If the other business method is in a CMT bean, use the container-managed transaction recipe. If an instance of `UserTransaction` was started in one method, it can be committed in a different method. Subsequent calls to `getUser-Transaction()` return the current transaction instance. Listing 5.9 shows a session bean that manages transactions in this manner.

Listing 5.9 SimpleBean.java

```
public class SimpleBean implements SessionBean
{
    public void businessMethodOne()
    {
        UserTransaction transaction = ejbContext.getUserTransaction();
        transaction.begin();
         //do some work
    }
    public void businessMethodTwo()
    {
        // do some work
        UserTransaction transaction = ejbContext.getUserTransaction();
        transaction.commit();
    }
}
```

◆ *Discussion*

This recipe does not apply to stateless session beans. Because stateless beans are shared across multiple clients, it does not make sense to share transactions across them. Per the EJB specification, one transaction cannot start in one stateless method or bean and complete in another. For stateless bean methods, transactions must be started and completed within the method invocation. This solution should therefore be applied only to stateful beans or entity beans as needed.

◆ *See also*

5.1—Tuning the container transaction control for your EJB

5.2—Handling transaction management without the container

5.13—Propagating a transaction to a nonEJB class

5.13 *Propagating a transaction to a nonEJB class*

◆ *Problem*

You want to involve a nonEJB class in the current transaction by propagating the transaction to the object.

◆ *Background*

Your EJB application makes use of session beans that call into data access objects (DAOs) rather than entity beans. If the data update from the DAO object fails, you want the transaction to roll back.

◆ *Recipe*

Two of the best ways to solve this problem are to catch a custom exception thrown by the DAO object (indicating a failed update), or to allow the DAO to throw a system exception upon the failed update.

The session bean in listing 5.10 uses a DAO pattern to update a database, and it catches the custom `BadUpdateException` thrown by the DAO. After catching the exception, it tells the container to roll back the transaction.

Listing 5.10 SimpleBean.java

```java
public class SimpleBean implements SessionBean
{
  public void businessMethod( Hashtable data )
  {
    BusinessDataAccessObject bdBean = getData();
    try
    {
      bdBean.updateData( parameters );
    }catch( BadUpdateException e )
    {
      //do some work before rolling back….

      ejbContext.setRollbackOnly();
    }
  }

  //remaining methods below
}
```

Alternatively, the DAO object could simply throw a system exception after telling its JDBC connection to roll back an update. The system exception will force a rollback of the current transaction. The data access object class in listing 5.11 demonstrates this concept.

Listing 5.11   BusinessDataAccessObject.java

```
public class BusinessDataAccessObject
{
   public void updateData( Hashtable parameters ) throws SQLException
   {
    Connection con = null;
    try{
      con = getConnection();
      con.setAutoCommit( false );
      PreparedStatement stmt = createStatement( con );
      stmt.executeUpdate();
      con.commit();

    }catch( Exception e )
    {
      con.rollback();
      throw new SystemException( e.getMessage() );
    }

   }
}
```

◆ *Discussion*

This recipe separates the actual transaction of the session bean and the JDBC transaction contained within the DAO object. The DAO uses a system exception in order to force the container to roll back the session bean's transaction upon an error in the update. This recipe works for CMT session beans; for BMT beans you could pass a reference to the UserTransaction instance to the DAO object for control. If you were using multiple DAO objects, each of which might possibly need rollbacks, it would be best to use a bean-managed transaction EJB, allowing you finer-grained control.

◆ *See also*

5.5—Forcing rollbacks before method completion

5.14 Starting a transaction in the client layer

◆ *Problem*

You want to start a transaction in the client layer of your application and propagate to an EJB.

◆ *Background*

You would like your application client to start a transaction with which to execute EJB methods. In this scenario, you want the client to propagate a transaction to the EJB container. This recipe should only be used with session beans.

◆ *Recipe*

To start a transaction in the client layer, first create an instance of the JNDI context and use it to acquire a `UserTransaction` instance (see listing 5.12).

Listing 5.12 Starting a transaction in the client layer

```
Properties props = new Properties();
//put any necessary vendor props...

Context myJNDIContext = new InitialContext( props );
UserTransaction transaction = (UserTransaction)
        myJNDIContext.lookup( "java:comp/env/UserTransaction" );
try
{
  transaction.begin();

    //do some work with EJBs

  transaction.commit();
}
catch( Exception e )
{
  transaction.rollback();
}
```

The EJB to be used should not declare its transaction level to be `RequiresNew`, `Never`, or `NotSupported`; anything else will work correctly (`Required`, `Supports`, or `Mandatory`).

◆ *Discussion*

Clients can make use of transactions like a BMT bean. From an initialized `Context` object, a client can acquire a new `UserTransaction` instance from the transaction system by looking up the JNDI name `java:comp/env/UserTransaction`. With a new instance in hand, the client can look up beans and execute their methods within the transaction. The transaction will be propagated to the beans for their use. The EJBs being used within the client transaction should not set the transaction level to `RequiresNew`, `Never`, or `NotSupported`. `RequiresNew` will force the container to create a new transaction for the bean and suspend the one started by the client. Using `Never` or `NotSupported` will tell the container that the bean should not be executed within a transaction, and an exception will be thrown.

When creating your `InitialContext` instance, be sure to check your vendor documentation for any specific properties you need to set in order for the lookup to function successfully.

Finally, keep in mind that you should apply this recipe only to session beans. In reality, you can apply it to entity beans, but it is accepted practice to avoid exposing entity beans to the client layer. You should use a session bean to wrap your data access. To include entity beans within a client-initiated transaction, use a session bean to wrap them—apply this recipe to the wrapping session bean. You can use the session bean to provide security, context, and better performance over the longevity of your application lifecycle.

If you are seriously considering starting a transaction on the client, you should attempt to first see if you can move that functionality to a session bean. Typically, you should start and complete transactions in the EJB layer in order to ensure that they are managed in the correct way.

◆ **See also**

> 3.17—Decreasing the number of calls to an entity bean
>
> 5.2—Handling transaction management without the container
>
> 5.15—Holding a transaction across multiple JavaServer Pages

5.15 *Holding a transaction across multiple JavaServer Pages*

◆ **Problem**

You want to hold a transaction across a series of JavaServer Pages.

◆ **Background**

You have a complex series of JSP pages that users interact with to complete a function, such as filling out a registration form or running a wizard. In order to provide your users with the best experience, you persist the collected information from each page (or *step*) of the process. Because many steps persist information, you want to span the entire process with a single transaction started and committed from your JSP.

NOTE   While spanning a JSP session with a single transaction is possible, it may not be the best solution. After examining this code, be sure to read the Discussion section for more information regarding the drawbacks of this approach.

◆ *Recipe*

To span a JSP session with a single transaction, create the transaction and store it in the `Session` object. Retrieve it from successive pages and commit or roll back when needed:

```
<%
    UserTransaction transaction = (UserTransaction)
            myJNDIContext.lookup( "java:comp/env/UserTransaction" );
    Session.setAttribute("CURRENT_TRANSACTION", transaction );
    transaction.begin();
      //do some work with EJBs
  %>
```

To retrieve the transaction, use this code:

```
<%
  UserTransaction transaction = ( UserTransaction )
            Session.getAttribute("CURRENT_TRANSACTION" );
    //do some work with EJBs
  %>
```

◆ *Discussion*

While this recipe will work, using it might indicate a possible need to re-architect your method of presenting a process to the end user. A better way of solving this problem, rather than carrying a transaction across multiple pages using the `Session`, is to store the user's progress in a stateful session bean. The sequence should move something like this:

1   The user starts the process and the JSP creates a stateful session bean for the user session.

2   For each process step, the JSP collects data and sends it to the user's session bean.

3 The process completes.

4 The JSP starts a transaction in the session bean, commits the data, and ends the transaction.

5 The JSP reports the status back to the user.

This method performs the same function and prevents database locks and long-lived transactions. In this manner you create a short transaction, and your system is better suited for multiple and long-lived sessions (alternatively, you could store state in the HTTP session of the user). You should use a form of this solution, rather than creating a long-lived transaction spanning a user session.

◆ **See also**

5.2—Handling transaction management without the container

5.14—Starting a transaction in the client layer

5.16 *Updating multiple databases in one transaction*

◆ *Problem*

You want to commit updates to two or more entity beans, persisting to different databases, in a single transaction. This is a two-phase commit.

◆ *Background*

One of the benefits of using EJBs for business logic and data persistence is the ability to trust the EJB container to properly manage complex transactional situations. For example, completing or rolling back a transaction that is involved in a two-phase commit is not easily managed by the programmer. When using container-managed transactions, you can easily perform a two-phase commit, updating two different databases in a single transaction.

◆ *Recipe*

Before you try a two-phase commit in your EJB application, you need to check the following:

1 Read your application server documentation to see if it supports two-phase commits with its transaction system.

2 Make sure your database driver supports the two-phase commit protocol for your connections. The database driver provider must include the classes `javax.sql.XAConnection` and `javax.sql.XADataSource`.

After meeting these requirements, you should not have any problems. For example, listing 5.13 contains a CMT session bean that updates two entity beans.

Listing 5.13   SampleBean.java

```java
public class SampleBean implements SessionBean
{
    private SampleEntityBean bean1;
    private SampleEntityBean bean2;

    /**
     * Sample business method executing in a single transaction.
     */
    public void commitMultipleEntities()
    {
      //look up 2 entity beans from separate data bases
        bean1 = getEntityDataFromDB1();
        bean2 = getEntityDataFromDB2();

        bean1.setMyAttribute( "abc" );
        bean2.setMyAttribute( "def" );
    }

    //session bean methods below not shown
}
```

Configure the method `commitMultipleEntities()` with the transaction attribute `Required`, `Mandatory`, or `RequiresNew`. The container will handle the commits or necessary rollback.

◆ *Discussion*

The entity beans used in the recipe solution (`bean1` and `bean2`) need to be configured separately to persist to separate databases. The entity beans should make use of an `XADataSource` in order for the distributed, two-phase commit to succeed. Check your application server documentation for setting up these beans.

Once configured, completing this type of transaction is no harder than any other type of transaction. The simple session bean just updates the two entity beans and completes the method. Once the method completes successfully, the EJB container's transaction manager will commit the transaction, telling the two different JDBC connections to commit. If both connections succeed, the transaction is considered a success.

◆ **See also**

3.2—Creating EJB 2.0 container-managed persistence

5.1—Tuning the container transaction control for your EJB

5.7—Combining entity updates into a single transaction

6 Messaging

"An army marches on its stomach."

—*Napoleon Bonaparte*

With the introduction of the message-driven bean in the EJB 2.0 specification, Enterprise JavaBean applications can now easily be integrated with messaging systems. Java 2 Platform Enterprise Edition (J2EE)-compliant application servers are required to provide messaging capabilities. Before the message-driven bean, EJB applications could still send Java Message Service (JMS) messages and listen for those messages by including a JMS listener object; however, messages had to be processed in a synchronous manner. Message-driven beans are now the ideal way to expose business logic to messaging applications.

This chapter primarily focuses on problems associated with message-driven bean development. In this chapter, you will find recipes dealing with these topics:

- Sending JMS messages
- Creating a message-driven EJB
- Processing messages first in, first out
- Putting business logic in message-driven beans
- Streaming data with JMS
- Triggering multiple message-driven beans
- Speeding up message delivery
- Using message selectors
- Handling errors in a message-driven bean
- Sending email asynchronously
- Handling rollbacks in a message-driven bean

6.1 Sending a publish/subscribe JMS message

♦ Problem

You want to send a JMS message to a message topic (known as *publish/subscribe* messaging).

♦ Background

Enterprise applications can now use the JMS to communicate to outside applications or other application servers. EJBs can use JMS to decouple communication with these other systems in an asynchronous manner using a publish/subscribe pattern. JMS message topics create a one (the sender) to many (the receiver) relationship between messaging partners. In addition, publish/subscribe topics can be used to store messages even when no entity is ready to retrieve them (referred to as *durable subscriptions*).

◆ *Recipe*

The code in listing 6.1 shows a private method, `publish()`, that can be used in any object that wishes to send a JMS message to a publish/subscribe topic.

Listing 6.1   The publish() method

```
private void publish(String subject, String content) {
    TopicConnection        topicConnection = null;
    TopicSession           topicSession = null;
    TopicPublisher         topicPublisher = null;
    Topic                  topic = null;
    TopicConnectionFactory topicFactory = null;

    try{
        Properties props = new Properties();
        props.put(Context.INITIAL_CONTEXT_FACTORY,
                "weblogic.jndi.WLInitialContextFactory");
        props.put(Context.PROVIDER_URL, url);
        InitialContext context = new InitialContext( props );

        topicFactory =
                    ( TopicConnectionFactory )
                    context.lookup("TopicFactory");

        topicConnection =
                    topicFactory.createTopicConnection();
        topicSession =
                    topicConnection.createTopicSession( false,
                            Session.AUTO_ACKNOWLEDGE );

        topic = ( Topic ) context.lookup( "ProcessorJMSTopic" );
        topicPublisher = topicSession.createPublisher(topic);

        MapMessage message = topicSession.createMapMessage();
        message.setString("Subject", subject );
        message.setString("Content", content);
        topicPublisher.publish(message);
    }catch(Exception e){
        e.printStackTrace();
    }
}
```

Creates an InitialContext for the Weblogic application server

Looks up the topic factory

Creates a topic connection and session

Finds the topic and builds a publisher

Builds and sends the message

◆ *Discussion*

Publish/subscribe messaging allows you to send a single message to many message listeners. In fact, you can create message Topic destinations as durable, allowing message listeners to retrieve messages that were sent before the listener subscribed to the topic.

To send a message to a JMS topic, you first need to create a Java Naming and Directory Interface (JNDI) context and retrieve the JMS connection factory for topics in the JMS environment. Next, you must create a topic connection in order to establish a topic session. Once you have a session, you can find the actual topic to which you want to send a message, and build a publisher object for transmission of your message. Finally, simply construct your message and send it using the publisher. For more about the JMS API, visit http://java.sun.com

◆ *See also*

6.2—Sending a point-to-point JMS message

6.3—Creating a message-driven Enterprise JavaBean

7.8—Securing a message-driven bean

6.2 Sending a point-to-point JMS message

◆ *Problem*

You want to send a point-to-point message.

◆ *Background*

Like the publish/subscribe messaging model shown in recipe 6.1, the point-to-point model allows applications to send messages asynchronously to remote message listeners. Point-to-point messaging differs in that it creates a one-to-one relationship between sender and receiver—that is, a single receiver consumes a single message. No message will be duplicated across multiple consumers.

◆ *Recipe*

The code in listing 6.2 shows a private method, send(), that can be used in any object that wishes to send a JMS point-to-point message.

Listing 6.2   The send() method

```
private void send(String subject, String content) {
  QueueConnection        queueConnection = null;
  QueueSession           queueSession=null;
  QueueSender            queueSender=null;
  Queue                  queue=null;
  QueueConnectionFactory queueFactory = null;

  try{
    Properties props = new Properties();
    props.put(Context.INITIAL_CONTEXT_FACTORY,
           "weblogic.jndi.WLInitialContextFactory");
    props.put(Context.PROVIDER_URL, url);
    InitialContext context = new InitialContext( props );

    queueFactory =
         (QueueConnectionFactory) context.lookup("QueueFactory");

    queueConnection = queueFactory.createQueueConnection();
    queueSession = queueConnection.createQueueSession(false,
                             Session.AUTO_ACKNOWLEDGE);
    queue = (Queue)context.lookup("BookJMSQueue");
    queueSender = queueSession.createSender(queue);

    MapMessage message =
       queueSession.createMapMessage();
    message.setString("Symbol",symbol);
    message.setString("Description",description);
    queueSender.send(message);

  }
  catch(Exception e){
    log("Error Publishing Message");
    e.printStackTrace();
  }
}
```

Annotations (right margin):
- **Creates an InitialContext for the Weblogic application server**
- **Looks up the topic factory**
- **Creates a topic connection and session**
- **Finds the topic and builds a sender**
- **Builds and sends the message**

◆ *Discussion*

To send a point-to-point message, you must send a message to a JMS message queue. To send the message, you first have to create a JNDI context and retrieve the JMS connection factory for a message queue in the JMS environment. Next, you must create a queue connection in order to establish a queue session. Once you have a session, you can find the actual queue to which you want to send a message, and build a sender object for transmission of your message. Finally, you simply construct your message and send it using the sender.

Message queues guarantee that messages are consumed by only one receiver and are never duplicated across multiple listeners (unlike a JMS topic). Message queues are ideal for messages that should be processed concurrently but only once. Many receivers can be pulling messages from a queue for processing at the same time, but each message will be sent to only one consumer.

◆ **See also**

6.1—Sending a publish/subscribe JMS message

6.3—Creating a message-driven Enterprise JavaBean

7.8—Securing a message-driven bean

6.3 *Creating a message-driven Enterprise JavaBean*

◆ **Problem**

You want to create a message-driven bean to contain business logic that will be triggered by a JMS message.

◆ **Background**

Message-driven beans (added to the EJB 2.0 specification) are assigned to receive messages from a particular JMS message destination. These EJBs are ideal for executing business logic asynchronously and for exposing EJB applications to enterprise messaging systems. Message-driven beans use the same transaction models (see chapter 5) and declarative security (see chapter 7) as do session and entity beans. Another advantage of message-driven beans is that they can be used to process messages concurrently. EJB containers can create a pool of identical message-driven beans that are able to process messages at the same time, generating a great deal of processing power.

◆ **Recipe**

This recipe illustrates how to build a simple message-driven bean and create its XML descriptor. The class in listing 6.3 defines a message-driven bean. It implements the required `MessageDrivenBean` interface and the necessary `MessageListener` interface that allows the bean to receive JMS messages.

Listing 6.3   SampleMDB.java

```java
public class SampleMDB implements MessageDrivenBean, MessageListener  ◁─┐
{                                                                    Implements the
  private MessageDrivenContext ctx;                            MessageDrivenBean and
                                                               MessageListener interfaces
  public void ejbRemove() { }

  public void ejbPassivate() {  }

  public void setMessageDrivenContext(MessageDrivenContext ctx) {
    this.ctx = ctx;
  }

  public void ejbCreate () throws CreateException {  }

  public void ejbActivate() {  }

  public void onMessage( Message msg ) {  ◁─┐ Handles
    MapMessage map = ( MapMessage ) msg;       incoming
                                               messages
    try {

       processMessage( map );
    }
    catch(Exception ex) {
      ex.printStackTrace();
    }
  }

  private void processMessage( MapMessage map ) throws Exception
  {
     //implementation not shown
  }

}
```

Listing 6.4 contains the partial deployment XML file for the bean; notice how it
indicates the source type of messages for the bean (either point-to-point or pub-
lish/subscribe).

Listing 6.4   Deployment descriptor

```xml
<ejb-jar>
 <enterprise-beans>

    <message-driven>
      <ejb-name>SampleMDB</ejb-name>
      <ejb-class>SampleMDB</ejb-class>
      <transaction-type>Container</transaction-type>
```

```
            <message-driven-destination>
                <destination-type>javax.jms.Topic</destination-type>
            </message-driven-destination>
        </message-driven>

    </enterprise-beans>

    <assembly-descriptor>
    </assembly-descriptor>

</ejb-jar>
```

**Describes the
messaging type
for this bean**

Finally, you must perform the vendor-specific steps to assign the bean to an actual
JMS message destination. The deployment XML describes only the type of messaging used by the message-driven bean, not the actual name of a topic or queue.
Consult your application server documentation for more information. For example, the following XML could be used for the Weblogic application server:

```
<weblogic-ejb-jar>

    <weblogic-enterprise-bean>
        <ejb-name>SampleMDB</ejb-name>
        <message-driven-descriptor>
            <destination-jndi-name>BookJMSTopic</destination-jndi-name>
        </message-driven-descriptor>
        <jndi-name>ejb/SampleMDB</jndi-name>
    </weblogic-enterprise-bean>

</weblogic-ejb-jar>
```

◆ *Discussion*

As with all other types of EJBs, security and transaction control is implemented in
the usual way. In some cases, transactions and security do have special considerations that you must take into account when dealing with message-driven beans.
For example, you need a good way to prevent unwanted clients from sending messages to your message-driven EJBs and triggering business logic, and you also need
to know how to handle rollbacks in the onMessage() method. In addition, you
should keep in mind that message-driven beans are stateless, and you should
therefore not attempt to keep any state information stored at a class level in-between onMessage() invocations.

The MessageDriveBean interface must be implemented in order to provide the
bean with the appropriate bean methods, such as ejbRemove() and ejbCreate().
The Context object set in the bean is an instance of the MessageDrivenContext,
which provides many of the methods found in the session and entity bean context
classes. However, due to the nature of the message-driven bean, many of the

context methods will throw an exception if used. Since a message-driven bean has no real EJB client (only the container that delivers the message), the getCaller-Principal() and isCallerInRole() methods throw a runtime exception. In addition, message-driven beans have no home interfaces (and therefore have no home objects), so getEJBHome() and getEJBLocalHome() also throw runtime exceptions if used. Finally, since no EJB clients exist for a message-driven bean, the transaction context for the start of the onMessage() method is started by the container in the case of container-managed transactions, or by the bean itself in the case of bean-managed transactions.

◆ *See also*

> 6.1—Sending a publish/subscribe JMS message
>
> 6.2—Sending a point-to-point JMS message
>
> 7.8—Securing a message-driven bean

6.4 *Processing messages in a FIFO manner from a message queue*

◆ *Problem*

You want to ensure that a message in a queue is processed only after any previous message has finished processing.

◆ *Background*

While some business logic operated by a message-driven bean can process messages in any order, other business functions might need messages supplied in a specific order. For instance, you might want to process incoming JMS messages according to the order in which they were received to preserve a specific data-driven workflow. Each message can be a step in a workflow, and the next step cannot begin without the previous one completing. Refer to recipe 6.2 for a discussion of using message queues.

◆ *Recipe*

The client shown in listing 6.5 publishes messages onto a message queue for a message-driven bean to pick up.

Listing 6.5   Client.java

```java
public class Client
{
  private QueueConnection          queueConnection = null;
  private QueueSession             queueSession = null;
  private QueueSender             queueSender = null;
  private Queue                    queue = null;
  private QueueConnectionFactory  queueFactory = null;
  private String                   url = getURL();

  public Client()throws JMSException, NamingException {
      Context context = getInitialContext();

      queueFactory = (QueueConnectionFactory)
                       context.lookup("BookJMSFactory");
      queueConnection = queueFactory.createQueueConnection();
      queueSession = queueConnection.createQueueSession(false,
                                      Session.AUTO_ACKNOWLEDGE);
      queue = (Queue) context.lookup("BookJMSQueue");
      queueSender = queueSession.createSender(queue);
  }

  public void send() throws JMSException {
    MapMessage message = null;

    for(int i=0;i<10;i++){
      message = queueSession.createMapMessage();
      message.setInt("Index",i);
      queueSender.send(message);
    }
  }

  public void close() throws JMSException {
    queueConnection.close();
  }

  public static void main(String[] args) {
    Client sender = null;

    try{
      sender = new Client();
      sender.send();
      sender.close();
    }
    catch(Exception ex) {
      ex.printStackTrace();
    }
  }
}
```

Notice that the client sends a counter value in the messages. The message-driven
bean will use that value to show that the messages are received and processed one
at a time. The message-driven bean shown in listing 6.6 picks up messages from
the message queue and prints out the counter value that each message contains.

Listing 6.6   MessageBean.java

```java
public class MessageBean implements MessageDrivenBean, MessageListener {

  private MessageDrivenContext ctx;

  public void onMessage( Message msg ) {
    MapMessage map = (MapMessage) msg;

    try {
      int index = map.getInt("Index");
      System.out.println( "Processing message: " + index );
    }
    catch(Exception ex) {
      ex.printStackTrace();
    }
  }

  //other bean methods not shown
}
```

Since we made use of a message queue, we are guaranteed that messages will be
removed from the queue in the order in which they were placed. To ensure that
one message is completely processed before the next message begins, you should
deploy only a single message-driven bean to remove messages from the queue.

Listing 6.7 contains the deployment XML for the bean; notice how it indicates
the source type of messages for the bean.

Listing 6.7   Deployment descriptor

```xml
<ejb-jar>
 <enterprise-beans>

   <message-driven>
     <ejb-name>fifoMDB</ejb-name>
     <ejb-class>fifo.MessageBean</ejb-class>
     <transaction-type>Container</transaction-type>
     <message-driven-destination>
       <destination-type>javax.jms.Queue</destination-type>
     </message-driven-destination>
   </message-driven>
```

```
</enterprise-beans>

<assembly-descriptor>
</assembly-descriptor>

</ejb-jar>
```

To ensure that the second message is not consumed before the first message processing has completed, you must have only one bean listening to the queue. This is set up in the vendor-specific deployment file. For example, you can use XML like that shown in listing 6.8 for the Weblogic application server.

Listing 6.8   Weblogic deployment descriptor

```
<weblogic-ejb-jar>

  <weblogic-enterprise-bean>                                    Creates the
    <ejb-name>fifoMDB</ejb-name>                                 message-
    <message-driven-descriptor>                               driven bean
      <pool>                                                  pool of size I
        <max-beans-in-free-pool>1</max-beans-in-free-pool>
        <initial-beans-in-free-pool>1</initial-beans-in-free-pool>
      </pool>
      <destination-jndi-name>BookJMSQueue</destination-jndi-name>
    </message-driven-descriptor>
    <jndi-name>fifo.MBD</jndi-name>
  </weblogic-enterprise-bean>

</weblogic-ejb-jar>
```

◆ *Discussion*

Message queues guarantee that only one consumer will process each single message. By limiting the number of consumers assigned to a queue to a single message-driven bean, you ensure that all the messages will be processed in the order in which they were received. In addition, using one consumer guarantees that each message will completely process before the next one begins processing. Otherwise, you can create a pool of message-driven beans (by increasing the pool size in a vendor-specific manner) to pull messages faster from the queue. Messages will still only be delivered to a single message-driven bean instance, but using many message-driven bean instances with the same queue results in faster message processing.

◆ *See also*

6.2—Sending a point-to-point JMS message

6.5 Insulating message-driven beans from business logic changes

♦ **Problem**

You want to prevent changing your message-driven EJB classes when the business logic they invoke changes.

♦ **Background**

Message-driven EJBs are ideal for executing business logic via JMS messages. However, when developing an enterprise application in a changing environment (or a shorter development cycle), you might find that you spend too much time upgrading the business logic contained in your message-driven beans. It would be ideal to encapsulate your business logic and insulate your message-driven beans from unnecessary changes.

♦ **Recipe**

To shield your message-driven beans from business logic changes, encapsulate the business logic with an intermediary object. The message-driven EJB shown in listing 6.9 uses an instance of the BusinessLogicBean class.

Listing 6.9   MessageBean.java

```
public class MessageBean implements MessageDrivenBean, MessageListener
{
  private MessageDrivenContext ctx;

  public void onMessage(Message msg) {
    MapMessage map=(MapMessage)msg;

    try {
      String symbol = map.getString("Symbol");
      String description = map.getString("Description");

      BusinessLogicBean bean =                                  Invokes the
            new BusinessLogicBean( symbol, description );       encapsulated
      bean.executeBusinessLogic();                             business logic
    }
    catch(Exception ex) {
      ex.printStackTrace();
    }
  }
}
```

◆ *Discussion*

The `BusinessLogicBean` class has a single purpose: to encapsulate business logic. This class is a simple object that allows the message-driven bean to execute business logic by passing in parameters and invoking a method. Using a class like this allows the EJB to shield itself from changes to the business logic. In addition, it is good practice to build business logic into reusable classes. An alternative to using a simple object is to invoke a session EJB that already encapsulates some business logic. By encapsulating all business logic with session beans, you ensure that the logic is available to both message-driven beans and any other EJB clients.

◆ *See also*

6.3—Creating a message-driven Enterprise JavaBean

6.6 *Streaming data to a message-driven EJB*

◆ *Problem*

You want to send a stream of data to a message-driven EJB.

◆ *Background*

Message-driven beans can receive all types of JMS messages. Because of that capability, you can use the most appropriate JMS message type for the data you want to send. For instance, when you want to send a large amount of binary data (like an image), you should stream the data to conserve bandwidth and memory. Refer to recipe 6.1 for more information on using message topics.

◆ *Recipe*

This solution demonstrates a client and a message-driven bean using streamed data. Listing 6.10 shows a client that streams a message containing data from a binary file to a message-driven EJB. It uses a message topic as a message destination.

Listing 6.10   Client.java

```java
public class Client
{
  private TopicConnection        topicConnection = null;
  private TopicSession           topicSession = null;
  private TopicPublisher         topicPublisher = null;
  private Topic                  topic = null;
  private TopicConnectionFactory topicFactory = null;
```

```
private String                   url= "http://myjndihost";

   public Client( String factoryJNDI, String topicJNDI )
                   throws JMSException, NamingException {

   // Get the initial context, implementation not shown
   Context context = getInitialContext();

   // Get the connection factory
   topicFactory = ( TopicConnectionFactory )
                           context.lookup( factoryJNDI );

   // Create the connection
   topicConnection = topicFactory.createTopicConnection();

   // Create the session
   topicSession=topicConnection.createTopicSession( false,
                           Session.AUTO_ACKNOWLEDGE );

   // Look up the destination
   topic = ( Topic ) context.lookup( topicJNDI );

   // Create a publisher
   topicPublisher = topicSession.createPublisher( topic );
}
public void sendToMDB( String filename ) throws JMSException
{
   byte[]           bytes = new byte[1024];
   FileInputStream istream = null;
   int             bytesRead = 0;

   try{
     BytesMessage message = topicSession.createBytesMessage();   ◁──┐  Creates the
     Istream = new FileInputStream(filename);                         BytesMessage
     while( (bytesRead = istream.read( bytes,0,bytes.length ) ) > 0 )  instance
     {
       message.writeBytes(bytes,0,bytesRead);   ◁──┐ Writes the data
     }                                               │ to the message
     istream.close();
     topicPublisher.publish(message);
   }
   catch(Exception e){
     e.printStackTrace();
   }
}
public void close() throws JMSException {
   topicSession.close();
   topicConnection.close();
}

public static void main(String[] args) {
   Client publisher = null;
   String filename = null;

   try{
```

```
      publisher = new Client( "BookJMSFactory", "BookJMSTopic" );
      System.out.println("Publishing message:");

      if( args.length > 0){
        filename = args[0];
        publisher.sendToMDB(filename);
        publisher.close();
      }
    }
    catch(Exception ex) {
      ex.printStackTrace();
    }
  }
}
```

Listing 6.11 shows the sample message-driven bean that receives data from a streamed message. This bean simply prints out the data it receives.

Listing 6.11   MessageBean.java

```
public class MessageBean implements MessageDrivenBean, MessageListener {

  private MessageDrivenContext ctx;

  public void ejbRemove() { }

  public void ejbPassivate() {   }

  public void setMessageDrivenContext(MessageDrivenContext ctx) {
    this.ctx = ctx;
  }

  public void ejbCreate () throws CreateException {   }

  public void ejbActivate() {   }

  public void onMessage( Message msg )
  {
    BytesMessage message = ( BytesMessage ) msg;
    int         bytesRead = 0;
    byte[]      bytes = new byte[1024];                  Reads the data
                                                         off the message
    try {
      while(  (bytesRead = message.readBytes(bytes, 1024) ) > 0 ){  ◁─
        System.out.println( new String( bytes, 0 , bytesRead ) );
      }
    }catch(Exception ex) {
      ex.printStackTrace();
    }
  }
}
```

◆ *Discussion*

Streaming large amounts of data helps you to avoid building a single large message. In addition, message streams are ideal for sending binary file data. By using message streams, you can more easily build messaging systems that can restart message transmission from the point of failure, rather than retransmit data. The client uses the `BytesMessage` message class. This message type is used specifically for sending large amounts of data to a message listener. The message-driven bean uses its `onMessage()` method to receive the message, as it would any other message type. The message-driven bean in this recipe only printed out the data it received from the streamed message, but it could instead store it in a database or create a new file containing the data.

◆ *See also*

> 6.1—Sending a publish/subscribe JMS message
>
> 6.3—Creating a message-driven Enterprise JavaBean

6.7 *Triggering two or more message-driven beans with a single JMS message*

◆ *Problem*

You want to start two or more business methods concurrently with a single JMS message.

◆ *Background*

Message-driven beans give other parts of an enterprise application the ability to execute business logic asynchronously. However, sending multiple JMS messages to execute multiple pieces of business logic can be time-consuming and redundant. To improve the efficiency of code, you should send a single message that triggers multiple message-driven beans.

◆ *Recipe*

To execute two pieces of business logic with a single message, you need only have two different message-driven beans listen for the same message. To do this, you must use a JMS message topic. Topics create a one-to-many relationship between sender and receiver(s). For this example, we will use two simple message-driven beans (listings 6.12 and 6.13). The `onMessage()` method simply prints out a statement indicating it has received a message.

Listing 6.12 MessageBean.java

```java
public class MessageBean implements MessageDrivenBean, MessageListener {

  public void onMessage(Message msg) {
    MapMessage map = ( MapMessage ) msg;

    try {
      String symbol = map.getString("Symbol");
      String description = map.getString("Description");

      System.out.println("MDB 1 received Symbol : " + symbol
          + " " + description );
    }
    catch(Exception ex) {
      ex.printStackTrace();
    }
  }
  //other bean methods not shown
}
```

Listing 6.13 MessageBean2.java

```java
public class MessageBean2 implements MessageDrivenBean, MessageListener {

  public void onMessage(Message msg) {
    MapMessage map=(MapMessage)msg;

    try {
      String symbol = map.getString("Symbol");
      String description = map.getString("Description");

      System.out.println("MDB 2 received Symbol : " + symbol
          + " " + description );
    }
    catch(Exception ex) {
      ex.printStackTrace();
    }
  }
}
```

Listing 6.14 contains the XML descriptor for these beans. As you can see, the descriptor indicates the JMS destination type.

Listing 6.14   Deployment descriptor

```
<enterprise-beans>

    <message-driven>
      <ejb-name>MDB</ejb-name>
      <ejb-class>multiSubscriber.MessageBean</ejb-class>
      <transaction-type>Container</transaction-type>
      <message-driven-destination>
        <destination-type>javax.jms.Topic</destination-type>     ◁
      </message-driven-destination>
    </message-driven>
                                                                      Assigns the
                                                                   message-driven
    <message-driven>                                             bean to a JMS topic
      <ejb-name>MDB2</ejb-name>
      <ejb-class>multiSubscriber.MessageBean2</ejb-class>
      <transaction-type>Container</transaction-type>
      <message-driven-destination>
        <destination-type>javax.jms.Topic</destination-type>     ◁
      </message-driven-destination>
    </message-driven>

</enterprise-beans>
```

The actual topic used by the message-driven beans is specified in a vendor-specific manner. For example, listing 6.15 shows the XML used by the Weblogic application server to specify the JMS topic for each bean.

Listing 6.15   Weblogic deployment descriptor

```
<weblogic-ejb-jar>

    <weblogic-enterprise-bean>              Assigns the message-driven bean
      <ejb-name>MDB</ejb-name>                 to the BookJMSTopic topic
      <message-driven-descriptor>
        <destination-jndi-name>BookJMSTopic</destination-jndi-name>   ◁
      </message-driven-descriptor>
      <jndi-name>multiSubscriber.MDB</jndi-name>
    </weblogic-enterprise-bean>

    <weblogic-enterprise-bean>
      <ejb-name>MDB2</ejb-name>
      <message-driven-descriptor>
        <destination-jndi-name>BookJMSTopic</destination-jndi-name>  |#1
      </message-driven-descriptor>
      <jndi-name>multiSubscriber2.MDB</jndi-name>
    </weblogic-enterprise-bean>

</weblogic-ejb-jar>
```

◆ *Discussion*

Recipe 6.1 provides more information on JMS topics. Since they allow multiple message-driven beans (even message-driven beans of different Java classes) to receive the same incoming message, you can use them to create concurrent processing for sections of business logic. Sending a single message, you can trigger two completely unrelated business functions to start processing at the same time.

In this recipe, each message-driven bean simply prints out a statement indicating it has received a message. However, in a practical application the two message-driven beans should each contain an important business function. To ensure that both message-driven beans receive the same message, they both need to subscribe to a JMS topic. For both beans to be triggered by a single message, both EJBs need to use the same topic.

◆ *See also*

6.1—Sending a publish/subscribe JMS message

6.3—Creating a message-driven Enterprise JavaBean

6.9—Filtering messages for a message-driven EJB

6.8 *Speeding up message delivery to a message-driven bean*

◆ *Problem*

You want to reduce the time it takes for a message to start processing in a message-driven bean.

◆ *Background*

In most enterprise situations, you want your asynchronous business functions to complete as quickly as possible. Since a message-driven bean processes a single message at a time, the waiting time for a single message increases as the number of messages delivered before it increases. In other words, if a single message takes a long period of time to complete, other messages experience a delay before processing. In critical applications, these messages should be processed as quickly as possible.

◆ *Recipe*

To speed up the consumption of messages, use a pool of message-driven beans. Each EJB is an instance of the single EJB class. With a pool of message-driven beans, you can consume more messages in a shorter time. Listing 6.16 shows a simple message-driven bean used to consume messages.

Listing 6.16   MessageBean.java

```java
public class MessageBean implements MessageDrivenBean, MessageListener {

  private MessageDrivenContext ctx;

  public void ejbRemove() {
  }

  public void ejbActivate() {
  }

  public void ejbPassivate() {
  }

  public void setMessageDrivenContext(MessageDrivenContext ctx) {
    this.ctx = ctx;
  }

  public void ejbCreate () throws CreateException {
  }

  public void onMessage(Message msg) {
    MapMessage map= (MapMessage) msg;

    try {
      String symbol = map.getString("Symbol");
      String description = map.getString("Description");

      System.out.println("MDB received Symbol : " + symbol
          + " " + description );
    }
    catch(Exception ex) {
      ex.printStackTrace();
    }
  }
}
```

To ensure a single message is not duplicated across instances in the message-driven bean pool, the message-driven bean instances should use a message queue as the destination type. Listing 6.17 contains the deployment descriptor for the bean.

Listing 6.17   Deployment descriptor

```
<enterprise-beans>

    <message-driven>
      <ejb-name>concurrentMDB</ejb-name>
      <ejb-class>concurrent.MessageBean</ejb-class>
      <transaction-type>Container</transaction-type>
      <message-driven-destination>
        <destination-type>javax.jms.Queue</destination-type>
      </message-driven-destination>
    </message-driven>

</enterprise-beans>
```

Message-driven bean instance pools are created in a vendor-specific manner. List-ing 6.18 shows how this is accomplished using the Weblogic application server. Notice the vendor XML creates a pool maximum size of five beans, with an initial size of two beans.

Listing 6.18   Weblogic deployment descriptor

```
<weblogic-ejb-jar>

  <weblogic-enterprise-bean>
    <ejb-name>concurrentMDB</ejb-name>                   Sets up the message-
    <message-driven-descriptor>                            driven bean pool
      <pool>
        <max-beans-in-free-pool>5</max-beans-in-free-pool>
        <initial-beans-in-free-pool>2</initial-beans-in-free-pool>
      </pool>
      <destination-jndi-name>BookJMSQueue</destination-jndi-name>
    </message-driven-descriptor>
    <jndi-name>concurrent.MBD</jndi-name>
  </weblogic-enterprise-bean>

</weblogic-ejb-jar>
```

◆ *Discussion*

Using a bean pool is a quick and dirty way to achieve concurrent processing of messages. The pool, combined with a message queue, provides a way to process many messages at once without duplicating messages across instances. Creating an environment like this allows messages to start processing instead of waiting for previous messages to complete. You should use this type of processing only when concurrent processing of messages will not cause problems in your business logic or invalid states in your data.

◆ **See also**

6.1—Sending a publish/subscribe JMS message

6.3—Creating a message-driven Enterprise JavaBean

6.9 *Filtering messages for a message-driven EJB*

◆ **Problem**

You want your message-driven beans to receive only the messages that they are intended to process.

◆ **Background**

Message-driven beans that subscribe to a topic or receive messages from a queue should be able to handle messages of the wrong type (which should not invoke the message-driven business logic). Beans should just politely discard these messages when they are encountered. This is especially true for message-driven beans that exist in an environment with many different beans that watch a single source for incoming messages. However, it would be more efficient to avoid the execution time used for discarding messages and instead avoid receiving unwanted messages.

◆ **Recipe**

To selectively deliver messages to a message-driven bean, the bean should be deployed with a *message selector*. The bean source needs no changes in order to use the message selector. Listing 6.19 shows a simple message-driven bean that only wants messages that contain an attribute UserRole set to "BuyerRole". The bean prints out the role of the incoming message for verification.

Listing 6.19   MessageBean.java

```
public class MessageBean implements MessageDrivenBean, MessageListener {

  private MessageDrivenContext ctx;

  public void onMessage(Message msg) {
    MapMessage map=(MapMessage)msg;

    try {
      String role = map.getString( "UserRole" );
```

```
      System.out.println("Received Message for Role: " + role);
      ProcessTheMessage( message );
    }
    catch(Exception ex) {
      ex.printStackTrace();
    }
  }
}
```

In the XML descriptor for the bean, you describe the message selector that filters undesired messages for the message-driven bean. Listing 6.20 shows the partial XML descriptor that describes the simple EJB and its message selector.

Listing 6.20   Deployment descriptor

```
<ejb-jar>
 <enterprise-beans>

  <message-driven>
    <ejb-name>MDB</ejb-name>
    <ejb-class>messageSelector.MessageBean</ejb-class>
    <transaction-type>Container</transaction-type>
    <message-selector>                              Specifies a
        <![CDATA[ UserRole = 'BuyerRole' ]]>        message
    </message-selector>                             selector
    <message-driven-destination>
      <destination-type>javax.jms.Topic</destination-type>
    </message-driven-destination>
  </message-driven>

 </enterprise-beans>
<ejb-jar>
```

Here is a simple publish method that appropriately creates messages for the message-driven bean message selector:

```
public void publish(String role) throws JMSException {

    MapMessage message = topicSession.createMapMessage();
    message.setString("UserRole",role);
    message.setStringProperty("UserRole",role);

    System.out.println( "Publishing message to Role:" + role );
    topicPublisher.publish(message);
}
```

◆ **Discussion**

When sending particular messages, we must assign a value to the property User-Role. The message selector will pick out the messages that meet its criteria and deliver them to the message-driven bean. Message selectors operate using the property values that are set in JMS messages. Any property that is set in the message can be examined by a message selector for filtering purposes.

Message selection strings can be any length and any combination of message property comparisons. The following is an example of a more complex message selector:

```
"DollarAmount < 100.00 OR (ShareCount < 100 AND ( CreditAmount
    - DollarAmount > 0 ) ) AND Role in ('Buyer', 'ADMIN' )"
```

You can make other familiar comparisons using the following operators as well: =, BETWEEN, and LIKE (using a % as a wildcard). As mentioned in the recipe, message selectors operate upon messages by examining the properties set in the message using its setStringProperty() method. If a property is not present in a message, the selector considers that a nonmatching message. To specify the message selector in the deployment XML, you must use the CDATA tag to avoid XML parsing errors due to the use of special characters like < or >.

◆ **See also**

6.3—Creating a message-driven Enterprise JavaBean

6.10 *Encapsulating error-handling code in a message-driven EJB*

◆ **Problem**

Rather than handle errors in a message-driven bean, you want your beans to off-load errors to an error-handling system.

◆ **Background**

Handling errors across all your message-driven beans should be consistent and exact. By keeping the error-handling code in your message-driven beans, you open your beans to tedious changes if your error-handling strategy changes. If you must change the error-handling code in one bean, you might have to change it in all your message-driven beans. Passing exceptions to an error-handling object or session bean allows you to avoid rollbacks and gracefully handle errors in a consistent manner.

◆ *Recipe*

Instead of acting upon any errors, the message-driven bean catches any exceptions and forwards them on to an error-handling session bean. The message-driven bean should be implemented as usual; the only new addition is the error-handling mechanism (see listing 6.21).

Listing 6.21   MessageBean.java

```java
public class MessageBean implements MessageDrivenBean, MessageListener {

  private MessageDrivenContext ctx;

  public void onMessage(Message msg) {
    MapMessage map = (MapMessage) msg;
    String     symbol = null;
    String     description = null;
    ErrorHome  errorHome = null;

    try {
      symbol = map.getString("Symbol");
      description = map.getString("Description");

      System.out.println("Received Symbol : " + symbol);
      System.out.println("Received Description : " + description);

      processEquityMessage( symbol, description );
    }
    catch(Exception e){
      e.printStackTrace();
      System.out.println("Error Creating Equity with Symbol:"+symbol);
      System.out.println("Consuming error and "
                        + "passing on to error Handler");
      try{
        handleError( e, msg );
      }
      catch(Exception errorExc){}
    }
  }

  private void handleError( Exception e, Message msg )
  {
    ErrorHandler handler = lookupErrorEJB();
    handler.handleMessageDrivenError( e.getMessage(), msg );
  }
}
```

Looks up and uses the error-handling session EJB

The handleError() method looks up a session EJB that handles specific errors. For example, the following remote interface could expose error-handling functionality to an entire EJB application:

```
public interface ErrorHandler extends javax.ejb.EJBObject
{
  public void handleMessageDrivenError( String message, Message mg );
  public void handleSessionError( Object errorMessage );
  public void handleEntityError( Object errorMessage );
}
```

◆ *Discussion*

The message-driven EJB shown in the recipe processes messages containing equity information. The actual message-processing logic is not shown, so instead let's examine the handleError() method invoked only when an exception occurs during message processing. The session EJB interface shown in the recipe declares methods for handling different types of errors. For example, the session bean has a specific way it can handle session bean errors, entity bean errors, and message-driven bean errors. Using an error-handling system like this does not have to take the place of a normal transactional system. Instead, it acts as a way to store information on errors occurring in your application—acting as a logger of errors, and possibly offloading them to a management system.

◆ *See also*

6.12—Handling rollbacks in a message-driven bean

6.11 Sending an email message asynchronously

◆ *Problem*

You want to provide your EJBs with the ability to send email in an asynchronous manner.

◆ *Background*

The ability to send email is an important part of many enterprise applications. Email can be used to send notifications, alerts, and general information, such as price quotes or contract information. When sending an email from an EJB, you should be able to continue processing without waiting for an email to be sent. Sending email using the Java mail package is a simple process.

◆ *Recipe*

Combining email-sending code with a message-driven bean provides the asynchronous behavior that is ideal for enterprise applications. Listing 6.22 contains a message-driven bean that sends email using property values passed to it via a JMS message.

Listing 6.22   EmailBean.java

```java
import javax.jms.*;

public class EmailBean implements MessageDrivenBean, MessageListener {

  private MessageDrivenContext ctx;

  public void onMessage( Message msg ) {
    MapMessage map = (MapMessage) msg;

    try {
      sendEmail( map.getProperty( "Recipient" ),
               map.getProperty("message" ) );     // Retrieves the email address
                                                   // and text from the JMS message
    }
    catch(Exception ex) {
      ex.printStackTrace();
    }
  }

  private void sendEmail(String recipient, String text)
                                           throws Exception {
    Session mailSession = null;
    javax.mail.Message msg = null;

    try{
      System.out.println( "Sending Email to: " + rcpt );

      mailSession = (Session) ctx.lookup("BookMailSession");

      msg = new MimeMessage(mailSession);
      msg.setFrom();
      msg.setRecipients(Message.RecipientType.TO,
                     InternetAddress.parse( recipient , false));
      msg.setSubject("Important Message");
      msg.setText(text);                     // Sends the email message
      Transport.send(msg);
      System.out.println("Sent Email to: "+rcpt);
    }
    catch(Exception e){
      e.printStackTrace();
    }
  }
}
```

◆ *Discussion*

When using a message-driven bean to send an email message, you need to be sure to send a JMS message with all the values that you need for the email. For instance, the solution in the recipe only retrieved the email address and text from the JMS message and populated the subject of the email with a hardcoded value.

Another improvement you can make to your message-driven email beans is to only send JMS messages that contain the email recipient address and the type of email to send. For instance, a message-driven bean can be initialized with standard email message texts to use for your various email needs in your enterprise application (purchase confirmation, error, contract status, etc.). This would include the subject and message. All your application needs to do is supply a valid email address and the type of email to send. This way, you won't have to transmit the body of an email message to the EJB. In addition, you could pass parameters to the EJB for formatting an already loaded email body.

◆ *See also*

4.5—Sending an email from an EJB

6.12—Handling rollbacks in a message-driven bean

6.12 *Handling rollbacks in a message-driven bean*

◆ *Problem*

When a transaction in a message-driven bean rolls back, the application server can be configured to resend the JMS message that started the transaction. If the error that caused the rollback keeps occurring, you could potentially cause an endless loop.

Background

Rollbacks in message-driven beans occur in the same way that they can happen in other beans—an error occurs in executing logic. However, in the case of a message-driven bean using a durable subscription, the application server will most likely attempt to redeliver the message that caused the rollback in the bean. If the error is not corrected, the rollback will continue on, consuming more processing time and memory. You need your message-driven beans to be insulated from rollback loops and able to handle error-causing messages without a rollback every time.

◆ *Recipe*

To handle rollbacks in a message-driven bean, keep track of the number of times a particular message has been delivered to the bean. Once a certain retry limit is reached, you want to discard the message from that point on. Listing 6.23 shows the onMessage() method from a message-driven bean that tracks and checks message redelivery attempts.

Listing 6.23   The onMessage() method

```
private HashMap previousMessages;
private int count = 0;

public void onMessage( Message incomingMsg )
{
   // get the unique message Id
   String msgId = incomingMsg.getJMSMessageID();        Checks for previous
                                                        attempts
   if ( previousMessages.containsKey(msgId) )   ◁───┘
      count = ( (Integer) msgMap.get(msgId) ).intValue();
   else
      count = 0;

   // if msg has been retried couple of times, discard it.
   //   and remove the stored id.
   if ( count < _MAX_REDLIVERY_CONST_ )   ◁── Checks the number of attempts
   {
      logMessage(incomingMsg);
      previousMessages.remove( msgId );
      return;
   }

   //perform business logic for message
   boolean error = doBusinessFunction();

   if ( error )                          Checks for
   {                                     necessary
     mdbContext.setRollBackOnly();       rollback
     previousMessages.put( msgId, new Integer(++count) );

   }
   else
   {
     if( previousMessages.containsKey( msgId ) )
        previousMessages.remove( msgId );
   }
}
```

◆ *Discussion*

Some application servers and some JMS vendors allow you to specify the redelivery count of a rolled-back message delivery to a message-driven bean. However, to ensure your message-driven EJBs are the most secure and portable, you can implement a simple message tracker like the one shown in the recipe. In this code, the EJB maintains a Map of message IDs and the number of times they have been delivered. If the delivered count for a particular message reaches a predefined constant value, the bean simply logs the message and returns. By returning successfully, the EJB ensures that the EJB container commits the transaction and the message will not be delivered again.

If the message makes it past the count check, the bean will attempt to perform its business function. After attempting the business logic, the EJB will check to see if it is necessary to mark the current transaction for rollback. If so, the EJB uses its `MessageDrivenContext` instance to mark the transaction and returns. The container will roll back the transaction and will attempt to redeliver the message. The `previousMessages` Hashtable will store only those message IDs that caused errors. If the message succeeds, no ID is stored (and any previously stored ID is removed).

◆ *See also*

Chapter 5, "Transactions"

7

Security

"Part of the secret of success in life is to eat what you like
and let the food fight it out inside."

— *Mark Twain*

J2EE security generally falls into three categories: authentication, authorization (or access control), and secure communication. Enterprise applications handle these three areas with different mechanisms. For instance, users are presented with a JSP form and must enter a username and password (authentication); EJBs map users to security roles in order to access business methods (access control); and the application server provides a secure socket layer (SSL) for communication.

EJBs are best suited for handling access control of clients. The EJB specification describes a system of specifying security roles that define the level of access to particular business methods and beans. This type of access control is a declarative security measure. Bean descriptors declare the roles that can access their methods, and the EJB container can map these logical roles to actual security realms within the application server. For example, when a user logs into a J2EE application, the application server matches the username to a security role called ADMIN. As the user attempts to execute code that performs a JNDI lookup of an EJB, the user's credentials (username and password) are passed to the EJB container. Before returning the bean, or before invoking bean methods, the container verifies that the user has sufficient access (as defined by the user's security role) to the bean.

The recipes contained in this chapter deal directly with security roles and access control (as well as a few other unique recipes). For information about mapping users to roles within an application server, you should consult the documentation from your vendor. After reading this chapter, you will be familiar with the following topics:

- Finding information about EJB clients
- Using client roles
- Passing client identity to EJBs
- Disabling EJB methods
- Using an EJB as a client
- Securing entity bean access
- Authenticating LDAP access
- Understanding message-driven bean security

7.1 Finding the identity and role of the caller inside an EJB method

◆ **Problem**

You want an EJB to be able to find the identity of the invoker of a bean method.

◆ **Background**

Many business situations require that decisions be made based on which user starts a process. For instance, depending on the permission of a user, an EJB may decide to limit functionality or validate input in a different manner. For example, if a user does not have Administrator permissions, you may allow that user to view data but not make any changes. Each EJB should be able to determine the EJB client in order to make such decisions if necessary.

◆ **Recipe**

To discover the EJB client's identity, use the security methods from the EJBContext instance set inside your EJB:

```
java.security.Principal principal = ejbContext.getCallerPrincipal();

System.out.println( "User name is: " + principal.getName() );

boolean inAdminRole = ejbContext.isCallerInRole( "ADMIN" );
```

◆ **Discussion**

Whether you are implementing methods inside an entity or session bean, the EJB container will provide you with an object that implements the EJBContext interface. Session beans will receive a SessionContext instance. Entity beans will receive an EntityContext instance. Since both instances implement the EJBContext interface, you can invoke the two methods shown in the recipe in both session and entity beans.

The getCallerPrincipal() method returns the Principal object associated with the caller of your EJB's method. With the Principal object, you can acquire the name of the invoker by using the Principal class's getName() method.

The isCallerInRole() method allows you to query the container for information about the caller's roles. For instance, the recipe is questioning whether the caller is in the ADMIN role. You can use this method to perform different implementations of an operation based on the role of the caller.

◆ **See also**

7.2—Assigning and determining EJB client security roles

7.3—Passing client credentials to the EJB container

7.4—Disabling methods for certain users

7.2 Assigning and determining EJB client security roles

◆ **Problem**

You want to assign logical roles to a client, and EJBs need to determine client roles at runtime.

◆ **Background**

In recipe 7.1, we showed how an EJB can determine the caller's identity (the username, for instance) and make informed decisions. In EJB applications, the application server has the ability to map a set of users to a logical role. By placing users into roles, you can programmatically assign permissions. For instance, you can limit application functionality based on the client's role.

◆ **Recipe**

To determine the client's role, use a method from the `EJBContext` instance set inside your EJB:

```
boolean inAdminRole = ejbContext.isCallerInRole( "Administrator" );
```

To create a logical role, use the `<security-role>` tag within the assembly descriptor section of the ejb-jar xml file:

```
<ejb-jar>
 <enterprise-beans>
  <entity>
   <!-- Bean data here -->
    <security-role>
      <description>
        The admin role
      </description>
      <role-name>
        ADMIN
      </role-name>
    </security-role>
  </entity>
 </enterprise-beans>
```

```
<assembly-descriptor >

</assembly-descriptor>

</ejb-jar>
```

Finally, you must reference this role for a particular EJB. You should place the following within the bean section of the deployment descriptor; it creates a logical role used by the EJB and maps it to a logical role in the assembly descriptor:

```
<security-role-ref>
    <description>
       Users with this role are in the Administrators group
    </description>
    <role-name>
       Administrator
    </role-name>
    <role-link>
       ADMIN
    </role-link>
</security-role-ref>
```

◆ *Discussion*

As stated in the chapter introduction, security roles are a declarative method of setting up client boundaries around an EJB. The <security-role> element of the assembly descriptor sets up logical roles used to group EJB clients. The <security-role-ref> element maps logical roles used by an EJB to a security role defined in the assembly descriptor or in the runtime environment. For instance, the recipe sets up a runtime role ADMIN and links it to users of the bean with the Administrator role.

The <role-link> tag is optional for the <security-role-ref> element, but if it is not provided to map to a <security-role> in the assembly descriptor, it must be mapped to a role in the runtime environment (see your vendor documentation). The logical roles set up in the deployment descriptor are just that: logical roles. They are only labels declared before runtime. Each role must be mapped to an existing security realm in the runtime environment. Again, this important step will differ across vendors, and you should consult your documentation for the exact process.

The isCallerInRole() method is used to determine the appropriate action of a method. Take the following implementation of a business method:

```
public void performImportantAction() throws NotAdminException
{
    boolean isAdmin = ejbContext.isCallerInRole( "ADMIN" );
    if( isAdmin )
       //perform the important function
```

```
    else
        throw new NotAdminException();
}
```

This example allows clients within the role ADMIN to perform the important function. Clients in other roles will cause a NotAdminException to be thrown if they try to invoke the method.

◆ See also

2.9—Specifying security roles in the bean source

7.1—Finding the identity and role of the caller inside an EJB method

7.3—Passing client credentials to the EJB container

7.4—Disabling methods for certain users

7.3 *Passing client credentials to the EJB container*

◆ Problem

You want your clients to pass along their security credentials to the EJB container when looking up or invoking an EJB.

◆ Background

Working within your application server, you have mapped certain users into specific logical roles. In addition, you have set up the security roles (see recipe 7.2) in the deployment descriptors for your EJBs. However, EJB clients must pass their security credentials to the EJB container in order for EJBs to acquire the user information.

◆ Recipe

To pass the client's credentials to the EJB container, create the JNDI InitialContext object using a set of properties that defines the client's credentials (listing 7.1).

Listing 7.1 Sample code initializing the InitialContext object with security credentials

```
Hashtable env = new Hashtable();

    //add security principal information into context environment
env.put( Context.SECURITY_AUTHENTICATION, "simple" );
env.put( Context.SECURITY_PRINCIPAL, "my_username" );
env.put( Context.SECURITY_CREDENTIALS, "my_password" );
```

```
//Optionally set any properties needed by your app server vendor…
/*
  env.put( "", "" );
*/
Context ctx = new InitialContext( env );

//Look up a particular EJB home interface
SampleBeanHome home = ( SampleBeanHome ) ctx.lookup( "ejb/SampleBean" );
```

The final step for this recipe resides in the documentation of your application server. You need to assign users to particular roles in the server (which are then mapped to logical roles in the bean's deployment XML).

◆ *Discussion*

The code in the recipe sets the username, password, and authentication mechanism for the client application. This information is passed to the container when the client attempts to look up or use a bean. The credentials are compared to a specific bean's security requirements to determine whether the client has enough privileges to use the bean. Additionally, beans can programmatically retrieve this information for use in method implementations to make flow decisions.

◆ *See also*

7.1—Finding the identity and role of the caller inside an EJB method

Chapter 1, "Client code"

7.4 *Disabling methods for certain users*

◆ *Problem*

You want to prevent certain clients from invoking certain EJB methods.

◆ *Background*

While you want to allow an EJB client to find and use a particular EJB, you want to expose only a limited set of methods to that client. Your goal is to hide a set of business methods, and possibly even particular home interface methods. For example, certain methods need to be available only to users in the Administrator role. Perhaps methods that make security changes, or critical data changes, should be hidden from normal users. EJBs use method permissions to further guarantee that the correct users are accessing methods.

◆ *Recipe*

To disable methods for users, you need to create a security role and configure the method access in the EJB deployment descriptor. Create security roles for your EJBs (see recipe 7.2 for more on this topic). Then, use the `<method-permission>` tag to set up method permissions for those roles. Assume an `EmployeeBean` contains getters and setters for the attributes `firstName` and `lastName`. The `Employee-Bean` has declared two roles, `ADMIN` and `READ_ONLY`, in its deployment descriptor. The code in listing 7.2 grants those with the `ADMIN` role access to all methods within an EJB.

Listing 7.2   Deployment descriptor

```
<ejb-jar>
  <enterprise-beans>
   <!-- Bean data here -->
  </enterprise-beans>

  <assembly-descriptor >
   <method-permission>
     <role-name>
        ADMIN
     </role-name>
     <method>
        <ejb-name>EmployeeBean</ejb-name>
        <method-name>*</method-name>
     </method>
   </method-permission>
  </assembly-descriptor>

</ejb-jar>
```

To map the `READ_ONLY` role to the correct method permissions (only allowing use of the getter methods), use the following:

```
<method-permission>
     <role-name>
        READ_ONLY
     </role-name>
     <method>
        <ejb-name>EmployeeBean</ejb-name>
        <method-name>getFirstName</method-name>
     </method>
     <method>
        <ejb-name>EmployeeBean</ejb-name>
        <method-name>getLastName</method-name>
     </method>
</method-permission>
```

To disable all security checks for all clients of an EJB for a particular method, use the <unchecked/> tag:

```
<method-permission>
    <unchecked/>
    <method>
        <ejb-name>EmployeeBean</ejb-name>
        <method-name>*</method-name>
    </method>
</method-permission>
```

◆ *Discussion*

Security roles are useful in and of themselves, but they would hardly be worth the trouble if you could use them only for the isCallerInRole() method from the EJBContext class. The EJB deployment descriptor also allows you to map security roles to actual EJB methods. The <method-permission> tag builds a many-to-many relationship between roles and methods, where a role is given access permission to certain methods.

The <method-permission> tag contains an optional <description> element, at least one <role-name> element, and at least one <method> element. To grant a role permission to use a method, you name the role in the <role-name> element, and name the method in the <method> element (using its <ejb-name> and <method-name> elements). The recipe demonstrates this in two ways. It names specific methods for the READ_ONLY role, allowing access only to getter methods. It also uses an * as a wildcard, indicating that the role ADMIN can access all methods within the EmployeeBean EJB. The only acceptable use of the wildcard is by itself. You cannot use something like get* for a method name; only a single * will work.

Finally, the recipe provides an example of the <unchecked/> method permission. If a method permission is declared unchecked, the method can be invoked by any client of any role. In other words, no security checks will occur when a client invokes the specified method. An unchecked method permission overrides all other permissions that might be specified for that method.

All methods from the EJB's remote, home, and super interfaces can be set up with permissions. Any method that is excluded from the method permissions list cannot be accessed by any role. In addition, the <method> element allows you to describe methods in more detail. This is important if your bean contains overloaded methods. Within the <method> element, you can use the <method-param> tag to specify parameter types, or use the <method-intf> tag to specify the interface (possible values are Home, Remote, LocalHome, or Local) in which the method is declared.

♦ **See also**

> 2.10—Generating and maintaining method permissions
>
> 7.2—Assigning and determining EJB client security roles

7.5 Assigning a role to an EJB

♦ **Problem**

All of your clients have been assigned a role, but now you need an EJB to run within a logical role in order to provide a more secure environment.

♦ **Background**

EJB clients don't always reside in the client layer. Many times, a client to an EJB is another EJB, and you need to ensure that the client EJB will have the necessary permission to access the methods on the second EJB. You need your client EJB to run as a particular role when interacting with a second EJB. Doing this allows you to avoid passing user credentials from bean to bean.

♦ **Recipe**

To assign a role to an EJB, use the `<security-identity>` tag within the bean section of the deployment descriptor, as shown in listing 7.3.

Listing 7.3   Deployment descriptor

```
<ejb-jar>
 <enterprise-beans>
  <entity>
   <!-- Bean data here -->

    <security-identity>
      <run-as>
       <role-name>
          ADMIN
       </role-name>
      </run-as>
    </security-identity>

   </entity>
  </enterprise-beans>

  <assembly-descriptor >

  </assembly-descriptor>

</ejb-jar>
```

◆ *Discussion*

The <run-as> functionality was reintroduced in the EJB 2.0 specification. Using the <security-identity> element lets you assign a role to an EJB. If and when the EJB becomes a client to another EJB, it assumes this role. This allows you to apply method permissions against the client EJB as well as other EJBs to ask for the client's role.

However, the identity role specified for this EJB does not have to be the identity that accesses the bean. For example, a client with the role READ_ONLY may access a session bean to obtain some data. That session bean has a security identity of ADMIN, which it uses to access other EJBs in order to complete the method invocation for its READ_ONLY client.

Alternatively, you can declare the security identity of an EJB to always be the identity of the EJB client. For example:

```
<security-identity>
   <use-caller-identity/>
</security-identity>
```

This entry makes the invoked EJB run under the identity of the client. If a READ_ONLY client invokes a bean with this type of identity (<use-caller-identity/>), the bean will also run under the role READ_ONLY.

◆ *See also*

2.9—Specifying security roles in the bean source

7.2—Assigning and determining EJB client security roles

7.6 *Preventing access to entity data*

◆ *Problem*

Even though you have assigned users to a role in order to allow limited access to your EJBs, you would like to further restrict a client's ability to find entity beans.

◆ *Background*

You need to ensure that users update only data that pertains to them. For example, users should be able to access and update their own user profile data but no other user profiles. A single bean class protects profile data, and this can be a problem because the method used to insert/update/delete user profile data is protected by a role. A member of the role has access to the method, but should be able to use it only to access certain data. Because of situations like these, you want to restrict a client's ability to access entity bean data.

◆ *Recipe*

For this recipe, we will use the example of a banking application that includes a session bean named `AccountAccessBean`, which contains methods like `withdraw()` and `deposit()`. You want only users with the role `BANK_CUSTOMER` to access these methods. However, you want customers to be able to access only their *own* accounts.

To solve this problem, create an additional session bean that has only one create method. The create method has a parameter for the account number, or user ID, or something similar. You can use this stateful bean to access all other data or methods based on the unique identifier. This recipe demonstrates the session facade pattern. The code in listing 7.4 shows the `AccountAccessBean`, a bean used to access the account data.

Listing 7.4   AccountAccessBean.java

```java
public class AccountAccessBean implements SessionBean
{
  public void create( String accountNumber )
  {
     this.account = accountNumber;
  }

  public void withdraw( double amount ) throws EJBException
  {
    withdrawFromAccount( account, amount );
  }

  public void deposit( double amount ) throws EJBException
  {
    depositToAccount( account, amount )
  }

  //remaining EJB and private methods not shown
}
```

The second part of this recipe is to create only local interfaces for your entity beans (this requires EJB 2.0 at a minimum). With only local interfaces for your entity beans, no remote clients have the ability to look up an entity bean and are forced to go through the session facade.

◆ *Discussion*

The point of this recipe is to highlight that good design can solve most of your EJB application problems. You should normally use a session bean as the only access to your entity bean layer. To ensure this, implement only local interfaces for your entity beans. To access the entity beans, a user must use the session bean, which can access the user's credentials and use custom finder methods on the entity beans to return those appropriate for the particular user only.

The EJB client passes its account number and credentials to the session facade, which uses the information in a finder method on the entity bean implemented to use the account number. This design ensures only the correct data is returned to the user.

By using only local interfaces for your entity beans, you deny any remote access to the beans. Combine the local entity beans with a session facade to the entity beans and you effectively wrap them with a security layer provided by a session bean. The session facade can use all the normal EJB security mechanisms, such as roles and method permissions, to protect your entity data.

7.7 Using EJBs to handle simple authentication with an LDAP source

◆ *Problem*

You want to use an EJB to authenticate users from a Lightweight Directory Access Protocol (LDAP) source.

◆ *Background*

You need to validate a user login from an LDAP source via an EJB call. Using an LDAP store is one of the quickest and most efficient ways to store user information for security and application permissions. Because of this, you might need to access an LDAP user store from an EJB managing logins.

◆ *Recipe*

Using JNDI from your EJB, you can successfully perform simple authentication to an LDAP source, as shown in listing 7.5.

Listing 7.5 Sample code showing LDAP authentication

```
Hashtable env = new Hashtable();

env.put( Context.PROVIDER_URL, "ldap://localhost:389/o=EJBCookbook" );
env.put( Context.INITIAL_CONTEXT_FACTORY,
            "com.sun.jndi.ldap.LdapCtxFactory" );

env.put( Context.SECURITY_PRINCIPAL,
            "cn=bsullins, ou=authors, o=EJBCookbook" );
env.put( Context.SECURITY_CREDENTIALS, "password" );
env.put( Context.SECURITY_AUTHENTICATION, "simple" );

//get the initial context
DirContext ctx = new InitialDirContext( env );
```

◆ *Discussion*

As you can see, the recipe code is not really EJB specific. If authentication fails, an
AuthenticationException will be thrown. The javax.naming package contains the
DirContext and AuthenticationException classes.

7.8 *Securing a message-driven bean*

◆ *Problem*

You need to provide more security for your message-driven beans.

◆ *Background*

A message-driven bean does not control user access with security roles or method
permissions. It receives JMS messages as the only form of access to the bean. Unauthorized (deceptive or phony) messages are a security problem encountered with
this type of bean. Your message-driven beans need the ability to authenticate messages that trigger their functionality.

◆ *Recipe*

Pass credentials in the messages sent to message-driven beans. In the onMessage()
method, retrieve the credentials for comparison. One way to pass the credentials
in the message is to set object properties in the message. The code in listing 7.6

demonstrates placing a JMS message on a message queue for a message-driven bean to retrieve—notice how it sets client credentials into the message.

Listing 7.6 Securing a JMS message

```
try
{
    Hashtable env = new Hashtable();
    env.put( Context.INITIAL_CONTEXT_FACTORY, getContextURL() );
    env.put( Context.PROVIDER_URL, getContextURL() );
    InitialContext jndi = new InitialContext( env );

    //create a JMS connection factory
    TopicConnectionFactory factory = ( TopicConnectionFactory )
                            jndi.lookup(
                                getConnectionFactoryClassName() );

    //creation a JMS connection
    TopicConnection connection = factory.createTopicConnection();
    TopicSession session = connection.createTopicSession(
                        false, Session.AUTO_ACKNOWLEDGE );

    //Look up  a JMS Topic
    Topic theTopic = ( Topic ) jndi.lookup( getTopicName() );
    TopicPublisher publisher = session.createPublisher( theTopic );
    connection.start();
    jndi.close();

    //publish a message
    javax.jms.Message message = session.createMessage();
    message.setObjectProperty( "USERNAME", getUserName() );
    message.setObjectProperty("PASSWORD", getPassword() );
    //add more to the message….

    publisher.publish( message );
}
catch( javax.naming.CommunicationException cex ){
    //handle error
}
catch( Exception e ){
    e.printStackTrace();
}
```

> **Set the username and password as properties**

After picking up a message, the message-driven bean must retrieve the client's credentials. The message-driven bean sample in listing 7.7 contains an `onMessage()` implementation that retrieves a username and password from a message.

Listing 7.7 SecureMDB.java

```
public class SecureMDB implements MessageDrivenBean,
                                  javax.jms.MessageListener
{

  public void setMessageDrivenContext(MessageDrivenContext mdc){
  }

  public void onMessage( Message msg ){
     String username = ( String ) msg.getObjectProperty( "USERNAME" );
     String password = ( String ) msg.getObjectProperty( "PASSWORD" );

     //verify username and password, perform actions…
  }
}
```

◆ *Discussion*

Before sending a JMS message, the creator of the message sets two object properties in the message. For example, the recipe retrieved the caller's username
using the key USERNAME and the client's password with the key PASSWORD. You
can develop your system to pass along actual user credentials, or you can pass
along a predefined message sending the username and password. This means
that clients creating messages for message-driven beans use a predefined username and password that message-driven beans can retrieve and verify before
executing any actions.

Part 3

Desserts

Part 3 concludes this book with the addition of two chapters. Chapter 8 covers application logging from Enterprise JavaBeans (EJB). Specifically, the chapter introduces the log4j framework from Apache. The log4j is an open source logging framework that is growing in popularity because of its modular, nonintrusive approach to logging. Chapter 9 covers problems encountered during the building, deployment, and testing of EJBs. Here we demonstrate using Ant to build, package, and deploy your EJBs. We also use Apache Cactus to build an EJB unit-testing framework. Cactus is another open source framework from Apache that helps you to unit-test server-side components, and chapter 9 shows you how to integrate Cactus tests into your Ant build system.

Logging

8

"Buzzards gotta eat ... same as worms."

—*Clint Eastwood as Josey Wales*
from the movie "The Outlaw Josey Wales"

Enterprise JavaBeans (EJB) deliver fantastic functionality, but also can make for difficult debugging and user tracking during runtime. A good logging framework remedies much of the complexity by allowing you to leave coded trails throughout your application. An experienced developer uses logging as a debugging tool and as a system to track application usage.

As Java moves increasingly into the enterprise, logging frameworks are becoming more important to enterprise applications. A large EJB application can push the limits of ordinary logging frameworks. Enterprise applications support many clients, run in clustered environments across many servers, and contain a multitude of transactions. All of these make an application more robust, but chip away at the usefulness of typical homegrown loggers.

The recipes in this chapter focus on using the log4j open source project to provide solutions to EJB logging problems. You will find the following topics in this chapter:

- Writing log messages with log4j
- Enhancing logging performance
- Creating a logging report
- Logging to a JMS destination
- Logging in XML format
- Viewing log files with a web browser
- Logging in a clustered environment
- Logging the life of an EJB
- Refreshing the logging setup
- Logging with many clients

A log4j appetizer

log4j is an excellent logging framework that is fast, lightweight, extensible, and easily configurable. To use log4j, perform the following steps:

1 Download log4j from http://jakarta.apache.org/log4j. (You can also find more information about log4j and the logging framework at this site.)

2 Include the log4j file in the application classpath. (See your application server vendor documentation for more information.)

3 Add the logger to your code.

4   In the properties file, set the logging level and assign an appender for each logger you reference in your code.

5   Initialize the logging framework with a configuration.

The best way to learn to use log4j is to go over a short example. The following example, combined with the various recipes, should be enough to get you going. After downloading and preparing your log4j installation, start by adding log statements to your code.

Adding a logger to your code

Since enterprise beans will eventually contain much of your business logic in an enterprise application, it is essential that you add logging messages to the bean code. For example, the AccountBean in listing 8.1 is an EJB used in a brokerage application.

Listing 8.1   AccountBean.java

```
import javax.ejb.SessionBean;          Imports
import org.apache.log4j.Logger;        log4j classes

public class AccountBean implements SessionBean
{
    private static final Logger logger = null;

    public void ejbCreate()
    {
        //instantiate a logger object                  Creates a
        logger = Logger.getLogger( "ejb.messages" );   Logger object

        //write an info message
        logger.info("Creating instance of AccountBean" );
    }

    public void ejbActivate()
                throws RemoteException, EJBException
    {
        logger = Logger.getLogger("ejb.messages" );
    }                                                   Writes
                                                        log
    public void buyStock( String symbol, int shares )   messages
                                    throws AccountException
    {
        //write a debug message
        logger.debug("Buying " + shares + " of " + symbol );
    }

    public void sellStock( String symbol, int shares )
                                    throws AccountException
    {
        logger.debug("Buying " + shares + " of " + symbol );
```

```
    }
    //remaining bean methods below
}
```

As you can see from the code, log4j is simple to use. For this example, the first thing we need to do is import the `Logger` class. The `Logger` class is the most used class in the logging framework; it provides the methods you use to write messages.

In the `ejbCreate()` and `ejbActivate()` methods, we acquired a reference to a new `Logger` instance, named `ejb.messages`. The `Logger` class is a factory for creating and finding `Logger` instances.

Setting up the properties file

Listing 8.2 shows the contents of the `logconfig.properties` configuration file associated with the brokerage application that contains the `AccountBean` (this can also be in an XML format).

> **Listing 8.2   Sample log4j configuration file**
>
> ```
> #set logger level and appenders
> log4j.rootLogger=DEBUG, stdout                    Sets the logging level and
> log4j.logger.ejb.messages=DEBUG, stdout           assigns appenders
>                                                                      Creates the
> #set logger appenders                                           stdout appender
> log4j.appender.stdout=org.apache.log4j.ConsoleAppender
> log4j.appender.stdout.layout=org.apache.log4j.PatternLayout
> log4j.appender.stdout.layout.ConversionPattern=%5p [%t] %F:%l - %m%n
> ```

To set up log4j, you need to set the logging level and assign an appender for each logger you reference in your code. In our case, we referenced the logger name `ejb.messages`. In the properties file, we first assigned the `rootLogger` and our logger to the DEBUG level, and assigned an appender named `stdout`. The root logger, which is always present, is the parent of all loggers you create. If our logger did not have an assigned level, it would fall back on the root logger's level. Configuring the root logger is optional. After setting these values, we need to configure the `stdout` appender that we assigned to our logger.

Appenders are assigned a class and a layout, plus any additional properties available to a particular type of appender. The `stdout` appender is assigned the class `org.apache.log4j.ConsoleAppender`, which routes log messages to the console window. Additionally, its layout is contained in the class `PatternLayout` of the same package. The `PatternLayout` class lets us assign a particular pattern to format a message. The specified format for the `stdout` appender produces the following output from the `AccountBean` when someone buys stock:

```
INFO [ejbCreate] AccountBean.java:12 - Creating instance of AccountBean
DEBUG [buyStock] AccountBean.java:17 - Buying 100 shares of WXYZ
```

You can create as many appenders as you need in a log configuration file, and you can assign as many appenders to a single logger as you want. Each appender is independent of any others assigned to the same logger; each log message is reproduced and sent through each appender on its list.

Initializing the logging framework

Before you can begin sending messages through the logging system, you must initialize the logging framework with a configuration. For example, to initialize the brokerage application with the previous configuration file, your application must use the `org.apache.log4j.PropertyConfigurator` class. The following code demonstrates:

```
Propertyconfigurator.configure( "logconfig.properties" );
```

You need only invoke the static configure method and pass in the name of the properties file that contains your logging configuration. You have to do this only once—by calling an initialization method on a static class from your EJBs. In addition, you can use the `configureAndWatch()` method to force the `log4j` framework to reload the configuration if you modify the properties file.

With this brief introduction, you are ready to start covering the recipes in this chapter. The recipes present only a subset of the log4j functionality, and generally focus on particular usage points beneficial to an EJB application rather than the log4j architecture or additional features.

8.1 Formatting log messages

◆ Problem

You want to alter the format of messages without changing your code.

◆ Background

You have already set up log4j for your EJB application and coded all the log messages that you need. Recording log events is only part of a good logging system. The final form of the message is as important as the message itself. Regardless of the final destination of your messages (file, database, JMS queue), you want to format them in a particular way without having to change any of your code.

◆ *Recipe*

When setting up an appender for the logger in question, use the `PatternLayout` class to format messages. For instance, you might set up a logger named `ejb.session` with an appender like this:

```
log4j.logger.ejb.session=DEBUG, myappender

#setup appender myappender
log4j.appender.myappender=org.apache.log4j.ConsoleAppender
log4j.appender.myappender.layout=org.apache.log4j.PatternLayout
log4j.appender.myappender.ConversionPattern=%5p [%t] - %m%n
```

After specifying the `PatternLayout` class as the formatter, also indicate the value of the `ConversionPattern` attribute for the appender. The `ConversionPattern` value tells the `PatternLayout` class how to format your message. Using this setup, the following shows output from some sample code:

```
public void testMethod(){
   Logger ejbSession = Logger.getLogger( "ejb.session" );
   ejbSession.debug("Writing statement 1" );
   ejbSession.debug("Writing statement 2" );
}
```

Invoking `testMethod()` produces the following output based on the appender setup for the logger `ejb.session`:

```
DEBUG [testMethod] - Writing statement 1
DEBUG [testMethod] - Writing statement 2
```

◆ *Discussion*

The conversion pattern value is composed of a set of conversion specifiers and any literal text you want. A conversion specifier starts with a `%` followed by an optional format modifier and then a conversion character. Format modifiers control spacing, justification, and so forth, and conversion characters specify the data to include with the message. In this example, the conversion pattern `%5p [%t] - %m%n` translates to *Logger level [thread name] – message\n*. Table 8.1 lists the possible conversion characters available to the `PatternLayout` class.

Table 8.1 shows you the data that log4j can add to the final message formatted by the `PatternLayout` class. Table 8.2 describes how you can format the individual pieces of data. This table contains several examples of formatting the message data (represented by `m`).

Table 8.1 All possible conversion characters for the `PatternLayout` class. Each character represents a piece of data that can be included in the conversion pattern. These characters allow you to add important information to the final form of the log message.

Character	Description
c	Outputs the name of the logger sending the message. Can be used with {} to substring logger names.
C	Outputs the fully qualified classname containing the message. Can be used with {} to substring the classname.
d	Outputs a timestamp for the logging event. Specify the format using {}. By default, ISO8601 format is used. Additionally, you can specify log4j formatters using `ABSOLUTE`, `DATE`, or `ISO8601`.
f	Outputs the filename of where the message was coded.
l	Outputs location information for the logging event. This varies by JVM implementation, but consists of a fully qualified classname, source filename, and line number.
L	Outputs the line number where the message was coded.
m	Outputs the message.
M	Outputs the method name of the occurrence.
n	Outputs a line separator for the execution platform.
p	Outputs the priority of the logging event.
r	Outputs the elapsed time since the start of the application (in milliseconds).
t	Outputs the thread name of the logging event.
x	Outputs the nested diagnostic context associated with the thread.
X	Outputs the mapped diagnostic context associated with a thread. Must be used with {} specifying a client number.
%	Use `%%` to output a single `%` character.

Table 8.2 Examples of formatting conversion characters. These are examples of applied formatting to the previous conversion characters. Each example uses the conversion character `m`.

Character	Description
%5m	The message (`m`) must be at least 5 characters long. To ensure this, the formatter will pad to the left if necessary.
%-5m	The message (`m`) must be at least 5 characters long. To ensure this, the formatter will pad to the right if necessary.
%.5m	The message (`m`) should be a maximum of 5 characters long. If necessary, the formatter will truncate it to 5 characters.

When formatting messages, you can combine format modifiers. For example, the modifier `%10.50c` adds padding to the left of the logger name if it contains fewer than 10 characters, and truncates it if it's longer than 50 characters.

◆ *See also*

8.2—Improving logging performance

8.2 Improving logging performance

◆ *Problem*

You want to enhance the performance of your logging system.

◆ *Background*

You have added logging code to your entire EJB application, but now you've noticed a performance degradation. Logging can affect the performance of your application in a number of ways. log4j is probably the fastest logger you can find, but depending on how you use it, you can hurt your application performance. The two most common areas that affect performance are the number of log messages and the construction of log messages.

◆ *Recipe*

There are four ways to improve the log4j performance:

- Adjust the logger level.
- Construct your messages economically.
- Use formatting with caution.
- Use a fast appender layout class.

Change the level of your loggers

A large application might have thousands of log messages of varying levels. Modify your logging configuration file to output only the absolutely necessary messages into your logs. Disabling messages will improve the overall performance of your application. For example, if you have tested your application in production, you might want to turn off the debugging statements that are no longer necessary.

Change the way you write messages

When you're outputting messages, performance is slowed not only by the actual act of logging, but also by the construction of the message. For instance, look at the following sections of code that contain log statements:

```
//first section
public String getValue()
{
  String returnValue = computeValue();
  Logger.debug( "Final value of action: " + action
                          + " is " + computeValue() );
  return returnValue;
}
```

Compare that code to the following:

```
//second statement
public String getValue()
{
  String returnValue = computeValue();

  if( logger.isDebugEnabled() ) //check for level enabled
  {
    logger.debug("Final value of action " +
                    action + " is " + returnValue ); //reuse computed value
  }
  return returnValue;
}
```

The first logging statement incurs the cost of an extra method call to com-puteValue() and string concatenation for the message even if the DEBUG level of the logging system is disabled. The second statement wisely reuses the return-Value object, and also constructs the log message only if the DEBUG level is enabled.

Change your conversion patterns

The PatternLayout class and ConversionPattern attribute comprise one of the most common configurations for log4j. However, many of the PatternLayout's formatting options can slow down your application. Table 8.3 lists the conversion characters you should use with caution—and really only if performance is not an issue with your application.

Change the layout class of an appender

Change the layout class to the org.apache.log4j.SimpleLayout class. This layout class produces messages that include only the log level and message of the logging event:

```
DEBUG - my message from the application
```

Table 8.3 Conversion characters that degrade overall application performance. The process that creates the data produced by these characters is time-consuming. Repeatedly using these characters will eventually degrade the performance of your application to a noticeable degree.

Character	Data acquired	Performance problem
C	Fully qualified classname	The logging framework must walk the stack trace in order to build the classname of the object sending the message.
d	Date of the logging event	If you use this character, use one of the log4j date formatters. For example, use ABSOLUTE, DATE or IISO8601 with a character like %d{ABSOLUTE}. The SimpleDateFormat from the JDK is much slower than the log4j formatters. See recipe 8.1 and log4j docs for more information.
F	Filename of the logging event	Same problems as using 'C'.
I	Location information	Suffers from having to walk the stack trace in order to gather information about class, file, and line number.
L	Line number	Same problems as 'I'.
M	Method name	Same problems as 'I'.

The SimpleLayout class is the fastest of the layout classes.

◆ *Discussion*

Regardless of the inherent speed of the log4j system, improving performance of your logging system relies on good programming practices and thoughtful message construction. For instance, the recipe shows a simple example of how reusing already acquired object values can decrease the time it takes to build a message. In addition, concatenating strings, converting primitive types to strings, and similar steps should be used only when necessary. If you must construct a message from various parts (which is common), you should at least test for the logger level to avoid unnecessary construction of the message.

When using the PatternLayout class to format your messages, always be concerned with the performance degradation of certain conversion characters. Refer to table 8.3 for these characters, but keep in mind that although they can provide useful data, they do so at a high cost of time. Finally, if performance is your utmost objective, switch to the SimpleLayout class for formatting messages. It provides only a simple message structure, but it performs the fastest of the layout classes.

◆ *See also*

8.1—Formatting log messages

8.3 *Using logging to generate reports*

◆ **Problem**

Without modifying your logging framework, you would like to generate reports based on the messages output by the logger.

◆ **Background**

In many production systems, the logging system is used to report critical errors to production support users. If your logging system outputs to a single file (or even multiple files), it can be difficult for users to work through a complex log file looking for particular messages. At specific times (for example, weekly or monthly), support personnel would like to summarize the errors or critical events of the previous cycle into a report.

◆ **Recipe**

To be able to generate logger reports, set up the JDBC appender for log4j in your log4j configuration file. For example, the following properties set up the appender for an Oracle database in a log4j properties file:

```
log4j.appender.myJDBC=org.apache.log4j.jdbc.JDBCAppender
log4j.appender.myJDBC.URL=jdbc:oracle:thin:@myhost:1521:mysid
log4j.appender.myJDBC.user=user
log4j.appender.myJDBC.password=password
log4j.appender.myJDBC.sql=INSERT INTO LogTable (date, logger_name, thread,
                          message ) VALUES ('%d', '%c', '%t' '%m')
log4j.appender.myJDBC.driver= oracle.jdbc.driver.OracleDriver
```

In addition, be sure to assign the new appender to an available logger:

```
log4j.logger.myLogger=DEBUG, myJDBC
```

◆ **Discussion**

By inserting log messages into a database table, you provide your application with an instant way to generate all types of reports. For example, you could log performance data, which could then be gathered to display performance of particular components of your application. In addition, log4j allows you to create multiple appenders and multiple loggers. Using a system as flexible as this lets you create separate database tables for many loggers, effectively separating messages as needed to better categorize your reporting.

As you can see in the recipe, log4j contains a JDBC appender. To create the appender, you need to provide it with a URL to a database, a username and password, a database driver classname, and an SQL statement. The appender invokes the SQL statement to insert a log message into a database table; notice that the message format is also specified in the SQL statement. You can use any of the conversion characters associated with formatting messages.

NOTE When sending messages to a JDBC appender, be careful not to send any characters in the message that would disrupt the SQL statement. For instance, sending a ' character would cause the SQL statement in the recipe to fail.

According to the log4j team, the JDBC appender will be replaced in the future with one that offers more features. For example, the current JDBC appender does not log exceptions. Please refer to the log4j documentation for updates to this appender.

◆ **See also**

8.1—Formatting log messages

8.4 *Sending log messages to a JMS topic*

◆ *Problem*

You want the ability to send certain log messages to a JMS topic.

◆ *Background*

Exposing your log messages to a JMS system lets you send logging events to any appropriately coded JMS listener. Sending your log messages to a JMS topic allows you to offload the process that stores the log messages. If your application runs in a clustered environment, you can use JMS to consolidate your log messages to a single repository.

◆ *Recipe*

To send log messages to a JMS topic, use the log4j JMS appender. The JMS appender will place messages on a queue according to a specified JMS topic. Objects look up a JMS topic using JNDI. Because of that, you must be aware of how you set up your log4j configuration file. If the logging system is initialized inside an EJB (see the chapter introduction), your appender setup should look similar to this:

```
log4j.appender.jmsappender=org.apache.log4j.net.JMSAppender
log4j.appender.jmsappender.TopicBindingName=LOGGING_TOPIC
```

The value `LOGGING_TOPIC` should be configured in the application server hosting your EJBs. See your vendor's documentation for more information.

If the logging system is initialized outside an EJB, you need to explicitly set up the initial context environment in the configuration properties. For example, use this code to look up a Weblogic context:

```
log4j.appender.jmsappender=org.apache.log4j.net.JMSAppender
log4j.appender.jmsappender.TopicBindingName=LOGGING_TOPIC
log4j.appender.jmsappender.InitialContextFactoryName=
    weblogic.jndi.WLInitialContextFactory
log4j.appender.jmsappender.ProviderURL=t3://localhost:7001
```

◆ Discussion

In order for the JMS appender to operate successfully, it must retrieve the JNDI `InitialContext` object for the operating environment. If the appender is initialized inside an EJB, it can make use of the `InitialContext` class's default constructor since the correct context is provided by the EJB container contract with the bean.

However, from outside the container, the appender will need to initialize the `InitialContext` with environment properties. The recipe provides an example of how this can be done through the log4j configuration properties. The additional properties shown are placed into a Hashtable and used to retrieve the `Initial-Context` for later use. Refer to the log4j API for more property information, and check your application server's documentation to learn about the required properties for the JNDI initial context.

8.5 Logging to an XML file

◆ Problem

You want your log messages to build an XML file.

◆ Background

Using XML is the best way to ensure that data is readable by a variety of clients. Creating a log file formatted as an XML document lets you transfer important information to a variety of applications.

◆ *Recipe*

To log to an XML file, use the log4j XML layout class with the rolling file appender. The following properties are a sample of a log4j properties configuration file that assigns a file appender with an XML layout to a logger:

```
#setup log level and assign appenders
log4j.logger.mylogger=DEBUG, xmlFileAppender

#setup xmlFileAppender appender
log4j.appender.xmlFileAppender=org.apache.log4j.RollingFileAppender
log4j.appender.xmlFileAppender.File=Log.xml
log4j.appender.xmlFileAppender.MaxFileSize=100KB
log4j.appender.xmlFileAppender.MaxBackupIndex=2
log4j.appender.xmlFileAppender.layout=org.apache.log4j.xml.XMLLayout
```

◆ *Discussion*

`RollingFileAppender` is an appender you can use to output messages to a file. In addition, the `RollingFileAppender` class will back up the log file when it reaches a certain size (which you specify). Not only that, but it will rename backup files as many times as you need. We set up this appender in order to provide the new XML layout in the file. Using the `org.apache.log4j.xml.XMLLayout` class, we placed each logging event in an XML tag. The following is a sample log message (event) capture in XML:

```
<log4j:event logger="test" timestamp="1037368796395" level="DEBUG"
thread="main">
<log4j:message><![CDATA[writing message number two]]></log4j:message>
</log4j:event>
```

The tags used by the layout correspond to the log4j.dtd file that comes with the log4j download. If you set the property `LocationInfo` to true, log4j will output location information about the message into the logs. You set the property with an additional line in the property configuration for the appender:

```
log4j.appender.xmlFileAppender.layout.LocationInfo=true
```

That line creates the following new output for logging events:

```
<log4j:event logger=
    "test" timestamp="1037369165731" level="DEBUG" thread="main">
<log4j:message><![CDATA[writing message number two]]></log4j:message>
<log4j:locationInfo class=
    "log4jTest" method="main" file="log4jTest.java" line="12"/>
</log4j:event>
```

XML output from log4j does not create a well-formed XML document. The data created is meant to be wrapped by a header and footer. See the log4j.dtd file and log4j documentation for more information.

◆ *See also*

8.2—Improving log performance

8.6 *Creating log file views for the web browser*

◆ *Problem*

You want to create log files that are easily readable with your web browser.

◆ *Background*

In most cases, capturing logging events is not the hardest task. Rather, it is the presentation of the message store in a meaningful and easy-to-interpret format that is more difficult. Log messages exist to enable us to analyze the behavior and lifecycle of applications. Creating a log file in HTML format is a quick and easy way of presenting log messages to a user.

◆ *Recipe*

To create a web browser view for your log files, use the log4j HTML layout class with the rolling file appender. The following properties are a sample of a log4j properties configuration file that assigns a file appender with an HTML layout to a logger:

```
log4j.logger.mylogger=DEBUG, htmlFileAppender

log4j.appender.htmlFileAppender =org.apache.log4j.RollingFileAppender
log4j.appender.htmlFileAppender.File=Log.html
log4j.appender.htmlFileAppender.MaxFileSize=100KB
log4j.appender.htmlFileAppender.MaxBackupIndex=2
log4j.appender.htmlFileAppender.layout=org.apache.log4j.HTMLLayout
log4j.appender.htmlFileAppender.layout.LocationInfo=true
```

◆ *Discussion*

The RollingFileAppender is an appender you can use to output messages to a file. In addition, the RollingFileAppender class will back up the log file when it reaches a certain size (which you specify). It will also rename backup files as many times as you need. We set up this appender in order to provide the new HTML layout in the file. Using the org.apache.log4j.HTMLLayout class (shown in the recipe), log4j builds an HTML table of logging events. The result of two application executions is shown in figure 8.1.

◆ *See also*

8.2—Improving logging performance

8.5—Logging to an XML file

Log session start time Fri Nov 15 07:26:42 MST 2002

Time	Thread	Level	Category	File Line	Message
0	main	DEBUG	test	Log4jTest.java:11	writing message number one
20	main	DEBUG	test	Log4jTest.java:12	writing message number two

Log session start time Fri Nov 15 07:28:29 MST 2002

Time	Thread	Level	Category	File Line	Message
0	main	DEBUG	test	Log4jTest.java:11	writing message number one
50	main	DEBUG	test	Log4jTest.java:12	writing message number two

Log session start time Fri Nov 15 16:20:46 MST 2002

Time	Thread	Level	Category	File Line	Message
0	main	DEBUG	test	Log4jTest.java:11	writing message number one
30	main	DEBUG	test	Log4jTest.java:12	writing message number two

Log session start time Mon Nov 18 07:26:56 MST 2002

Time	Thread	Level	Category	File Line	Message
0	main	DEBUG	test	Log4jTest.java:11	writing message number one
40	main	DEBUG	test	Log4jTest.java:12	writing message number two

Log session start time Mon Nov 18 07:42:14 MST 2002

Time	Thread	Level	Category	File Line	Message
0	main	DEBUG	test	Log4jTest.java:12	writing message number one

Figure 8.1   The HTML view generated by log4j

8.7 Creating a centralized log file
in a clustered environment

◆ **Problem**

In your clustered environment, you would like to consolidate your log messages
into a single, centralized location.

◆ **Background**

As application servers grow easier to use, it also becomes easier to cluster your
enterprise applications. Once you begin to cluster your applications, you might be
faced with the problem of consolidating your log files. When each member of the
cluster creates its own log file, you will have an increasingly difficult time tracking
user sessions and critical events.

◆ **Recipe**

To set up a centralized log file, create in your cluster a new EJB application consist-
ing of only a single message-driven bean. In the other members of the cluster, create a JMS appender for the logging framework that publishes messages to a topic
that the message-driven bean uses to acquire messages. The single message-driven
bean writes out the messages as needed. The code in listing 8.3 shows a sample
message-driven bean class.

Listing 8.3   LogConsolidatorBean.java

```java
import javax.ejb.*;
import javax.jms.*;
import org.apache.log4j.*;

public class LogConsolidatorBean implements MessageDrivenBean,
    MessageListener
{
  private static final Logger logger = null;

  public void setMessageDrivenContext(MessageDrivenContext mdc){
  }

  public void ejbCreate()
  {
    logger = Logger.getLogger( "app.consolidated" );    ◁─┐ Creates the
  }                                                          Logger object
```

```
    public void ejbRemove()
    {
      LogManager.shutdown();
    }
    public void onMessage( Message msg )
    {
      LoggingEvent event;
      Logger tempLogger;

      try
      {
        ObjectMessage objectMessage = ( ObjectMessage ) message;
        event = (LoggingEvent) objectMessage.getObject();
        tempLogger = Logger.getLogger( event.getLoggerName() );
        tempLogger.callAppenders( event );

      }
      catch( JMSException jmse )
      {
        logger.error("Cannot log incoming message", jmse);
      }
    }
  }
```

**Invokes
appenders for
the logger**

When deploying this bean, you must also provide a log4j configuration file with
all the logger names that are found in the other cluster members. Provide a single
appender across all the named loggers in order to achieve a single, consolidated
log repository.

◆ *Discussion*

The important parts of this recipe are the onMessage() method of the message-
driven bean LogConsolidatorBean and its log4j configuration file. Examining the
onMessage() call, you might be asking yourself why we did not simply call the
event.getMessage() method and send it to a new logger for formatting. Well, we
could have done that, but the log message would have lost all of its format and
context information. For instance, all the messages sent to a new logger would
have a new thread, timestamp, classname, and so forth. Instead, we preserve logging event context information by sending the event itself to a logger. To actually
persist the log message (to a file, for example), we need to invoke the appenders
associated with the retrieved logger.

The key to this recipe is duplicating all the logger names specified in the cluster into the log4j configuration file used by the message-driven bean JVM. It is not
necessary to duplicate all of the appender setup—just the loggers. In the new

log4j configuration file, you need just one appender for all the loggers, which ensures that all the messages are routed to a single location. For information about sending log messages to a JMS queue (from each of the cluster members), see recipe 8.4.

◆ **See also**

6.3—Creating a message-driven Enterprise JavaBean

8.1—Formatting log messages

8.4—Sending log messages to a JMS topic

8.10—Sorting log messages by client

8.8 *Tracking the lifecycle of an EJB*

◆ **Problem**

You want to use your logging framework to track the lifecycle of your EJBs.

◆ **Background**

When tuning an EJB application for production, it is useful to know how the container manages instances of your EJBs. You would like to see how your EJBs move through their lifecycle in your application. This information can allow you to tune the EJB container or provide metrics of client usage, container tuning, performance, and more.

◆ **Recipe**

To track the lifecycle of an EJB, you should create a particular Logger instance and place log messages in the lifecycle methods of the EJB.

Create a logger in the creation method for each EJB deployed and name the logger using the EJB classname. In the various lifecycle methods, such as ejbCreate() and ejbRemove(), log a message indicating that the method is executing. In the log4j configuration file, format your log messages so that they include the logger name, timestamp, method name, and message. For example, the following portion of a log4j configuration properties file sets up a logger for a sample EJB. The appender should be shared among all loggers.

```
#setup log level and assign appenders
#this logger is named after an EJB classname
log4j.logger.cookbook.ch8.SampleBean=DEBUG, output
```

```
#setup output appender
log4j.appender.output =org.apache.log4j.RollingFileAppender
log4j.appender.output.layout=org.apache.log4j.PatternLayout
log4j.appender.output.layout.ConversionPattern=%c; %d{HH:mm:ss}; %M; %m%n
```

When creating the logger in the bean, use the classname as the logger name. Finally, in each bean, create a unique ID by using a random number (or something similar) that identifies the life of the particular EJB. Send this ID as the message to the logging framework. For instance, examine the code for the bean cookbook.ch8.SampleBean in listing 8.4.

Listing 8.4   SampleBean.java

```
package cookbook.ch8;

import javax.ejb.*;
import org.apache.log4j.*;

public class SampleBean implements SessionBean
{
    private static final Logger logger = null;
    private String beanID = null;

    public ejbCreate()
    {                                                   ⟵  Creates the
        logger = Logger.get( SampleBean.class );  ⟵    Logger object
        Random random = new Random();
        beanID = random.nextInt() + "SampleBean";        Creates a unique ID
        logger.debug( beanID );                          for this bean
    }

    public ejbRemove()
    {
     logger.debug( beanID );
    }                                   Logs the ID at
                                        critical points
    public void ejbPassivate()
    {
        logger.debug( beanID );
    }

    public void ejbActivate()
    {
     logger.debug( beanID );
    }

    //business methods below
}
```

The code in listing 8.4 shows a sample session EJB that logs messages with an ID identifying the bean and tracks its lifecycle. The output would look something similar to this:

```
cookbook.ch8.SampleBean; 07:20:53; ejbCreate; 986751959SampleBean
cookbook.ch8.SampleBean; 07:20:54; ejbPassivate; 986751959SampleBean
cookbook.ch8.SampleBean; 07:20:55; ejbActivate; 986751959SampleBean
cookbook.ch8.SampleBean; 07:20:56; ejbRemove; 986751959SampleBean
```

◆ Discussion

We used the EJB classname as the logger name in order to better sort the resulting log file created with multiple bean entries. Since we used a semicolon to separate the portions of the formatted message, we can open the log file in Microsoft Excel and sort messages by timestamp, logger name, and message (the unique ID). The unique ID lets us pull the exact log events for an EJB session lifecycle. We don't have to specify anything else in the message to the logger because we are pulling the method name from the logging event.

◆ See also

8.1—Formatting log messages

8.2—Improving logging performance

8.9 Using a different configuration at runtime

◆ Problem

You would like to specify which logging configuration file to load, or even switch configurations during runtime of your EJB application.

◆ Background

While log4j lets you create multiple destinations and formats for your log messages, you would like to change the log4j configuration after your application has started. For instance, after testing your application in production, you need to turn down the logging level from a debug level to a normal operating level. You can improve performance by including only logging messages that are absolutely necessary.

◆ *Recipe*

To update the log4j configuration for the JVM running your EJB application, deploy a servlet to that JVM that has the ability to refresh the log4j system. For instance, the servlet shown in listing 8.5 initializes the logging framework as it is deployed, and its doGet() method can be used to reset the logging framework after a configuration file has been replaced or modified.

Listing 8.5   LoggerInitializationServlet

```java
import javax.servlet.*;
import org.apache.log4j.PropertyConfigurator;
import java.io.*;

public class LoggerInitializationServlet extends HttpServlet
{

  private static String file = null;

  public void init()                                              Retrieves the
  {                                                               configuration
    file = getInitParameter( "CONFIGURATION_FILE" );   ◁──┘      filename
    initialize( file );
  }

  private void initialize( String filename )
  {
    if( filename != null )
    {
      this.file = filename;
    }

    PropertyConfigurator.configure( getServletContext().getRealPath("/")
                  + file ) );                    Initializes the logging system
  }

  public void doGet( HttpServletRequest reg, HttpServletResponse res )
  {
   String filename = getFileName( req );
    initialize( filename );                     Initializes the logging system at
  }                                             any servlet request

  public void doPost( HttpServletRequest reg, HttpServletResponse res )
  {
    String filename = getFileName( req );
    initialize( filename );
  }
}
```

The servlet example in listing 8.5 does not show the `getFileName()` method. You must implement this method to retrieve a configuration filename from the servlet request. To deploy this servlet, add the following to your web.xml file:

```
<servlet>
  <servlet-name>init-servlet</servlet-name>
  <servlet-class>LoggerInitializationServlet</servlet-class>

  <init-param>
    <param-name>CONFIGURATION_FILE</param-name>
    <param-value>WEB-INF/classes/logconfig.properties</param-value>
  </init-param>
</servlet>
```

◆ *Discussion*

The initialization servlet is a flexible way of resetting your logger configuration at runtime. You can develop the servlet to accept parameters, such as new filenames, to control how the logger is reset. Essentially, the servlet opens a runtime window to the logger configuration, and with an open place to add code, you can do anything you need.

Alternatively, if your application server contains a JMX MBean server, you could write an MBean to expose the logging configuration to a management console. For more information on JMX (Java Management Extensions), read *JMX in Action* (2002, Manning Publications).

8.10 *Sorting log messages by client*

◆ *Problem*

You would like your log files to be sortable by user session. More important, you need to sort a user's session log events in the order they occurred, separated from other sessions.

◆ *Background*

An enterprise application usually allows access from a group of users. In web applications, each user is usually mapped to a single session. A user session may touch many pieces of the application. When an application allows access to simultaneous user sessions, the log store becomes a confusion of interlayered log events from different users.

To solve this problem, you can use the log4j NDC class. NDC stands for Nested Diagnostic Context. By using this class, you can have log4j retrieve information about a client (its context information) and display that information in the log message repository, allowing log readers to make sense of multiclient environments.

◆ *Recipe*

To identify a single client in a multiclient log file, push client-specific information onto the NDC stack. Then, using the pattern layout in your configuration file, retrieve the NDC information and use it to identify log messages. For example, for each new client, pick a unique characteristic (username, hostname, ID, etc.) and push it onto the NDC stack. The following code does this:

```
//starting client thread session inside bean
NDC.push( username );
logger.debug("a message written to the log" );

//more messages and code…
```

When work for the (client) thread is complete, clean up the NDC stack object:

```
NDC.pop();
NDC.remove();
```

To configure an appender to use the NDC information to identify a client, configure one similar to the following:

```
log4j.appender.myappender =org.apache.log4j.ConsoleAppender
log4j.appender.myappender.layout=org.apache.log4j.PatternLayout
log4j.appender.myappender.layout.ConversionPattern=%x %5p [%t] - %m%n
```

In the conversion pattern, %x refers to the NDC stack for the particular thread sending the log message. log4j retrieves any information pushed onto the stack and includes it in the output. See recipe 8.1 for formatting questions.

◆ *Discussion*

The NDC class acts as a stack for each thread. log4j provides a stack for each new thread context that executes. The NDC operates a stack on a per-thread basis. That is, each new thread gets its own stack to use. In the EJB environment, a single user session may span several threads during its lifetime. If you are trying to tie log messages back to a user session, you need to push context information onto the NDC for each user thread. For instance, if you are using the username of a client as context information, you must make sure the username is available in each thread.

Before exiting a thread, you should call the `remove()` method on the NDC class, as you can see in the recipe. This method cleans up memory allocated for the thread and ensures the garbage collector can perform its duties.

EJBs can always retrieve the security `Principal` of callers through their `EJBContext` instance set during their creation. For example, the following code retrieves the username of an EJB client:

```
String username = ejbContext.getPrincipal().getName();
```

During the design of your application, you will need to consider how you want to track the user's session across nested EJB calls. EJBs can choose to run under a client's identity using the `<use-caller-identity/>` tag in the EJB deployment descriptor.

An alternative to the NDC class is the MDC class (Mapped Diagnostic Context). The MDC operates in much the same manner as the NDC, but it is a map instead of a stack. A map allows you store and retrieve information about a client in a more controlled fashion. For instance, even though you may place many items about a client in the map, you can choose to only retrieve a single item. You make use of the MDC by placing thread context information in the map using a key:

```
MDC.put("username", userNameVariable );
logger.debug("writing a log message" );
```

An appender set up to use the MDC information is similar to the previous NDC example:

```
log4j.appender.myappender =org.apache.log4j.ConsoleAppender
log4j.appender.myappender.layout=org.apache.log4j.PatternLayout
log4j.appender.myappender.layout.ConversionPattern=%X{username} %5p [%t]-
    %m%n
```

When using the MDC, you retrieve information with the `%X{key}` conversion character.

◆ **See also**

7.1—Finding the identity and role of a caller inside an EJB method

7.5—Assigning a role to an EJB

8.1—Formatting log messages

8.2—Improving logging performance

Deploying and unit testing

"There can be no question, my dear Watson, of the value of exercise before breakfast."

—*Sherlock Holmes*

A good build system can be a developer's best friend. Apache Ant provides the perfect combination of power and flexibility to meet all of your application building and deployment needs. Another important tool the EJB developer needs is a comprehensive testing utility. Apache Cactus, an open source framework, lets you build unit tests for your EJB functionality. In addition, you can use Ant to build a good regression test system with your unit tests. The recipes in this chapter demonstrate how to use Ant to build and deploy your EJBs and how to use Cactus for testing your EJBs.

You will find recipes for the following topics in this chapter:

- Using Ant for compilation
- Packaging beans into an ejb.jar file
- Generating stub classes
- Unit-testing stateless session beans
- Unit-testing stateful session beans
- Unit-testing an entity bean
- Automating test cases
- Executing test cases

A deployment and testing appetizer

After all your work developing your EJB applications, you're ready to send them out into the world. Using two open source Apache projects, you can build and test your EJBs. Apache Ant is an excellent tool for creating and automating a build system for your EJB application; Apache Cactus provides an equally excellent system for building and running EJB unit tests.

Apache Ant

Put simply, Ant executes tasks described in a build.xml file. These Ant tasks are implemented in Java classes and perform such tasks as class compilation and JAR file creation. Ant allows you to build your own tasks, as well as use the many tasks it already includes. In this chapter, we demonstrate how to use Ant to build, package, and deploy your EJBs.

The build.xml file defines an Ant project. The project contains different targets, each of which define a task that Ant will accomplish (such as compiling, copying files, or making directories). You will see how to create these Ant tasks as you read through the Ant recipes in this chapter. If, after examining the recipes, you need more information about Ant, refer to "Second helpings: Additional resources," at the end of this book.

Apache Cactus

In this book, we have focused on a few open source tools. For testing EJBs, we chose to use another open source framework, Apache Cactus. Cactus lets you build and execute test cases for server-side components like servlets and EJBs. Cactus uses JUnit (a popular unit testing framework) and extends it.

We might have chosen other testing frameworks for this chapter. In fact, you can test EJBs using simple JUnit test cases. Instead, we chose Cactus for a few main reasons:

- Cactus executes tests within the EJB container.

- Cactus can test EJBs that use only local interfaces.

- Cactus tests run in the same environment as your production environment. This means test execution occurs the same way a production EJB call would.

- You can use Ant to automate your Cactus tests to build a rigorous regression testing system.

Using Cactus, you build test cases for all of your session bean business logic and entity bean data access. Cactus redirects test cases using the process illustrated in figure 9.1. It redirects test cases invoked on the client side by a JUnit test runner to server-side test cases.

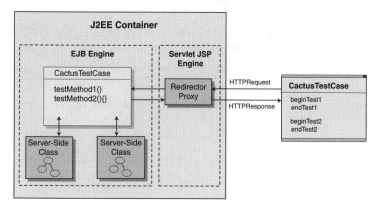

Figure 9.1 A Cactus test case. Test cases are started on the client side by a JUnit test runner and passed to the Cactus test redirector servlet in the server-side container, where actual test cases are executed.

To download and install Cactus, acquire the latest build from Apache at http://jakarta.apache.org/cactus. Cactus doesn't require installation per se; it's only a framework, and as such, the necessary Cactus JAR files need only be in the classpath of your application. Extracting the downloaded file to a working directory, you should notice several JAR files and documentation. You can place the JAR files into the classpath of your application in two ways: either include the files in the classpath of the application server running your EJB application, or package them in the enterprise archive (EAR) or web archive (WAR) file containing your application. The following JAR files come with the Cactus binary download (their names may vary depending on the version number):

- cactus.jar
- cactus-ant.jar
- httpclient.jar
- junit.jar
- aspectj.jar
- commons-logging.jar
- log4j.jar

All of the JAR files listed should be placed in the application server classpath, or simply in the classpath of your application (its WAR or EAR file, for instance). In addition, these JAR files are needed for the execution of the test client, and you must include them in the classpath of your Ant setup and JUnit test runner, as illustrated by recipes 9.7 and 9.8.

In order to actually execute the test cases you write for your EJBs, you must deploy the test case classes and the Cactus servlets into your application server. Cactus has several servlets used to execute various server-side tests. The following sample web.xml file shows how you would deploy the Cactus servlets with your web application. You would need to do this for each of your applications.

```
<web-app>
  <welcome-file-list>
    <welcome-file>index.html</welcome-file>
  </welcome-file-list>

  <!-- =======[ Remainder is set up for Cactus Test Suite
    ]========= -->
  <servlet>
    <servlet-name>ServletTestRunner</servlet-name>
    <servlet-class>
        org.apache.cactus.server.runner.ServletTestRunner
```

```
    </servlet-class>
  </servlet>

  <servlet-mapping>
    <servlet-name>ServletTestRunner</servlet-name>
    <url-pattern>/ServletTestRunner</url-pattern>
  </servlet-mapping>

  <filter>
      <filter-name>FilterRedirector</filter-name>
      <filter-class>org.apache.cactus.server.FilterTestRedirector
       </filter-class>
  </filter>

  <filter-mapping>
      <filter-name>FilterRedirector</filter-name>
      <url-pattern>/FilterRedirector</url-pattern>
  </filter-mapping>

  <servlet>
      <servlet-name>ServletRedirector</servlet-name>
      <servlet-class>
              org.apache.cactus.server.ServletTestRedirector
      </servlet-class>
  </servlet>

  <servlet>
      <servlet-name>JspRedirector</servlet-name>
      <jsp-file>/jspRedirector.jsp</jsp-file>
  </servlet>

  <servlet-mapping>
      <servlet-name>ServletRedirector</servlet-name>
      <url-pattern>/ServletRedirector</url-pattern>
  </servlet-mapping>

  <servlet-mapping>
      <servlet-name>JspRedirector</servlet-name>
      <url-pattern>/JspRedirector</url-pattern>
  </servlet-mapping>

</web-app>
```

The servlet classes and their dependent classes (contained in the JAR files listed in recipe 9.1) should already be in the classpath, as described earlier.

With that brief introduction to Cactus, you're prepared to start writing and executing EJB test cases (see recipes 9.4–9.8). While Cactus has many features, the recipes in this chapter focus on using Cactus for testing EJBs. You should consult the full Cactus documentation to learn about its other features and abilities.

9.1 Compiling Enterprise JavaBeans

◆ **Problem**

You want to use Apache Ant to build your EJB source files.

◆ **Background**

The first step in a good build system is to successfully manage the compilation of source files. You need a build system that is fast, reliable, and easy to use. With Apache Ant, compiling your source file is a straightforward task. After following this recipe for building your EJB source files, you can proceed to the next recipes, which focus on packaging your EJBs and building stub classes. Since this is the first of several recipes using Ant to create a build and deploy systems, we need to set up some basic files.

◆ **Recipe**

We will be using two files for these build recipes. The first is a properties file that contains some environment variables used by Ant to successfully build our EJBs. For this recipe, the properties file (listing 9.1) defines variables describing the source directory and build directory, among other things.

> **Listing 9.1 The build.properties file**

```
#choose classic, modern, jikes, or jvc
JAVAC=modern

#The Ant project name                    Names the
PROJECT_NAME=ejbCookbook  ◁┘  Ant project

#-------------[ Point to the J2EE JAR for includes ]--------------
EJB_JAR=C:/j2sdkee1.4/lib/j2ee.jar  ◁┐  Describes external JARs needed for compiling

#-------------[ Where do all the source files live ]--------------
EJB_SOURCE=ejbs              Names the source
META_SOURCE=META-INF    directories

#-------------[ Where do all the class/build files live ]----------
BUILD=build                  Names the build
EJB_BUILD=${BUILD}/ejbs    directories
```

The second file Ant needs for this recipe is the build.xml file, shown in listing 9.2. As we move on to the next recipes, we will be adding to this file to accomplish different build tasks. For now, this build file only sets up the classpath, compiles the sources, and cleans the build directory.

Listing 9.2   The build.xml file used to compile and package an EJB application

```
<project name="${PROJECT_NAME}" default="all" basedir=".">

  <!-- set global properties for this build -->
  <property environment="env"/>
  <property file="build_ejb.properties"/>           Loads the build
                                                     properties file

 <target name="all" depends="init, compile_ejb, jar_ejb,
                   ejbc, deploy_jar">
    <echo>---------[ Project name: ${PROJECT_NAME} Completed ]----
    </echo>
 </target>                                          Executes the build system

  <!--
    ============================================================
        Setup ready for build.
        Create all the necessary Directories
    ============================================================
  -->
  <target name="init">
    <tstamp/>
    <echo>----[ Creating all Directories and copying XML files ]-
    </echo>
    <mkdir dir="${BUILD}"/>
    <mkdir dir="${EJB_BUILD}"/>
    <mkdir dir="${EJB_BUILD}/META-INF"/>            Creates necessary
  </target>                                                directories

  <!--
    =================================================
        Clean the files up
    =================================================
   -->
  <target name="clean">
    <tstamp/>
    <echo>---[ Cleaning the Compiled and Deployed Files ]-----
    </echo>
    <delete dir="${BUILD}"/>                        Deletes the build
  </target>                                        directory and contents

  <!—
    =================================================
        Compile the EJB Source Files
    =================================================
  -->
```

```
<target name="compile_ejb" depends="init">
<tstamp/>
<echo>---[ Compiling EJB Source Files ]------------</echo>
<javac srcdir="${EJB_SOURCE}" destdir="${EJB_BUILD}" >
  <classpath>
    <pathelement location="${EJB_JAR}"/>
    <pathelement location="${INCLUDE_JARS}"/>
  </classpath>
</javac>                                         Builds the EJB
</target>                                           class files

</project>
```

After creating these two files, make sure you put them in the directory structure that is described by the project. For instance, in this recipe, they should be in the same directory, one level above the source directory. From a command prompt, change to the directory and execute the following command:

```
prompt> ant all
```

◆ *Discussion*

Obviously, you should modify the build properties file to represent your particular folder structure for both source and build directories. After running Ant with this setup, you should see the class file in your build directory. Without executing the clean target, successive runs of Ant will compile any source files that have changed since the previous execution.

◆ *See also*

9.2—Building the ejb.jar file

9.3—Building Enterprise JavaBean stub classes

9.2 *Building the ejb.jar file*

◆ *Problem*

After compiling the EJB source files, you want Ant to also package the new class files into an ejb.jar file.

◆ *Background*

After building class files, you need to package them into an ejb.jar file along with the XML deployment descriptor that describes your EJBs. The JDK includes a JAR tool that will package all of your class files along with the descriptor, but it's cumbersome to manually execute it after every source compilation. You should automate the JAR execution along with the generation of class files.

◆ *Recipe*

For this step, no changes are necessary to the build properties file (created in recipe 9.1). We only need to add a dependent target to the build.xml file. The changes are shown in bold in listing 9.3.

Listing 9.3 build.xml

```
<project name="${PROJECT_NAME}" default="all" basedir=".">

  <!-- set global properties for this build -->
  <property environment="env"/>
  <property file="build_ejb.properties"/>

  <target name="all" depends="init, compile_ejb, jar_ejb">
      <echo>---------[ Project name: ${PROJECT_NAME} Completed ]---
      </echo>
  </target>                        Adds the new jar_ejb target to the depends list

  <!--
      ===================================================
          Setup ready for build.
          Create all the necessary Directories
      ===================================================
  -->
  <target name="init">
    <tstamp/>
    <echo>---[ Creating all Directories and copying XML files ]--
    </echo>
    <mkdir dir="${BUILD}"/>
    <mkdir dir="${EJB_BUILD}"/>
    <mkdir dir="${EJB_BUILD}/META-INF"/>
  </target>

  <!--
      ===========================================
          Clean the files up
      ===========================================
   -->
  <target name="clean">
    <tstamp/>
    <echo>----[ Cleaning the Compiled and Deployed Files ]-------
    </echo>
    <delete dir="${BUILD}"/>
  </target>

  <!—
```

```
     =================================================
          Compile the EJB Source Files
     =================================================
-->

  <target name="compile_ejb" depends="init">
  <tstamp/>
  <echo>---------[ Compiling EJB Source Files ]------</echo>
  <javac srcdir="${EJB_SOURCE}" destdir="${EJB_BUILD}" >
    <classpath>
      <pathelement location="${EJB_JAR}"/>
      <pathelement location="${INCLUDE_JARS}"/>
    </classpath>
  </javac>
</target>

<!--
    =======================================
        Create the EJB JAR File
    =======================================
-->
<target name="jar_ejb" depends="compile_ejb">
  <tstamp/>
  <echo>--[ Copying META-INF Files ]--------------</echo>
  <copy todir="${EJB_BUILD}/META-INF">
    <fileset dir="${META_SOURCE}">
      <include name="*.xml"/>
    </fileset>
  </copy>
  <echo>---------[ Creating EJB JAR File ]-------</echo>
  <jar jarfile="${BUILD}/${PROJECT_NAME}.jar" basedir="${EJB_BUILD}" />
</target>

</project>
```

> **Describes the task that will create the ejb.jar file**

◆ *Discussion*

This recipe adds a new target to the build.xml file. The jar_ejb target sets up and executes the JAR tool against the newly created class files (from the compile command). Notice, in fact, that it depends on the compile_ejb target before it executes. This ensures that class files are present for the JAR tool. Before setting up the <fileset> tag, the target copies all available EJB XML files into a META-INF folder under the build directory. Next the <fileset> tag tells the target where to find the class files for the JAR tool. Finally, the <jar> command builds a JAR file named after the project.

◆ **See also**

9.1—Compiling Enterprise JavaBeans

9.3—Building Enterprise JavaBean stub classes

9.3 Building Enterprise JavaBean stub classes

◆ **Problem**

After building class files from your EJB source files, you want to automate the generation of your EJB stub classes.

◆ **Background**

After you generate the class file for your EJBs, you also need to generate the stub classes for deploying the beans into a specific EJB container. Generating stub classes requires you to run an EJB compiler tool provided by the vendor. This tool will generate stub source files and automatically compile them. Using Ant, you can automate the use of this tool.

◆ **Recipe**

For this recipe, we will generate stub classes for deploying EJBs into the Weblogic EJB container. The properties file in listing 9.4 shows the changes needed for this step in our build system. The changes from the previous recipe are shown in bold.

Listing 9.4   The modified build.properties file for generating stubs

```
#choose classic, modern, jikes, or jvc
JAVAC=modern

PROJECT_NAME=ejbCookbook

#-------------[ Point to the J2EE JAR for includes ]------------------
EJB_JAR=C:/j2sdkee1.4/lib/j2ee.jar
INCLUDE_JARS=C:/bea/wlserver6.1/lib/weblogic.jar    ⊲─┤ Used to add the weblogic.jar
                                                        to the classpath
#-------------[ Where do all the source files live ]------------------
EJB_SOURCE=ejbs
META_SOURCE=META-INF

#-------------[ Where do all the class/build files live ]------------------
BUILD=build
EJB_BUILD=${BUILD}/ejbs

#-------------[ This is specific to the Weblogic container for us ]-------
WL_HOME=C:/bea/wlserver6.1   ⊲─┐ Used to store the BEA Weblogic home directory
```

Listing 9.5 shows the build.xml file, also taken from the previous recipe. In this version of the file, we added a new target that builds the stub files. Notice that the `all` target now also depends on the new target. The differences are highlighted in bold.

Listing 9.5 The modified build.xml file

```xml
<project name="${PROJECT_NAME}" default="all" basedir=".">

  <!-- set global properties for this build -->
  <property environment="env"/>
  <property file="build_ejb.properties"/>

  <target name="all" depends="init, compile_ejb, jar_ejb, ejbc">
    <echo>---------[ Project name: ${PROJECT_NAME} Completed ]---
    </echo>
  </target>
```
> Adds the ejbc target
> to the depends list

```xml
  <!--
      ==========================================
           Setup ready for build.
           Create all the necessary Directories
      ==========================================
  -->
  <target name="init">
    <tstamp/>
    <echo>--[ Creating all Directories and copying XML files ]---
    </echo>
    <mkdir dir="${BUILD}"/>
    <mkdir dir="${EJB_BUILD}"/>
    <mkdir dir="${EJB_BUILD}/META-INF"/>
  </target>

  <!--
      ==========================================
           Clean the files up
      ==========================================
  -->
  <target name="clean">
    <tstamp/>
    <echo>---[ Cleaning the Compiled and Deployed Files ]--------
    </echo>
    <delete dir="${BUILD}"/>
  </target>

  <!--
      ===============================================================
           Compile the EJB Source Files
      ===============================================================
  -->

    <target name="compile_ejb" depends="init">
    <tstamp/>
```

```
      <echo>----[ Compiling EJB Source Files ]----------</echo>
      <javac srcdir="${EJB_SOURCE}" destdir="${EJB_BUILD}" >
        <classpath>
          <pathelement location="${EJB_JAR}"/>
          <pathelement location="${INCLUDE_JARS}"/>
        </classpath>
      </javac>
   </target>

   <!--
      =================================================
         Create the EJB JAR File
      =================================================
   -->
   <target name="jar_ejb" depends="compile_ejb">
     <tstamp/>
     <echo>---[ Copying META-INF Files ]--------------</echo>
     <copy todir="${EJB_BUILD}/META-INF">
       <fileset dir="${META_SOURCE}">
         <include name="*.xml"/>
       </fileset>
     </copy>
     <echo>---------[ Creating EJB JAR File ]--------------</echo>
     <jar jarfile="${BUILD}/${PROJECT_NAME}.jar" basedir="${EJB_BUILD}" />
   </target>

   <!--
      ================================================================
         Run EJBC for Weblogic Container Deployment Descriptors
      ================================================================
   -->
   <target name="ejbc" depends="jar_ejb">
     <tstamp/>
     <echo>---------[ Creating Deployable Jar File using EJBC ]---
     </echo>
     <copy tofile="${BUILD}/wl_${PROJECT_NAME}.jar"
             file="${BUILD}/${PROJECT_NAME}.jar" />
     <java classpath="${CLASSPATH}" classname="weblogic.ejbc"
         fork="yes">
       <sysproperty key="weblogic.home" value="${WL_HOME}"/>
       <arg line="-compiler javac ${BUILD}/wl_${PROJECT_NAME}.jar
             ${BUILD}/${PROJECT_NAME}.jar"/>
       <classpath>
         <pathelement path=
         "${WL_HOME}/lib/weblogic_sp.jar;${WL_HOME}/lib/weblogic.jar"/>
       </classpath>
     </java>
     <delete file="${BUILD}/wl_${PROJECT_NAME}.jar"/>
   </target>

</project>
```

Describes the task that will generate the EJB stubs

◆ *Discussion*

The new addition to the build.xml is the `ejbc` target. This target sets up and executes a Java command that runs the EJB stub compiler for the Weblogic container. In the build properties file, we added the weblogic.jar file to a variable so that we can add it to the classpath for this execution. Examining the new target, notice that it does three things:

1   It copies the ejb.jar file to a temporary JAR file.
2   It executes the weblogic.ejbc class file using a JVM.
3   It deletes the temporary JAR file.

Since this target depends on the target that creates the ejb.jar file, it can assume that a JAR file (with the project name) exists. Using the `<copy>` tag, the target creates a temporary JAR file. Next, the `<java>` tag sets up the classpath, names the class to execute (the `weblogic.ejbc` class), and also uses the `<arg>` tag to add arguments to the execution of the Java class. These arguments are specific to the EJB compiler needed by the EJB container. Once the execution is complete, the target completes execution by deleting the temporary JAR file it used as input to the EJB compiler. The execution of the EJB compiler produced a new JAR file, again named after the project.

◆ *See also*

9.1—Compiling Enterprise JavaBeans
9.2—Building the ejb.jar file

9.4 *Creating a stateless session bean unit test*

◆ *Problem*

You want to create a unit test for your stateless session Enterprise JavaBeans.

◆ *Background*

Unit-testing stateless session beans helps you catch errors in your business logic before moving your application to the next phase: application or user testing. Using Cactus, you can create tests that execute in the EJB container in order to test not only the business logic, but also the deployment of the EJBs in the EJB container. This integration testing helps prevent deployment errors long before it's time to move the application into other environments.

◆ *Recipe*

In order to create unit tests with Cactus, you need to extend a test-case base class provided by Cactus. For our test cases, we will be extending the `ServletTestCase` class. Test cases have the following requirements:

1   Import the `org.apache.cactus` and `junit.framework` packages.
2   Extend a Cactus test case base class.
3   Include a constructor that accepts the test name as a `String` parameter (a one-argument constructor).
4   Include at least one `testXXX()` method, where *XXX* is a name of your choosing describing the functionality.

Optionally, your test cases can provide a `suite()` method that will list the available `testXXX()` methods contained in the test case class, and a `main()` method that will allow the test case to be executed from a command line. The `testXXX()` methods have only a few responsibilities:

1   Instantiating or obtaining the object to test
2   Invoking methods upon the test object
3   Using the JUnit `assert()` methods to determine the test results

The sample test case class in listing 9.6 instantiates `TestStateless` EJBs and creates two test methods—`testPositiveResponse()` and `testNegativeResponse()`—that test return values from sample business methods on the bean.

Listing 9.6   TestStateless.java

```
import org.apache.org.*;
import junit.framework.*;

public class TestStateless
                              extends ServletTestCase{

    public TestStateless (String theName){
        super( theName );        ←┐ Initializes the test
    }                               │ class with a name

    public static Test suite(){                          │ Creates and returns
        return new TestSuite(TestServlet.class);    ←┘ a suite class
    }

    public void testPositiveResponse(){

        try{
            TestStatelessHome home = lookupHome();
            TestStateless session = createSession(home);
```

```
      boolean value = session.positiveResponse();
      assertEquals(true,value);      ⟵⌐ Tests an equals-true
    }                                      comparison
    catch(Exception e){
        e.printStackTrace();
        System.out.println("Failed Finding Session:"
            + e.getMessage());
    }

}

public void testNegativeResponse(){

    try{
      TestStatelessHome home=lookupHome();
      TestStateless session=createSession(home);
      boolean value=session.negativeResponse();
      assertEquals(false,value);     ⟵⌐ Tests an equals-false
    }                                      comparison
    catch(Exception e){
        e.printStackTrace();
        System.out.println("Failed Finding Session:"
                +e.getMessage());
    }

}
                                           Creates a session bean
/** private methods below **/                from a home object

private TestStateless createSession( TestStatelessHome home )   ⟵⌐
        throws ObjectNotFoundException,
                CreateException,RemoteException {

  TestStateless session = null;

  System.out.println("Creating Session");
  session = (TestStateless) PortableRemoteObject.narrow(
                            home.create(),
                            TestStateless.class);

  System.out.println("Created Session ");
  return session;                          Looks up a home object
}                                            for a session bean

private TestStatelessHome lookupHome() throws NamingException{   ⟵⌐
  Context ctx = new InitialContext();

   System.out.println("Looking up Home:");
  TestStatelessHome home = (TestStatelessHome)
                            ctx.lookup("testStateless");
  home = (TestStatelessHome) PortableRemoteObject.narrow(
                        home,
                        TestStatelessHome.class);
  return home;
}
}
```

◆ *Discussion*

Running tests against stateless session beans is a simple matter of looking up the bean and executing its business methods. You can choose to either catch exceptions or evaluate return values to determine if the test is successful. Notice that both test methods in our recipe invoke private methods to create an instance of the stateless session bean. To save time and improve the performance of your tests, you can factor out the EJB lookup by storing the bean reference in a local class member variable. Each test method can then check the member variable for an existing reference before performing another EJB lookup.

Notice that the test methods use assert*XXX*() methods to perform test comparisons to determine success or failure conditions for the tested business logic. Test cases inherit these methods from the JUnit `Assert` class. Table 9.1 lists additional assert*XXX*() methods that are available in the JUnit API.

Table 9.1 The various `assert`*XXX*`()` methods that test methods can use to evaluate pass/fail conditions of tested business logic

Method	Description
assertEquals()	Many versions of this method exist to compare many types of objects and basic data types for equality.
assertSame()	These methods test to see if two references point to the same object.
assertFalse()	Tests a condition for a false value.
assertTrue()	Tests a condition for a true value.
assertNotNull()	Tests an object reference for a null value.
assertNotSame()	Tests that two references point to different objects.
assertNull()	Tests that a reference is a null value.

◆ *See also*

9.5—Creating a stateful session bean unit test

9.6—Creating an entity bean unit test

9.7—Automating test case execution

9.8—Executing test cases using a UI

9.5 *Creating a stateful session bean unit test*

◆ **Problem**

You want to create a unit test for a stateful session Enterprise JavaBean.

◆ **Background**

Unit-testing stateful session beans helps you to catch errors in your business logic and integration with other resources. Using Cactus, you can create tests that execute in the EJB container in order to test not only the business logic, but also the deployment of the EJBs in the EJB container. Testing stateful session beans using Cactus helps you test an EJB's dependencies on the application server. For example, a stateful session bean might use a data source or other EJB. Please read recipe 9.4 for the common requirements for building a Cactus test case class.

◆ **Recipe**

The test case class in listing 9.7 provides a single test method, `testIncrement()`, that tests a business method upon a stateful session bean.

Listing 9.7   TestStateful.java

```java
import org.apache.org.*;
import junit.framework.*;

public class TestStateful extends ServletTestCase{

public TestStateful(String theName){
  super(theName);            ⟵ Initializes the test
}                                class with a name
public static Test suite(){
  return new TestSuite(TestServlet.class);  ⟵ Creates and
}                                              returns a suite class
public void testIncrement(){
  int count = 0;

  try{
  TestStatefulHome home = lookupHome();
  TestStateful session = createSession(home);

  session.increment();
  count++;
  assertEquals(count,session.getCurrentCount());  ⟵ Tests a comparison
                                                      with a counted value
  session.increment();
  count++;
  assertEquals(count,session.getCurrentCount());
```

```
session.increment();
count++;
assertEquals(count,session.getCurrentCount());

}
catch(Exception e){
e.printStackTrace();
System.out.println("Failed Working with Session:"
+e.getMessage());
}

}

private TestStateful createSession( TestStatefulHome home )
  throws ObjectNotFoundException,
CreateException,RemoteException {

TestStateful session = null;

System.out.println("Creating Session");
Session = (TestStateful) PortableRemoteObject.narrow(
home.create(),
TestStateful.class);

System.out.println("Created Session");
return session;
}

private TestStatefulHome lookupHome() throws NamingException{
    Context ctx = new InitialContext();

     System.out.println("Looking up Home");
    TestStatefulHome home = (TestStatefulHome)
    ctx.lookup("testStateful");
    Home = (TestStatefulHome) PortableRemoteObject.narrow(
    home,
    TestStatefulHome.class);
    return home;
}
}
```

Creates a session bean
from a home object

Looks up a home object
for a session bean

◆ *Discussion*

Executing tests against a stateful session bean is similar to running tests against a stateless session bean. In the case of stateful beans, you have the added ability of storing and retrieving state information during a test. Therefore, you should construct your tests with this in mind. As we also discussed in the previous recipe, you can factor out the EJB lookup in each test method by storing a reference to the bean in a local member variable. In the case of stateful bean tests, use the local variable to test the state of the EJB.

◆ **See also**

9.4—Creating a stateless session bean unit test

9.6—Creating an entity bean unit test

9.7—Automating test case execution

9.8—Executing test cases using a UI

9.6 *Creating an entity bean unit test*

◆ **Problem**

You want to create a unit test for an entity Enterprise JavaBean.

◆ **Background**

Unit-testing entity Enterprise JavaBeans means testing not only business logic, but also database access and schema mappings. Unit-testing your entity beans lets you test for incorrect column names, finder methods, and overall database usage. This is especially important when using bean-managed persistence, where errors are more likely to exist. Please read recipes 9.4 and 9.5 before using this recipe; they provide the foundation for building Cactus test cases.

◆ **Recipe**

This recipe tests the ability to create and find a particular entity bean. Here we are testing the entity schema and the integration with the application server. The test case class in listing 9.8 provides two test methods—one that tests the ability to create an entity bean, and one that tests the ability to find a bean.

Listing 9.8   TestEntity.java

```
import org.apache.org.*;
import junit.framework.*;

public class TestEntity extends ServletTestCase{

    public TestEntity(String theName){
        super(theName);          ◁─┐ Initializes the test
    }                                class with a name

    public static Test suite(){                          ┐ Creates and returns
        return new TestSuite(TestEntity.class);  ◁─┘ a suite class
    }
                                           ┐ Tests the creation of
    public void testCreateEntity(){  ◁─┘ an entity bean
```

```
    try{
      TestEntityHome home = lookupHome();
      TestEntity entity = createEntity("This is a test",home);
    }
    catch(Exception e){
      e.printStackTrace();
      System.out.println("Failed Finding Entity:"+e.getMessage());
    }
  }

public void testFindEntity(){
    Integer id = null;

    try{
      TestEntityHome home = lookupHome();

      //---------[ Create the entity ]--------------//
      TestEntity entity = createEntity("This is a test",home);
      id = entity.getEntityId();
      System.out.println("Created Entity with ID:"
                              +id.intValue());

      //---------[ Find the entity ]--------------//
      entity = findEntity(id, home);

      //---------[ Check the id to be identical ]-----------//
      assertEquals(id, entity.getEntityId());   ◁┐  Tests the entity of a
    }                                                created and found
    catch(Exception e){
      e.printStackTrace();
      System.out.println("Failed Finding Entity:"+e.getMessage());
    }
  }

private TestEntity createEntity(String txt, TestEntityHome home)  ◁─
        throws ObjectNotFoundException,                   Creates the test
              CreateException,RemoteException {            entity bean

    TestEntity entity = null;
    Integer    id = null;

    System.out.println("Creating Entity with ID: "+txt);
    entity = (TestEntity) PortableRemoteObject.narrow(
                        home.create(txt),
                        TestEntity.class);
    id = entity.getEntityId();

    System.out.println("Created Entity with ID: "+id.intValue());
    return entity;
  }

private TestEntity findEntity(Integer id, TestEntityHome home)  ◁─
  throws ObjectNotFoundException, FinderException,
              CreateException, RemoteException {        Finds the test
                                                        entity bean
```

```
    System.out.println( "Trying to find Entity with ID: "+id);
    return (TestEntity) PortableRemoteObject.narrow(
                home.findByPrimaryKey(id), TestEntity.class);
}

private TestEntityHome lookupHome() throws NamingException{
    Context ctx = new InitialContext();

    System.out.println("Looking up Home:");
    TestEntityHome home = (TestEntityHome)
                    ctx.lookup("testEntity");
    home = (TestEntityHome) PortableRemoteObject.narrow(home,
                    TestEntityHome.class);
    return home;
}
}
```

◆ *Discussion*

Notice that the test method testCreateEntity() does not use an assert() method to evaluate any test conditions. However, it does catch and throw an exception if something goes wrong while trying to create an instance of the test entity bean. If an exception is thrown from a test method, Cactus will recognize the test as a failure. You can use this Cactus feature to test business logic that is evaluated without the basis of return values. Business methods that throw exceptions as a method of validation and a way to indicate errors can be quickly tested using methods that pass along the exceptions to the Cactus framework.

◆ *See also*

9.4—Creating a stateless session bean unit test

9.5—Creating a stateful session bean unit test

9.7—Automating test case execution

9.8—Executing test cases using a UI

9.7 *Automating test case execution*

◆ *Problem*

You want to automate the execution of your test cases. Specifically, you want to avoid executing them manually (potentially one at a time).

◆ Background

After creating numerous unit test cases with Cactus, you need a good system of executing them. In addition, you should create a system that lets you quickly re-execute test cases after changes in your EJBs. Creating an automated testing system will help you create a quickly executed and effective test regression framework. Using Ant to execute your test cases is a good way to integrate unit testing into your build system. With Ant executing your test, you can quickly build a robust regression test system for your EJB layer.

Making this task easier is the Cactus framework itself. Cactus provides a custom Ant task that allows you to develop a step-by-step testing system. With the Cactus Ant task, you can deploy your tests, start your EJB container, execute the tests, and stop your EJB container. For the task to execute successfully, you must provide information about your application server. Fortunately, Cactus also includes the Ant tasks for many popular application servers.

◆ Recipe

This recipe shows the additions you should make to your Ant build.xml file in order to integrate Cactus into your build system. The first item to add is the setup of the new Cactus Ant task. The following `initcactus` target defines the new task, `runservertests`:

```
<target name="initCactus" description="Initialize Cactus">
 <taskdef name="runservertests"
         classname="org.apache.cactus.ant.RunServerTestsTask">
    <classpath>
        <pathelement location="${CACTUS_ANT_JAR}"/>
    </classpath>
 </taskdef>
</target>
```

The second target you need to add to your build.xml file is a test target that executes the newly defined `runservertests` task provided by Cactus. The following test target illustrates the invocation of the Cactus task:

```
<target name="test" depends="initCactus"
                   description="Run tests using Cactus">
    <runservertests
      testURL=
 "http://localhost:7001/${PROJECT_NAME}/
   ServletRedirector?Cactus_Service=RUN_TEST"
        startTarget="start.weblogic.61"
        stopTarget="stop.weblogic.61"
```

```
        testTarget="runCactusTest"
      />
   </target>
```

After defining the previous target, you must also define the targets it depends on. This includes the targets you name in the startTarget, stopTarget, and testTarget parameters. This target definition, testTarget, is responsible for actually running the Cactus tests:

```
<target name="runCactusTest">
    <junit printsummary="yes" haltonfailure="yes" haltonerror="yes"
    fork="yes">
      <classpath>
        <pathelement location="${PROJECT_LOCATION}/build/tests"/>
        <pathelement location="${PROJECT_LOCATION}/build/ejbs"/>
        <pathelement location="C:/cactus/lib/cactus-1.4.1.jar"/>
        <pathelement location="C:/j2sdkee1.4/lib/j2ee.jar"/>
        <pathelement
          location="C:/jakarta-ant-1.5-cactus/lib/aspectjrt-1.0.5.jar"/>
        <pathelement
        location="C:/jakarta-ant-1.5-cactus/lib/commons-collection-2.0.jar"/>
        <pathelement
        location="C:/cactus/lib/commons-httpclient-2.0alpha1-20020606.jar" />
        <pathelement location="." />
      </classpath>

      <formatter type="plain" usefile="false"/>
      <test name="${PROJECT_NAME}.TestStateless"/>
    </junit>

</target>
```

A test is executed for each <test> element present in the target. Each <test> target specifies a classname of a test case in which to invoke. The following target is for starting the server; this is the target that was specified in the startTarget parameter of the Cactus task. This target definition has been taken exactly from the Cactus distribution. The distribution contains target definitions for most of the popular application servers available today. This one is for the Weblogic application server:

```
<target name="start.weblogic.61">
  <echo>deploy location=${DEPLOY_LOCATION}</echo>
  <java classname="weblogic.Server" fork="yes" dir="${DEPLOY_LOCATION}">

    <classpath>
      <pathelement
          location="${WL_HOME}/wlserver6.1/lib/weblogic.sp.jar"/>
      <pathelement location="${WL_HOME}/wlserver6.1/lib/weblogic.jar"/>
      <pathelement location="${junit.jar}"/>
    </classpath>
```

```
            <jvmarg value="-hotspot"/>
            <jvmarg value="-ms64m"/>
            <jvmarg value="-mx64m"/>
            <jvmarg
value="-Djava.library.path=${java.library.path};${WL_HOME}/wlserver6.1/bin"
            />
            <jvmarg value="-Dweblogic.RootDirectory=."/>
            <jvmarg value="-Dweblogic.Domain=bookdomain"/>
            <jvmarg value="-Dweblogic.Name=myserver"/>
            <jvmarg value="-Dbea.home=${WL_HOME}"/>
            <jvmarg value="-Dweblogic.management.password=dietcoke"/>
            <jvmarg value="-Djava.security.policy==./lib/weblogic.policy"/>

        </java>

    </target>
```

Finally, the following target illustrates the `stopTarget` task supplied to the Cactus test. Like the previous target, this one is also supplied in the Cactus distribution. For both the start and stop targets, you need only supply pertinent parameter values.

```
    <target name="stop.weblogic.61">

        <java classname="weblogic.Admin" fork="yes">

        <classpath>
          <pathelement
             location="${WL_HOME}/wlserver6.1/lib/weblogic.sp.jar"/>
          <pathelement location="${WL_HOME}/wlserver6.1/lib/weblogic.jar"/>
        </classpath>

        <arg line="-url t3://localhost:${test.port}"/>
        <arg line="-username system"/>
        <arg line="-password dietcoke"/>
        <arg value="SHUTDOWN"/>

        </java>

    </target>
```

◆ *Discussion*

To execute the task, you need to specify a few arguments: a URL to the server, and three other target names that can be executed by the Cactus task in order to stop or start your application server and to actually execute test cases.

The <runservertests> task will want to check whether the application server is already running before invoking the target that starts the server. It does this by examining the cactus.properties file found in the classpath. In this properties file (if it exists), the Cactus task will find a URL to the application server it can use to test whether it is running. If the application server is already running, it will not attempt to start it. Once the server is running, the Cactus task will invoke the test target, and then the stop server target. For example, if you choose to provide a cactus.properties file, it might contain something like the following:

```
cactus.contextURL=http://localhost:7001/myDomain
```

◆ See also

9.4—Creating a stateless session bean unit test

9.5—Creating a stateful session bean unit test

9.6—Creating an entity bean unit test

9.8—Executing test cases using a UI

9.8 Executing test cases using a UI

◆ Problem

You want more ways of executing tests, not always using Ant.

◆ Background

After creating a multitude of Cactus tests, and setting up Ant to execute your tests, you may find yourself wanting a few other methods of executing your tests. For instance, you may have set up Ant to run all your tests, or a few specific tests, but you also want the ability to execute only a single test when needed. Basically, your Ant build.xml file is a static resource that describes which test cases to run, and you want the ability to run single tests at a moment's notice.

◆ Recipe

Your Cactus tests can be run from a web browser, from Apache Ant, or by Cactus UI classes included in the Cactus distribution. This recipe illustrates executing test cases from a web browser and the Cactus UI classes.

Executing unit tests from a web browser

To execute a unit test from a web browser, contact the Cactus servlet (the test redirector) with a specific URL. Create the URL directly to the Cactus servlet, and pass the test name as a parameter. For example, to execute a test case encapsulated by the class examples.cactus.Test1, use the following URL (your URL might differ by hostname, port, and servlet location):

```
http://localhost:7001/ServletTestRunner?suite=examples.cactus.Test1
```

Notice that the single URL parameter `suite` includes the fully qualified classname of a test case. Opening the URL will produce something similar to the following XML output:

```
<?xml version="1.0" encoding="UTF-8" ?>
<testsuites>
  <testsuite name="examples.cactus.Test1"
             tests="2" failures="0"
             errors="0" time="0.07">
    <testcase name="testPositiveResponse" time="0.02" />
    <testcase name="testNegativeResponse" time="0.04" />
  </testsuite>
</testsuites>
```

To return HTML instead of pure XML, indicate to the test redirector servlet that it should use an XSL style sheet. Here is the modified URL:

```
http://localhost:7001/ServletTestRunner?suite=
examples.cactus.Test1&xsl=junit-noframes.xsl
```

In order for this to work successfully, you need to make sure you deploy the XSL style sheet where the servlet can find it. Consult the Cactus documentation if you have any problems. In figure 9.2, we've captured the test case output in the browser.

Executing unit tests from UI classes

Each of the test cases we wrote in previous recipes contained a `main()` method that lets you execute it from a command line using the Java runtime environment. These `main()` methods make use of a utility class provided by the JUnit framework for executing test cases visually. The following is a sample `main()` method from one of our test cases:

```
public static void main(String[] theArgs)
{
    junit.swingui.TestRunner.main(new String[]
               {TestServlet.class.getName()});
}
```

The UI shown in figure 9.3 allows you to run available tests provided in the test case class and to view their results.

◆ Discussion

Combining the two methods for executing test cases shown in this recipe with the ability to execute tests with Ant provides you with a robust test evaluation system. Using Ant to build a regression system in the build process provides long-term

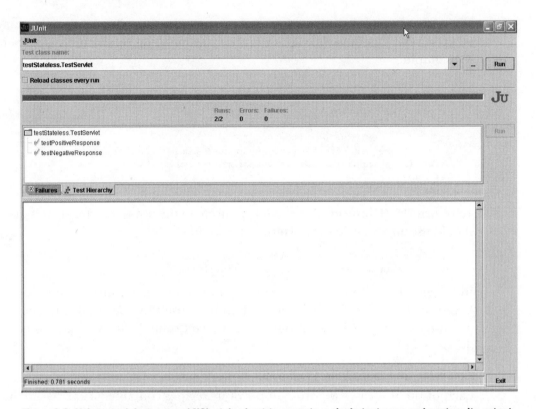

Figure 9.2 Using a web browser and XSL style sheet to execute a single test case and capture its output

unit testing of your EJBs. By executing test cases from a web browser, or by invoking them directly, you can spot-check your EJBs or quickly verify newly developed code. In addition, if your Ant system executes only a subset of tests, you can use either of these new methods to evaluate code that is not frequently tested.

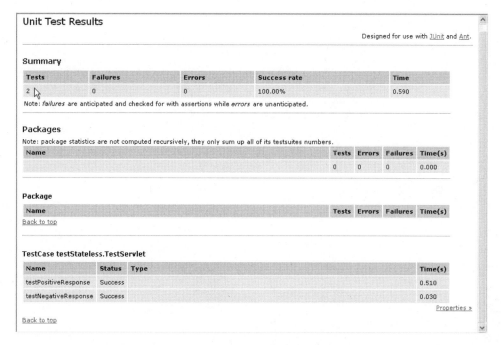

Figure 9.3 The JUnit UI lets you execute tests and view the results.

◆ *See also*

9.4—Creating a stateless session bean unit test

9.5—Creating a stateful session bean unit test

9.6—Creating an entity bean unit test

9.7—Automating test case execution

Mixing it up: related recipes

Chapter 1 • Client code

1.1   Invoking a local EJB from another EJB   4
     1.1—Invoking a local EJB from another EJB   4
     1.12—Improving your client-side EJB lookup code   31
     2.1—Generating home, remote, local, and local home interfaces   37
     2.7—Facilitating bean lookup with a utility object   58
     7.6—Preventing access to entity data   239

1.2   Invoking a remote EJB from another EJB   6
     1.2—Invoking a remote EJB from another EJB   6
     1.12—Improving your client-side EJB lookup code   31
     2.1—Generating home, remote, local, and local home interfaces   37
     4.1—Retrieving an environment variable   134

1.3   Accessing EJBs from a servlet   8
     1.4—Invoking an EJB from a JavaServer Page   12
     1.12—Improving your client-side EJB lookup code   31
     2.1—Generating home, remote, local, and local home interfaces   37
     2.7—Facilitating bean lookup with a utility object   58

1.4   Invoking an EJB from a JavaServer Page   12
     1.3—Accessing EJBs from a servlet   8
     3.15—Creating an interface to your entity data   120
     5.15—Holding a transaction across multiple JavaServer Pages   191

1.5   Invoking EJB business logic from a JMS system   15

1.6   Persisting a reference to an EJB instance   18
     1.7—Retrieving and using a persisted EJB reference   20
     1.8—Persisting a home object reference   21

1.7   Retrieving and using a persisted EJB reference   20
     1.6—Persisting a reference to an EJB instance   18
     1.8—Persisting a home object reference   21

1.8   Persisting a home object reference   21
     1.6—Persisting a reference to an EJB instance   18
     1.7—Retrieving and using a persisted EJB reference   20
     1.12—Improving your client-side EJB lookup code   31

1.9   Comparing two EJB references for equality   23

1.10   Using reflection with an EJB   25

1.11   Invoking an EJB from an applet   27
     1.2—Invoking a remote EJB from another EJB   6
     1.3—Accessing EJBs from a servlet   8
     1.4—Invoking an EJB from a JavaServer Page   12

1.12 Improving your client-side EJB lookup code   31
    2.2—Adding and customizing the JNDI name for the home interface   43
    2.7—Facilitating bean lookup with a utility object   58

Chapter 2 • Code generation with XDoclet

2.1 Generating home, remote, local, and local home interfaces   37
    2.2—Adding and customizing the JNDI name for the home interface   43
    2.5—Generating a primary key class   53
    2.11—Generating finder methods for entity home interfaces   66

2.2 Adding and customizing the JNDI name for the home interface   43
    2.1—Generating home, remote, local, and local home interfaces   37

2.3 Keeping your EJB deployment descriptor current   45
    2.8—Generating vendor-specific deployment descriptors   62

2.4 Creating value objects for your entity beans   47
    2.1—Generating home, remote, local, and local home interfaces   37
    2.2—Adding and customizing the JNDI name for the home interface   43
    2.5—Generating a primary key class   53

2.5 Generating a primary key class   53
    2.1—Generating home, remote, local, and local home interfaces   37

2.6 Avoiding hardcoded XDoclet tag values   56
    2.1—Generating home, remote, local, and local home interfaces   37
    2.2—Adding and customizing the JNDI name for the home interface   43
    2.3—Keeping your EJB deployment descriptor current   45

2.7 Facilitating bean lookup with a utility object   58
    2.1—Generating home, remote, local, and local home interfaces   37
    2.2—Adding and customizing the JNDI name for the home interface   43

2.8 Generating vendor-specific deployment descriptors   62
    2.3—Keeping your EJB deployment descriptor current   45

2.9 Specifying security roles in the bean source   63
    2.3—Keeping your EJB deployment descriptor current   45
    2.8—Generating vendor-specific deployment descriptors   62
    2.10—Generating and maintaining method permissions   64

2.10 Generating and maintaining method permissions   64
    2.1—Generating home, remote, local, and local home interfaces   37
    2.3—Keeping your EJB deployment descriptor current   45
    2.8—Generating vendor-specific deployment descriptors   62
    2.9—Specifying security roles in the bean source   63

2.11 Generating finder methods for entity home interfaces 66
2.1—Generating home, remote, local, and local home interfaces 37

2.12 Generating the ejbSelect method XML 67
2.3—Keeping your EJB deployment descriptor current 45

2.13 Adding a home method to generated home interfaces 68
2.1—Generating home, remote, local, and local home interfaces 37

2.14 Adding entity relation XML to the deployment descriptor 70
2.3—Keeping your EJB deployment descriptor current 45
3.7—Modeling one-to-one entity data relationships 97

2.15 Adding the destination type to a message-driven bean deployment descriptor 71
2.3—Keeping your EJB deployment descriptor current 45
2.16—Adding message selectors to a message-driven bean deployment
descriptor 73

2.16 Adding message selectors to a message-driven bean deployment descriptor 73
2.3—Keeping your EJB deployment descriptor current 45
2.15—Adding the destination type to a message-driven bean deployment
descriptor 71

Chapter 3 • Working with data

3.1 Using a data source 78
4.1—Retrieving an environment variable 134

3.2 Creating EJB 2.0 container-managed persistence 81
2.3—Keeping your EJB deployment descriptor current 45
3.4—Using a database sequence to generate primary key values for entity beans 88
3.5—Using a compound primary key for your entity beans 92

3.3 Using different data sources for different users 85
3.1—Using a data source 78
7.1—Finding the identity and role of the caller inside an EJB method 231

3.4 Using a database sequence to generate primary key values for entity beans 88
2.5—Generating a primary key class 53
3.1—Using a data source 78
3.2—Creating EJB 2.0 container-managed persistence 81
3.5—Using a compound primary key for your entity beans 92

3.5 Using a compound primary key for your entity beans 92
2.5—Generating a primary key class 53
3.1—Using a data source 78
3.2—Creating EJB 2.0 container-managed persistence 81
3.4—Using a database sequence to generate primary key values for entity beans 88

3.6   Retrieving multiple entity beans in a single step   95
        3.1—Using a data source   78
        3.12—Using EJB-QL to create custom finder methods   111

3.7   Modeling one-to-one entity data relationships   97
        2.14—Adding entity relation XML to the deployment descriptor   70
        3.2—Creating EJB 2.0 container-managed persistence   81
        3.8—Creating a one-to-many relationship for entity beans   101
        3.9—Using entity relationships to create a cascading delete   104
        3.10—Developing noncreatable, read-only entity beans   107

3.8   Creating a one-to-many relationship for entity beans   101
        2.14—Adding entity relation XML to the deployment descriptor   70
        3.7—Modeling one-to-one entity data relationships   97
        3.9—Using entity relationships to create a cascading delete   104
        3.10—Developing noncreatable, read-only entity beans   107

3.9   Using entity relationships to create a cascading delete   104
        3.2—Creating EJB 2.0 container-managed persistence   81
        3.10—Developing noncreatable, read-only entity beans   107

3.10   Developing noncreatable, read-only entity beans   107
        3.2—Creating EJB 2.0 container-managed persistence   81
        3.7—Modeling one-to-one entity data relationships   97
        3.8—Creating a one-to-many relationship for entity beans   101
        7.6—Preventing access to entity data   239

3.11   Invoking a stored procedure from an EJB   109
        3.1—Using a data source   78

3.12   Using EJB-QL to create custom finder methods   111
        2.11—Generating finder methods for entity home interfaces   66
        3.2—Creating EJB 2.0 container-managed persistence   81

3.13   Persisting entity data into a database view   115
        3.2—Creating EJB 2.0 container-managed persistence   81

3.14   Sending notifications upon entity data changes   117

3.15   Creating an interface to your entity data   120
        3.2—Creating EJB 2.0 container-managed persistence   81
        7.6—Preventing access to entity data   239

3.16   Retrieving information about entity data sets   122

3.17   Decreasing the number of calls to an entity bean   124

3.18   Paging through large result sets   126

Chapter 4 • EJB activities

4.1   Retrieving an environment variable   134
        3.1—Using a data source   78

4.2   Implementing toString() functionality for an EJB   136

4.3   Providing common methods for all your EJBs   137
        2.1—Generating home, remote, local, and local home interfaces   37
        2.4—Creating value objects for your entity beans   47
        3.17—Decreasing the number of calls to an entity bean   124
        4.1—Retrieving an environment variable   134
        4.4—Reducing the clutter of unimplemented bean methods   139

4.4   Reducing the clutter of unimplemented bean methods   139
        4.3—Providing common methods for all your EJBs   137

4.5   Sending an email from an EJB   144
        6.11—Sending an email message asynchronously   223

4.6   Using the EJB 2.1 timer service   145
        4.11—Insulating an EJB from service class implementations   157

4.7   Sending a JMS message from an EJB   147

4.8   Using an EJB as a web service   149

4.9   Creating asynchronous behavior for an EJB client   151
        4.7—Sending a JMS message from an EJB   147
        4.10—Creating asynchronous behavior without message-driven beans   156

4.10   Creating asynchronous behavior without message-driven beans   156
        4.1—Retrieving an environment variable   134
        4.5—Sending an email from an EJB   144
        4.6—Using the EJB 2.1 timer service   145

4.11   Insulating an EJB from service class implementations   157
        4.1—Retrieving an environment variable   134

4.12   Creating a batch process mechanism   159
        4.9—Creating asynchronous behavior for an EJB client   151
        4.10—Creating asynchronous behavior without message-driven beans   156
        4.11—Insulating an EJB from service class implementations   157

Chapter 5 • Transactions

5.1   Tuning the container transaction control for your EJB   166

5.2   Handling transaction management without the container   169
            5.1—Tuning the container transaction control for your EJB   166

5.3   Rolling back the current transaction   170
            5.4—Attempting error recovery to avoid a rollback   172
            5.5—Forcing rollbacks before method completion   175
            5.8—Managing EJB state at transaction boundaries   179
            5.10—Managing EJB state after a rollback   183

5.4   Attempting error recovery to avoid a rollback   172
            5.2—Handling transaction management without the container   169
            5.3—Rolling back the current transaction   170
            5.8—Managing EJB state at transaction boundaries   179
            5.10—Managing EJB state after a rollback   183

5.5   Forcing rollbacks before method completion   175
            5.3—Rolling back the current transaction   170
            5.8—Managing EJB state at transaction boundaries   179
            5.10—Managing EJB state after a rollback   183

5.6   Imposing time limits on transactions   176
            5.2—Handling transaction management without the container   169
            5.5—Forcing rollbacks before method completion   175
            5.8—Managing EJB state at transaction boundaries   179
            5.10—Managing EJB state after a rollback   183

5.7   Combining entity updates into a single transaction   177
            5.1—Tuning the container transaction control for your EJB   166
            5.16—Updating multiple databases in one transaction   193

5.8   Managing EJB state at transaction boundaries   179
            5.2—Handling transaction management without the container   169
            5.4—Attempting error recovery to avoid a rollback   172
            5.5—Forcing rollbacks before method completion   175
            5.10—Managing EJB state after a rollback   183

5.9   Using more than one transaction in a method   181
            5.1—Tuning the container transaction control for your EJB   166
            5.12—Propagating a transaction to another EJB business method   186
            5.13—Propagating a transaction to a nonEJB class   188

5.10   Managing EJB state after a rollback   183

5.11   Throwing exceptions without causing a rollback   184
       5.5—Forcing rollbacks before method completion   175

5.12   Propagating a transaction to another EJB business method   186
       5.1—Tuning the container transaction control for your EJB   166
       5.2—Handling transaction management without the container   169
       5.13—Propagating a transaction to a nonEJB class   188

5.13   Propagating a transaction to a nonEJB class   188
       5.5—Forcing rollbacks before method completion   175

5.14   Starting a transaction in the client layer   190
       3.17—Decreasing the number of calls to an entity bean   124
       5.2—Handling transaction management without the container   169
       5.15—Holding a transaction across multiple JavaServer Pages   191

5.15   Holding a transaction across multiple JavaServer Pages   191
       5.2—Handling transaction management without the container   169
       5.14—Starting a transaction in the client layer   190

5.16   Updating multiple databases in one transaction   193
       3.2—Creating EJB 2.0 container-managed persistence   81
       5.1—Tuning the container transaction control for your EJB   166
       5.7—Combining entity updates into a single transaction   177

Chapter 6 • Messaging

6.1   Sending a publish/subscribe JMS message   198
       6.2—Sending a point-to-point JMS message   200
       6.3—Creating a message-driven Enterprise JavaBean   202
       7.8—Securing a message-driven bean   242

6.2   Sending a point-to-point JMS message   200
       6.1—Sending a publish/subscribe JMS message   198
       6.3—Creating a message-driven Enterprise JavaBean   202
       7.8—Securing a message-driven bean   242

6.3   Creating a message-driven Enterprise JavaBean   202
       6.1—Sending a publish/subscribe JMS message   198
       6.2—Sending a point-to-point JMS message   200
       7.8—Securing a message-driven bean   242

6.4   Processing messages in a FIFO manner from a message queue   205
       6.2—Sending a point-to-point JMS message   200

6.5   Insulating message-driven beans from business logic changes   209
          6.3—Creating a message-driven Enterprise JavaBean   202

6.6   Streaming data to a message-driven EJB   210
          6.1—Sending a publish/subscribe JMS message   198
          6.3—Creating a message-driven Enterprise JavaBean   202

6.7   Triggering two or more message-driven beans with a single JMS message   213
          6.1—Sending a publish/subscribe JMS message   198
          6.3—Creating a message-driven Enterprise JavaBean   202
          6.9—Filtering messages for a message-driven EJB   219

6.8   Speeding up message delivery to a message-driven bean   216
          6.1—Sending a publish/subscribe JMS message   198
          6.3—Creating a message-driven Enterprise JavaBean   202

6.9   Filtering messages for a message-driven EJB   219
          6.3—Creating a message-driven Enterprise JavaBean   202

6.10   Encapsulating error-handling code in a message-driven EJB   221
          6.12—Handling rollbacks in a message-driven bean   225

6.11   Sending an email message asynchronously   223
          4.5—Sending an email from an EJB   144
          6.12—Handling rollbacks in a message-driven bean   225

6.12   Handling rollbacks in a message-driven bean   225

Chapter 7 • Security

7.1   Finding the identity and role of the caller inside an EJB method   231
          7.2—Assigning and determining EJB client security roles   232
          7.3—Passing client credentials to the EJB container   234
          7.4—Disabling methods for certain users   235

7.2   Assigning and determining EJB client security roles   232
          2.9—Specifying security roles in the bean source   63
          7.1—Finding the identity and role of the caller inside an EJB method   231
          7.3—Passing client credentials to the EJB container   234
          7.4—Disabling methods for certain users   235

7.3   Passing client credentials to the EJB container   234
          7.1—Finding the identity and role of the caller inside an EJB method   231

7.4   Disabling methods for certain users   235
          2.10—Generating and maintaining method permissions   64
          7.2—Assigning and determining EJB client security roles   232

7.5   Assigning a role to an EJB   238
  2.9—Specifying security roles in the bean source   63
  7.2—Assigning and determining EJB client security roles   232

7.6   Preventing access to entity data   239

7.7   Using EJBs to handle simple authentication with an LDAP source   241

7.8   Securing a message-driven bean   242

Chapter 8 • Logging

8.1   Formatting log messages   251
  8.2—Improving logging performance   254

8.2   Improving logging performance   254
  8.1—Formatting log messages   251

8.3   Using logging to generate reports   257
  8.1—Formatting log messages   251

8.4   Sending log messages to a JMS topic   258

8.5   Logging to an XML file   259
  8.2—Improving logging performance   254

8.6   Creating log file views for the web browser   261
  8.2—Improving logging performance   254
  8.5—Logging to an XML file   259

8.7   Creating a centralized log file in a clustered environment   263
  6.3—Creating a message-driven Enterprise JavaBean   202
  8.1—Formatting log messages   251
  8.4—Sending log messages to a JMS topic   258
  8.10—Sorting log messages by client   269

8.8   Tracking the lifecycle of an EJB   265
  8.1—Formatting log messages   251
  8.2—Improving logging performance   254

8.9   Using a different configuration at runtime   267

8.10   Sorting log messages by client   269
  7.1—Finding the identity and role of the caller inside an EJB method   231
  7.5—Assigning a role to an EJB   238
  8.1—Formatting log messages   251
  8.2—Improving logging performance   254

Chapter 9 • Deploying and unit testing

9.1   Compiling Enterprise JavaBeans   278
      9.2—Building the ejb.jar file   280
      9.3—Building Enterprise JavaBean stub classes   283

9.2   Building the ejb.jar file   280
      9.1—Compiling Enterprise JavaBeans   278
      9.3—Building Enterprise JavaBean stub classes   283

9.3   Building Enterprise JavaBean stub classes   283
      9.1—Compiling Enterprise JavaBeans   278
      9.2—Building the ejb.jar file   280

9.4   Creating a stateless session bean unit test   286
      9.5—Creating a stateful session bean unit test   290
      9.6—Creating an entity bean unit test   292
      9.7—Automating test case execution   294
      9.8—Executing test cases using a UI   298

9.5   Creating a stateful session bean unit test   290
      9.4—Creating a stateless session bean unit test   286
      9.6—Creating an entity bean unit test   292
      9.7—Automating test case execution   294
      9.8—Executing test cases using a UI   298

9.6   Creating an entity bean unit test   292
      9.4—Creating a stateless session bean unit test   286
      9.5—Creating a stateful session bean unit test   290
      9.7—Automating test case execution   294
      9.8—Executing test cases using a UI   298

9.7   Automating test case execution   294
      9.4—Creating a stateless session bean unit test   286
      9.5—Creating a stateful session bean unit test   290
      9.6—Creating an entity bean unit test   292
      9.8—Executing test cases using a UI   298

9.8   Executing test cases using a UI   298
      9.4—Creating a stateless session bean unit test   286
      9.5—Creating a stateful session bean unit test   290
      9.6—Creating an entity bean unit test   292
      9.7—Automating test case execution   294

Second helpings:
additional resources

We've covered so many different topics in this book—we hope you aren't suffering from indigestion! Several chapters have focused on a particular open source tool that we used to write many of our recipes. If in the process of reading our recipes you were left with some unanswered questions, use the following resources to find more information. The list contains a few web links to many of the topics covered in this book. However, keep in mind that links tend to change, so some of them may not work by the time you try them.

Apache Ant
  http://ant.apache.org/index.html
  Java Development with Ant (Manning, 2002), by Erik Hatcher
  and Steve Loughran

Apache Cactus
  http://jakarta.apache.org/cactus
  JUnit in Action (Manning, 2003), by Vincent Massol and Ted Husted

Apache log4j
  http://jakarta.apache.org/log4j/docs/index.html

EJB 2.1 specification
  http://java.sun.com/products/ejb/docs.html#specs
  Bitter EJB (Manning, 2003), by Bruce Tate, et al.

J2EE tutorial
  http://java.sun.com/j2ee/download.html#tutorial

JDBC
  http://developer.java.sun.com/developer/onlineTraining/Database/
  JDBC20Intro/

XDoclet
  http://xdoclet.sourceforge.net/
  XDoclet in Action (Manning, 2003), by Craig Walls and Norman Richards

Also, please visit our Author Online forum at www.manning.com/sullins2. We wish you the best of luck with your future EJB development!

index

A

access control 230
accessing EJBs from a servlet 8
AccountAccessBean 240
AccountBean 249
ACID 165
adding a home method to generated home interfaces 68
adding entity relation XML to the deployment descriptor 70–71, 73
adding log messages 249
AddressBean 98
afterBegin 179–180, 183
afterCompletion 180, 184
Ant 274, 278
   automating tests 294
   building stubs 283
   building the ejb.jar 280
   compiling EJB source 278
   properties 56
   properties with XDoclet 57
   setting up for build 278
   with Cactus 294
   See also build.xml
Apache
   Ant 274
   Cactus 275
appenders
   html 261
   JDBC 257
   JMS 258
   rolling file 260
   XML 259
Applet 27

<arg> 286
assert 287, 289
assertEquals 289
assertFalse 289
assertNotNull 289
assertNotSame 289
assertNull 289
assertSame 289
assertTrue 289
assigning a role to an EJB 238
assigning and determining EJB client security roles 232
AsynchBean 156
asynchronous business logic 202
asynchronous email 223
asynchronous processes 151
   without message-driven bean 156
asynchronous timer 145
AsyncProcessBean 151
atomic 165
attempting error recovery to avoid a rollback 172
authentication 230
AuthenticationException 242
authorization 230
automate development 34
<automatic-key-generation> 91
automating test cases 274
   execution 294
automation, building EJB stubs 283
avoiding a rollback 172
   in a BMT bean 173
   in a CMT bean 173
avoiding hard-coded XDoclet tag values 56

B

batch processes 159
BatchProcessBean 160
bean adapter 139
bean-managed transactions 166, 169
beforeCompletion 179–180, 183
BETWEEN 221
binary data messages 210
BMP
   switching to CMP 81
BMT 170
BookJMSQueue 208
build.properties 278, 283
build.xml 35–38, 40, 44, 49, 62, 64, 66–68
   for building ejb.jar 281
   for generating deployment descriptor 46
   for generating interfaces 40
   for XDoclet 36
   generating EJB interfaces 41
   generating stubs 284
   generating utility objects 59
   generating XML 45
   using Ant properties 57–58
building 278
   EJB stubs 283
   ejb.jar file 280
building Enterprise JavaBean stub classes 283
business logic insulation 209
BusinessDataAccessObject 189
BusinessLogicBean 209
BytesMessage 211, 213

C

Cactus
  automating tests 294
  building test cases 286
  introduction 275
  jar files 276
  servlets 276
  testing entity beans 292
  unit test for a stateful
      bean 290
  unit test for session bean 286
  with a UI 298
cactus.jar 276
cactus.properties 297
CallableStatement 111
106
cascading deletes 104
CDATA 220–221
centralize logging 263
change the level of your
    loggers 254
change the way you write
    messages 255
change your conversion
    patterns 255
class files
  packaging 280
client 210
  applet 27
  assigning security role 232
  categories 4
  credentials 234
  EJBs finding identity 231
  JMS 15
  JSP 12
  other EJBs 4
  remote EJB 6
  servlets 8
  sorting log messages 269
  starting asynchronous
      processes 151
  starting transactions 190
  streaming 210
  using large result sets 126
Client.java 206
  using reflection 25
ClientLoader 20
ClientSaver 18
cluster, centralize logging 263

CMP 81, 84
  EJB-QL 111
  generating primary keys 88
84
CMR XML
  generating 70
104
CMT 165–169, 173, 181, 194
code finder methods
  generating 66
code generation 33
  CMR XML 70
  deployment descriptor 45
  EJB interfaces 37
  finder methods 66
  JMS XML 71
  primary key class 53
  utility objects 58
  value objects 47
code value objects 47
Collection 96
combining entity updates into a
    single transaction 177
commitMultipleEntities 178
common interfaces 137
COMP_NAME 44, 60–61
comparing two EJB references
    for equality 23
compile_ejb target 282
compiling Enterprise
    JavaBeans 278
compound primary keys 92
consistent 165
ConsoleAppender 250, 252,
    270–271
constant values 134
CONTACT_URL 135
  env var 135
container-managed
    persistence 81
container-managed
    transactions 165, 186
  multiples in a method 181
  propagating to another
      method 186–187
  rollback 173–174
  throwing exceptions 184
  timeout 177
<container-transaction> 167
Context.SECURITY_
    AUTHENTICATION 234

Context.SECURITY_
    CREDENTIALS 234
Context.SECURITY_
    PRINCIPAL 234
continuous integration 34
conversion characters 253
  formatting 253
conversion specifiers 252
ConversionPattern 252
  performance 255
createServiceInstance 158
creating a batch process
    mechanism 159
creating a centralized log file in
    a clustered environment 263
creating a message-driven
    Enterprise JavaBean 202
creating a one-to-many relation-
    ship for entity beans 101
creating a stateful session bean
    unit test 290
creating a stateless session bean
    unit test 286
creating an entity bean unit
    test 292
creating an interface to your
    entity data 120
creating asynchronous behavior
    for an EJB client 151
  without message-driven
      beans 156
creating EJB 2.0 container-
    managed persistence 81
creating log file views for the
    web browser 261

D

DAO 188
data source 78
  for different users 85
database
  logging 257
  view 115
database sequence 88
  for BMP 88
  for CMP 90
DataBean 39
DataSource 79
  EJB deployment descriptor 79

decreasing hardcoded
  values 134
decreasing the number of calls
  to an entity bean 124
deployment descriptor 65
  cascading deletes 106
  CMP 83
  CMR 1 to 1 99
  CMR 1 to many 102
  datasource 79
  for a CMP bean 83
  for BMT 169
  for CMP primary key
    generation 90
  for message-driven bean 203
  one-to-one relationship 99
  setting transaction
    control 166
  showing a data source 79
  showing environment
    variable 135
  vendor specific 62
  weblogic for message-driven
    bean 204
<deploymentdescriptor/> 45,
  47, 66, 68
<description> 135
<destination-jndi-name> 215
<destination-type> 204
developing noncreatable, read-
  only entity beans 107
disabling methods for certain
  users 235
distributed transactions 193
Durable 72
durable subscriptions 165, 199

E

EJB 18
  2.0 specification 5, 202
  2.1 149
  2.1 specification 145
  See also Enterprise JavaBeans
EJB clients, using Timer
  service 146
EJB Container. getting client
  credentials 234
EJB credentials 234
EJB equality 23

EJB handle 19–21
EJB interfaces
  generating 37
  inheritance 137
EJB lifecycle 265
EJB lifecycle methods 139
EJB references 23
@ejb.bean 38–39, 44, 46, 53–54,
  57, 59, 64–65, 67–68
  properties 41
@ejb.finder 41, 66–67
@ejb.home-method 41, 69
ejb.jar 280
  using Ant 280
@ejb.permission 65
@ejb.persistence 48–49, 54
@ejb.pk 41, 48–49, 53–54, 56
@ejb.pk-field 41, 48–49,
  53–54, 56
@ejb.security-identity 64
@ejb.select 41, 67–68
ejb.session 252
@ejb.util 59, 61
@ejb.value-object 48
ejbActivate, inheriting 139
EJBApplet 28
EJBApplet.java 28
ejbBookDataSource 80
ejbc 285–286
EJBContext 169–172, 174,
  177, 231
  identity methods 231–232
<ejbdoclet/> 35–38, 40, 62, 64
  generating a primary key
    class 53
  generating a value object 52
  generating EJB interfaces 40
  generating interfaces 42
  generating XML 45
  sample usage 37
  using Ant properties 57
  utility objects 59
  vendor XML 62
ejbFindByPortfolioName 96
ejbHomeGetCountOfSymbols
  123
<ejb-jar/> 83
ejb-jar.xml 47
  generating 45
ejbLoad 180, 184

EJBLocalHome 23
EJBMetaData 25–27
EJBObject 19
ejbPassivate, inheriting 139
EJB-QL 68, 111
<ejb-ql> 114
<ejb-relation/> 99–100
<ejb-relation-name> 99
ejbTimeout 146–147, 157, 160
ejbToString 136–137
EJBWebService 149
EJBWebServiceBean 150
@ejb.security-role-ref 64
email 144
  asynchronous 223
  synchronous 144
EmailBean 224
encapsulate business logic 210
encapsulating error-handling
  code in a message-driven
  EJB 221
Enterprise JavaBeans
  as a web service 149
  building stubs 283
  cascading deletes 104
  CMP 81
  compiling 278
  creating a message-driven
    bean 202
  disabling methods 235
  email 223
  error handling in an
    MDB 221
  examining with reflection 25
  faster lookup 31
  finding client identity 231
  finding client role 232
  generating code 34
  generating interfaces 37
  handling rollbacks in an
    MDB 225
  invoking another EJB
    (local) 4
  invoking another EJB
    (remote) 6
  logging in a cluster 263
  logging with many clients 269
  looking up with JNDI 43
  one-to-many relationships 101
  one-to-one relationships 97
  packaging 280

Enterprise JavaBeans *(continued)*
  retreiving a persisted
      reference 20
  saving a home object
      reference 21
  saving a reference 18
  security 230
  security role identity 238
  sending JMS messages 147
  stateful unit test 290
  superclass 139
  testing for equality 23
  toString method 136
  tracking the lifecycle 265
  2.1 timer service 145
  using a data source 78
  using environment
      variables 134
  with applets 27
  with JMS 202
  with JSP 12
  with no create method 107
  with servlets 8
entity bean
  cascading deletes 104
  compound primary key 92
  decreasing calls 124
  EJB-QL 111
  finder methods 95
  from a database view 115
  generating interfaces 39
  generating primary keys 88
  primary key classes 95
  security 239
  select methods 122
  session facade 120
  superclass 140
  unit test 292
  value objects 124
  with JMS 117
entity deletes 104
entity relationships
  generating 70
  generating XML 45
EntityBeanTemplate 140
53
<env-entry> 135
<env-entry-name> 135
<env-entry-type> 135
<env-entry-value> 135
environment entry, data
    types 135

environment variables 134
equality 23
equals 23
EquityBean 7, 24, 81, 137
  sample toString 137
  with a database view 115
EquityHome 6
equityPriceView 115
EquityVO 125
error handling
  message-driven beans 221
  rollbacks in a message-driven
      bean 225
ErrorHandler 223
executing test cases 274
  using a UI 298
executing unit tests
  from a web browser 298
  from UI classes 299

F

facilitating bean lookup with a
    utility object 58
FIFO 205
37, 282
filtering messages for a message-
    driven EJB 219
findByPortfolioName 96
findByPrimaryKey 96
finder methods 95
  EJB-QL 111
findHighPriced 112
findHighPricedLowPE 112
finding a remote EJB 6
finding the identity and role of
    the caller inside an EJB
    method 231
forcing rollbacks before method
    completion 172, 175, 177,
    180, 185, 189
formatting log messages 251
FROM 114

G

generating a primary key
    class 53
generating and maintaining
    method permissions 64
generating finder methods for
    entity home interfaces 66

generating primary key
    values 88
generating stub classes 274
generating the ejbSelect method
    XML 67
generating vendor XML 62
generating vendor-specific
    deployment descriptors 62
getCallerPrincipal 205, 231
getCodeBase 30
getConnection 85
getCountOfSymbols 122, 124
getEJBMetaData 25
getEJBObject 21
getEquityHome 6
getHandle 19
getHomeHandle 22–23
getPasswordHome 5
getPrincipal 271
getRollbackOnly 172
getRow 131
getStoredProcPrice 110
getUserTransaction 169–170,
    173, 177, 181–182, 187
Google xv

H

Handle 18
Handle class 18
handleMessageDrivenError 222
handling rollbacks in a message-
    driven bean 225
handling transaction manage-
    ment without the
    container 169
HelperBean 121
holding a transaction across
    multiple Java Server
    Pages 191
HoldingKey 92
home interfaces
  caching 61
  generating 37
  JNDI name variable 44
home methods, generating 68
home object reference,
    persisting 21
HomeHandle 23
how to format log4j
    messages 251

HTML 29
  as a log format 261
  converter 29
  layout 261
htmlFileAppender 261
HTMLLayout 261

I

IIOP 8, 11
IllegalStateException 169, 171
implementing toString functionality for an EJB 136
imposing time limits on
  transactions 176
improving logging
  performance 254
improving your client-side EJB
  lookup code 31
inheritance
  EJB superclass 139
  interfaces 137
<initial-beans-in-free-pool> 208
InitialContext 170, 190–191
  configuring JMS
    appender 259
  finding a remote EJB 6
  finding environment
    entries 135
  initializing 6
  with a servlet 12
  with a utility object 32
  with JSP 13
<init-param> 269
insulating an EJB from service
  class implementations 157
insulating message-driven beans
  from business logic
  changes 209
insulation 157, 209
invoking a local EJB from
  another EJB 4
invoking a remote EJB from
  another EJB 6
invoking a stored procedure
  from an EJB 109
invoking an EJB from a Java-
  Server Page 12
invoking an EJB from an
  applet 27
invoking EJB business logic from
  a JMS system 15

invoking EJBs in the same
  container 4
isCallerInRole 231, 233, 237
isDebugEnabled 255
isIdentical 24–25
Isolated 165
isPasswordValid 120
ItemBean 48, 53, 67–68
ItemBeanPK 54
ItemBeanPK.java 54
ItemBeanValue 49
ItemBeanValue.java 49

J

J2EE 1.4 156
jar_ejb target 282
<java> 286
Java Message Service. See JMS
Java plug-in 29
java.util.Collection 95, 103–104,
  106
JavaServer Page. See JSP
javax.mail 144
javax.rmi.PortableRemoteObject
  8, 10–11, 26, 31
62
JDBC 78
  appender 257
  data source 78, 85
  invoking a stored
    procedure 109
  log4j 257
  opening a connection 81
  using a database view 115
  with large result sets 126
JMS 15, 147
  appender 258
  decouple communication 198
  FIFO 205
  for centralizing logging 263
  for clustered logging 263
  generating XML 71
  invoking an EJB 15
  logging 258
  message destination 202
  message selectors 73
  security 242
  sending messages to many
    consumers 200
  sending to a JMS topic 198

sending to a queue 200
  speeding up message
    delivery 216
  streaming data 210
  topic 198
  triggering multiple MDBs 213
  using message selectors 219
  with entity beans 119
JMSAppender 259
JMSPublisher 117
JMX
  to refresh log4j 269
JNDI 8, 42, 44, 170, 190, 241
  avoiding repeated
    lookups 18, 21
  finder methods 95
  finding env variables 135
  home interface JNDI
    variable 43
  name added to the home
    interface 42
  static member variable 44
  with JMS 200–201
  with log4j JMS appender 258
JNDI_NAME 45
join 116
63
63
JSP xix, 12, 191
  calling an EJB 12
  calling local EJB 13
  calling remote EJB 14
JUnit 275
junit.framework 287

L

LDAP 241
lifecycle methods 139
LIKE 221
loadReference 20, 22
local interfaces 5
  generating 37
LocationInfo 260
log level 254
log4j 248
  conversion characters 253
  formatting messages 251
  in a cluster 263
  initialization 251
  introduction 248–249
  isDebugEnabled 255

log4j *(continued)*
  jdbc 257
  JDBC appender 257
  Location Info 252
  making reports 257
  performance 254
  refreshing configuration 267
  rolling file appender 260
  sample configuration 250
  sorting messages by client 269
  to HTML 261
  to JMS 258
  XML file log 259
logconfig.properties 250
LogConsolidatorBean 263
Logger.getLogger 249
LoggerInitializationServlet 268
logging 247
  format characters 253
  formatting messages 251
  making reports 257
  performance 254
  to a database 257
  to an XML file 259
  to HTML 261
  to JMS 258
  to XML 259
  tracking EJB lifecycle 265
LoginBean 8
LoginHome 13
LoginServlet 9–10
lookup 135
  env vars 135

M

managing EJB state after a
    rollback 183
managing EJB state at transac-
    tion boundaries 179
Mandatory 168
Map 126
MapMessage 199
Mapped Diagnostic Context 271
<max-beans-in-free-pool> 208
MDC 271
message filters 219
message queue 200
message selectors 73, 219
MessageBean 16–17, 154, 207,
    209, 214, 217, 219, 222

MessageBean2 214
MessageBeanTemplate 142
MessageDriveBean 204
<message-driven> 202–203
message-driven beans
  business logic 209
  creating 202
  deployment descriptor 203
  email 223
  error handling 221
  for centralizing logging 263
  handling rollbacks 225
  pool of 208
  security 204, 242
  superclass 142
  using message selectors 219
MessageDrivenBean 203
MessageDrivenContext 203
<message-driven-
    descriptor> 215
<message-driven-
    destination> 204
MessageListener 15, 203
<message-selector> 220
method permissions 64, 235
  generating XML 45
method that compares EJB
    references 24
<method-intf> 237
<method-permission> 236–237
Microsoft Excel 267
modeling one-to-one entity data
    relationships 97
MyService 158

N

NDC 270
Nested Diagnostic Context 270
nested transactions 182
Never 168
next 127
NonDurable 72
NotAdminException 233
NotSupported 168

O

one-to-many 101
one-to-one 97

onMessage 203, 242–243
  handling rollbacks 226
  security 242
org.apache.cactus.server.runner.
    ServletTestRunner 276
org.apache.cactus.server.Servlet
    TestRedirector 277
<orion/> 63
OwnerBean 70, 98, 101

P

packaging beans into an ejb.jar
    file 274
PaginationBean 127
paging through large result
    sets 126
passing client credentials to the
    EJB container 234
PasswordBean 108, 121
PasswordHome 5
PatternLayout 250, 252
  performance 255
patterns
  bean adapter 139
  session facade 120
performance
  JMS message delivery 216
  logging 254
  repeated lookups 31
permissions 235
persisting a home object
    reference 21
persisting a reference to an EJB
    instance 18
persisting entity data into a data-
    base view 115
point-to-point 200
pool
  of MDB 208
PortableRemoteObject 7, 10,
    18, 20, 28, 32
PortfolioBean 101–102, 104
PortfolioHolding 95
PortfolioHoldingBean 93, 96
PortfolioHoldingHome 95
<pramati/> 63
prepareCall 111
preventing access to entity
    data 239
previous 127
PricingBean 110

primary key class 92
   generating 53
   requirements 94
primary keys
   compound 92
   custom classes 94
   from a database sequence 88
processing messages 205
   in a FIFO manner from a message queue 205
propagating transactions 165, 186, 190
   to a nonEJB class 188
   to another EJB business method 186
Propertyconfigurator 251
providing common methods for all your EJBs 137
publish 148, 199
publish/subscribe 198
publishMessage 119

Q

<query> 113–114
<query-method> 114
queue 201, 205
   for FIFO messaging 205
QueueConnection 201
QueueConnectionFactory 201
QueueSender 201
QueueSession 201

R

read-only entity beans 107
reducing the clutter of unimplemented bean methods 139
reference, EJB 18
reflection 25
registerOutParameter 111
<relationship/> 100
<relationship-role-source> 100
<relationships> 99
relationships
   cascading deletes 104
   one-to-many 101
   one-to-one 97
remote interfaces
   generated sample 42
   generating 37

reports 257
Required 168
RequiredLocalException 168
RequiresNew 167–168
<resin-ejb-xml/> 63
<resource-ref>
   for a data source 80
<resource-ref/> 80
result sets 126
retrieving an environment variable 134
retrieving and using a persisted EJB reference 20
retrieving information about entity data sets 122
retrieving multiple entity beans in a single step 95
RMI 5
<role-link> 233
<role-name> 66, 232, 236
rollback 171, 173–174, 182, 189–190
rollback recovery 174
rollbacks 170
   message-driven bean 225
rolling back the current transaction 170
RollingFileAppender 260–261
rootLogger 250
<run-as> 239
runCactusTest 296
<runservertests> 295, 297
RuntimeException 176, 185

S

sample JSP looking up a remote EJB 14
sample JSP using a local EJB 13
sample log output 251
SampleBean 178
SampleDataSourceBean 79
   deployment descriptor 79
SampleMDB 203
saveHomeReference 22
saveReference 18
saving an EJB reference 18
SecureMDB 244
securing a message-driven bean 242
security 230
   credentials 234

disabling methods 235
entity beans 239
LDAP 241
local interfaces 240
MDB 242
message-driven beans 204
passing credentials to the EJB container 234
roles 238
security roles 232
   for an EJB 238
   generating XML 45
SecurityException 171
<security-identity> 238–239
<security-role> 232–233
<security-role-ref> 233
SELECT 114
select methods 67, 122
   generating 67
selector 221
send 201
sendEmail 144–145, 224
SendEmailBean.java 144
sending a JMS message from an EJB 147
sending a point-to-point JMS message 200
sending a publish/subscribe JMS message 198
sending an email from an EJB 144
sending an email message asynchronously 223
sending notifications upon entity data changes 117
SequenceBean 89
   CMP 90
serializable 18
   EJB handles 18
service classes 157, 209
serviceMethod 151
servlets
   as EJB clients 8
   calling local EJB 8
   calling remote EJB 10
   initialization parameters 11
   refreshing log4j 263
ServletTestCase 287, 290, 292
session beans
   facade 5
   generating interfaces 38

session beans (continued)
  invoking a stored
      procedure 109
  paging through data 126
  sending email 144
  session facade 120
  superclass 141
  unit test 286
session facade 120, 241
SessionBeanTemplate 141
SessionSynchronization 177,
    179–180, 183–184
setRollbackOnly 171–172,
    174, 188
setTransactionTimeout 177
simple lookup method 5
SimpleDateFormat 256
SimpleLayout 256
sorting log messages by
    client 269
source files
  compiling 278
specifying security roles in the
    bean source 63
speeding up message delivery to
    a message-driven bean 216
start.weblogic.61 296
starting a transaction in the cli-
    ent layer 190
startProcess 156
startTarget 296
startTimer 146
StatusBean 153
stdout appender 250
stop.weblogic.61 297
stopTarget 296
store procedure 109
Streaming 210
streaming data to a message-
    driven EJB 210
stub classes 283
super interface 139
Supports 168
Swing 29
SystemException 171–172, 177

T

test_sequence 88
testCreateEntity 294
TestEntity 292
TestEntityBean 141

testIncrement 290
testing 274
  automating tests 294
  entity bean 292
  from a browser 298
  from Swing 299
  statefull session 290
  stateless session 286
  with a UI 298
testNegativeResponse 287
testPositiveResponse 287
TestStateful 290
TestStateless 287
testTarget 296
throwing exceptions without
    causing a rollback 184
TimedObject 146–147
timeouts 176
Timer 145
timer service
  to create asynchronous
      process 156
TimerHandle 147
TimerService 146
TimerSession 146
TimerSessionBean 146
topic 199
  logging to JMS 258
TopicBindingName 259
TopicConnection 199
TopicConnectionFactory 199
TopicPublisher 199
TopicSession 199
toString 136
tracking the lifecycle of an
    EJB 265
transaction attribute
  Mandatory 167
  Never 167
  NotSupported 167
  Required 167
  Supports 167
transaction behavior 166
transaction boundaries 179
TransactionRequiredException
    168
transactions 164
  avoiding rollbacks 172
  distributed 193
  forcing rollbacks 175
  introduction to 165
  JSP 191

managing state 179
nested 182
progating to nonEJB 188
propagating to an EJB 186
restoring state after
    rollback 183
rollback the current
    transaction 170
throwing exceptions 184
timeouts 176
updating multiple entity
    beans 177
using more than one per
    method 181
170, 181
<trans-attribute> 167
triggering two or more message-
    driven beans with a single
    JMS message 213
trivial implementations 139
tuning the container transac-
    tion control for your EJB 166
2 phase commit 193
TYPE_SCROLL_INSENSITIVE
    131

U

<unchecked> 65, 237
unit tests
  an entity bean 274
  automation 294
  entity 292
  executing 298
  stateful session 290
  stateful session beans 274
  stateless session 286
  stateless session beans 274
Updating multiple databases in
    one transaction 193
239
UserBean 31, 38, 44, 46, 57, 59,
    64–65
  sample ejb-jar.xml 46
  utility object 59
UserSpecificDB
  deployment descriptor 86
UserSpecificDBBean 85
UserTransaction 169–171,
    173–174, 177, 181, 187,
    189–190, 192

UserUtil 31
UserUtil.java 31
using a compound primary key
    for your entity beans 92
using a data source 78
using a database sequence to
    generate primary key values
    for entity beans 88
using a different configuration
    at runtime 267
using an EJB as a web
    service 149
using Ant for compilation 274
using different data sources for
    different users 85
using EJB-QL to create custom
    finder methods 111
using EJBs to handle simple
    authentication with an LDAP
    source 241
using entity relationships to cre-
    ate a cascading delete 104
using environment
    variables 134
using more than one transaction
    in a method 181
using reflection with an EJB 25
using the EJB 2.1 timer
    service 145
UtilInterface 138
<utilityobject> 59

V

value objects 124
    generating 47
<valueobject> 49

W

web browser
    viewing log files 261
    with a UI 298
web service config.xml 150
web services 149
web.xml
    for cactus 276
Weblogic
    ejbc 286
    finding remote EJBs 7
    stubs 283
Weblogic deployment
    descriptor 17
    for message-driven bean 204
    generating primary keys 91
    MDB pool 208
63
WHERE 114
wildcard 237
wscompile 150

X

XAConnection 194
XADataSource 194
XDoclet 34–35, 37, 44, 66
    40
    adding home methods 69
    continuous integration 34
    customizing home
        interfaces 44
    deployment descriptor 46–47
    generating a primary key
        class 53
    generating EJB interfaces 38
    generating interfaces 41
    generating utility objects 58
    generating vendor XML 62
    generating XML 67
    generating XML file 62
    installing 35
    introduction to 34
    jar dependencies 36, 168
    JNDI names 42
    method permissions 64
    security roles 63
    using Ant properties 56, 58
    value objects 52
    vendor XML subtasks 62
    website 37
XDoclet tags
    @ejb
        create-method 38
    @ejb.bean 38
    @ejb.create-method 39, 41,
        48, 53, 65–66
    @ejb.interface-method 38–
        41, 49, 54, 65–66, 70
    @ejb.util 59
    @ejb-relation 70
    @ejb-value-object 48
    generating EJB interfaces 41
XML 84, 259
    as log file 259
    descriptor for Servlet EJB
        client 11
    layout 259
    message selectors 221

MORE JAVA TITLES FROM MANNING

Bitter Java
    by Bruce Tate
    ISBN: 1-930110-43-X
    368 pages
    $44.95
    March 2002

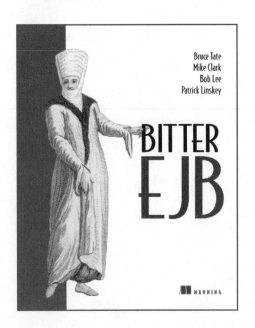

Bitter EJB
    by Bruce Tate, Mike Clark, Bob Lee,
       Patrick Linskey
    ISBN: 1-930110-95-2
    450 pages
    $44.95
    June 2003

For ordering information go to www.manning.com

Eclipse in Action: A Guide for Java Developers
   by David Gallardo, Ed Burnette,
     Robert McGovern
   ISBN: 1-930110-96-0
   416 pages
   $44.95
   May 2003

JUnit in Action
   by Vincent Massol and Ted Husted
   ISBN: 1930110-99-5
   300 pages
   $39.95
   September 2003

For ordering information go to www.manning.com

MORE JAVA TITLES FROM MANNING

Java Development with Ant
   by Erik Hatcher and Steve Loughran
   ISBN: 1-930110-58-8
   672 pages
   $44.95
   August 2002

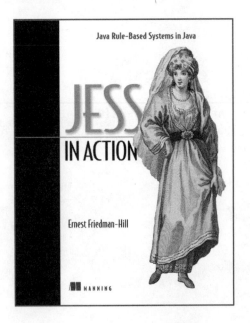

Jess in Action: Java Rule-based Systems
   by Robert Friedman-Hill
   ISBN: 1-930110-89-8
   525 pages
   $44.95
   July 2003

For ordering information go to www.manning.com